WHAT IT'S
LIKE TO
LIVE NOW

WHAT IT'S
LIKE TO
LIVE NOW

Meredith Maran

BANTAM BOOKS
New York   Toronto   London   Sydney   Auckland

Grateful acknowledgment is made for permission to reprint from "Wooden Ships," by Stephen Stills, David Crosby, and Paul Kantner © 1969 Gold Hill Music, Inc. (ASCAP) and Guerilla Music and Icebag Music Corp. (BMI). All rights administered by Almo Music Corp. (ASCAP) on behalf of Gold Hill Music, Inc. (ASCAP) for the world. All rights administered by Irving Music, Inc. (BMI) on behalf of Guerilla Music and Icebag Music Corp. (BMI) for the world. All rights reserved. International © secured. Used by permission.

Some names and identifying details have been changed for privacy's sake, but the people in this book and the events it depicts are real.

WHAT IT'S LIKE TO LIVE NOW

A Bantam Book / April 1995

Book design by Donna Sinisgalli

Library of Congress Cataloging-in-Publication Data

Maran, Meredith.
    What it's like to live now / Meredith Maran.
        p.   cm.
    ISBN 0-553-09600-1
    1. Maran, Meredith.   2. Lesbians—California—San Francisco—Biography.   3. Lesbian mothers—California—San Francisco—Biography.   4. Divorced mothers—California—San Francisco—Biography.   I. Title.
    HQ75.4.M327A3   1995   94-22688
    306.874'3'092—092dc20   CIP

Published simultaneously in the United States and Canada

Bantam Books are published by Bantam Books, a division of Bantam Doubleday Dell Publishing Group, Inc. Its trademark, consisting of the words "Bantam Books" and the portrayal of a rooster, is Registered in U.S. Patent and Trademark Office and in other countries. Marca Registrada. Bantam Books, 1540 Broadway, New York, New York 10036.

PRINTED IN THE UNITED STATES OF AMERICA

BVG   0 9 8 7 6 5 4 3 2 1

For Annie, my first and only.

And for Peter, pure heart.
And Jesse, rare soul.

Love makes a family; nothing else, nothing less.

Contents

WHAT IT'S LIKE TO LIVE NOW

MARCH 1992

This is how it usually starts: I see a headline in the paper or one of our cars gets broken into or I'm in bed overhearing an argument on the street and wondering whether or when to call 911. Then my throat constricts and the thought erupts: I want to move away from here, and then I'm moving all right, off and running.

This is how it started this morning: the kids and I walked together to the Ashby BART station, them to take the Fremont train to school; me to board the San Francisco train I take every day to work. Inside the station, two BART cops are talking to a boy twelve or thirteen, about Peter's age. The boy is crying and covering one eye with his hand. He looks as embarrassed to be crying in public as Peter or Jesse would be, all the briefcase people staring as they herd themselves through the turnstiles.

"He got beat up," Peter says flatly, slicing through my denial of that same thought. I see that he's got that studied "Shit Happens" look on his downy little face. Jesse's big brown eyes get bigger; he gives me one of those surreptitious sidelooks that says, simultaneously, "Don't get over-protective; I'm eleven years old; don't embarrass me," and, "Are you my mother? Are you protecting me?" The cops take notes as the kid talks in bursts through the sobs that keep collapsing his swollen face.

"At eight o'clock in the *morning,*" I mutter, and immediately regret my words. Peter exhales loudly, shakes his flat-topped head, and gives me a long-suffering frown. "Mom," he begins, and I know I'm in for it. "People get beat up here all the time. Teenagers hang around in the parking lot and wait for younger kids to beat up on. We're used to it. Why do you make such a big deal out of every little thing?"

My heart aches. I'm torn, as always in these interactions, between hanging on to my self, whether my kids like her responses or not ("My babies! This world is too harsh for my babies . . .") and the cool, detached, streetwise Mom who mimics, and therefore is acceptable to, my children ("Shit Happens").

I try for a compromise between the two. "What do you guys do to protect yourselves?" I don't know why I always say "you guys"; it's Peter, the shop steward for the younger half of our family, who invariably provides the answer, while Jesse silently and attentively fact-checks his brother's response. "Run," Peter says without hesitation, the tightening around his downcast eyes the only hint of emotion. Jesse focuses on me intently, then quickly looks away.

This is how it starts, the self-berating that builds on its own momentum. I can't believe I'm raising my kids like this. How can I call myself a mother when I can't even keep my kids safe? How can they turn out to be the sweet, sensitive men I promised myself I'd produce when the life I've given them requires such callousness, such denial, such smooth detached responses to fear? I moved to California to raise my kids so they wouldn't grow up to be crime-glazed New Yorkers. Now they're more jaded than I am. How did I let this happen—to them, to me?

The kids' train pulls in. I squeeze Jesse's arm good-bye, the most affection I am permitted to display in public, and look longingly down the platform where Peter stands (so as not to be seen in the presence of his mother). I'm in luck today: graced with a glance from my firstborn son. Peter's curt nod in my general direction satisfies me, because it has to. Jesse lets his hand graze mine as he steps away from me into the crowd. They do love me.

I watch my children whiz by me in the silver train: Jesse looking young and tall and innocent; two cars back Peter looking nearly man-sized and bored. All that work, all their lives, to teach them to know their own feelings. Will *I* ever again be allowed to know what they feel?

If I'd raised them on a farm in Petaluma, a hilltop in Marin, in a commune in North Berkeley, would they be as open with me on a subway platform as they are in their bedrooms in the dark, way past their bedtimes when they keep me up way past mine, so I can scratch their velvety backs and inhale their puppy scents while they talk to me for hours about making out with girls at parties, and how outraged and afraid they were after the Rodney King verdict, and whether it's entrepreneurial or unethical that Peter rents out his "Fuck Authority" button for a dollar a period at school, and the likelihood of Jesse's making a living someday as a comic-book artist, and—nine years after the fact—why their dad and I got a divorce?

If I'd sent them to private school? If they were girls? If I wasn't a lesbian? If the women's movement had succeeded?

Moments later I embark the San Francisco train, alone.

When I get like this, the world around me tends to cooperate. Today's morning newspaper headline announces: "Seven Murders in 24 Hours Jolt Oakland." Oakland, I remind myself needlessly, is where I have entrenched myself—where I own a house and pay taxes and send my children to school. I imagine my richer, wiser, and infinitely more fortunate friends in Mill Valley, Menlo Park, North Berkeley reading that headline and wondering what Meredith's problem is, anyway. When will she ever get over that outdated commitment to raising her kids in a "mixed" (meaning: mostly black and poor) neighborhood and move somewhere *safe*, already?

The train pulls into the West Oakland station, which is outdoors and elevated, providing me a sweeping view of the past two years' worth of East Bay disasters. Just a few feet in front of me is what the '89 earthquake left behind after it compressed forty-five people into specks of bone and blood on the Cypress freeway: two cement platforms suspended 100 feet above the ground, neatly sliced off by the demolition crews that cleared the crushed cars, rebar, and people from the shattered interchange throughout the weeks of aftershocks. Looking back toward Berkeley I see the hills, once landscaped with million-dollar homes and stands of silvery eucalyptus, now scorched, with blackened chimneys towering above the ashes and rubble like elongated gravestones.

My fellow commuters are buried behind their newspapers and blank faces. I wonder, as I do daily, why I'm the only one who stares out the window when this view is spread before us like a color still from some grade-B disaster movie. Why they don't take this moment to reflect on the lessons we all learned the hard way—in October of 1989, when our chimneys came crashing down, and again in October of 1991, when chimneys were all that was left standing?

Since the earthquake, since the week after it when I moved with my lover and my children into our still-shuddering dream house on the fault line, every moment of stillness has felt to me like a warning, a gathering of the forces of disaster preparing for the next strike: a brief cease-fire between the sounds of overpowered undermufflered American cars screaming through the streets with cop cars in hot pursuit; between diagnoses of AIDS and cancer in people I count on for my happiness; between dark rainy nights when my kids come home a few minutes late to find me shaking with terror and rage, between earthquakes and firestorms.

This is how it goes on from here: "I've got to get away from Oakland, get safe. I'll put the kids in private school, convince their father to move to New Mexico, Vermont, Marin . . ."

Eight years ago I uprooted my children, and eventually my joint-custodial ex-husband, from suburban San Jose, where we never locked our doors and a car break-in was a gossip-worthy neighborhood event. I wanted to raise my kids in what I then referred to as "the real world." I wanted them to know people who weren't white. I wanted neighbors who didn't wear bras. I wanted to walk to demonstrations at Sproul Plaza and Mime Troupe plays in the park.

And so, after five years of sociopolitical deprivation and emotional isolation in the stucco tracts of San Jose, I put my $10,000 divorce settlement down on an $80,000 cottage on the Berkeley-Oakland border and hurtled myself and my kids into the closest thing to a sixties life I could construct.

I put Peter and Jesse in an Oakland public school and went to endless meetings to make sure their education was politically, if not academically, correct. I rode my bicycle to the market and rode home with my backpack full of exotic lettuces and tomato-basil baguettes. I helped organize our Neighborhood Watch Association. I took my kids to puppet shows about Nicaragua at the neighborhood community center, whose walls were papered with flyers announcing solidarity marches, multicultural day care centers, and incest survivor support groups.

I got to know my neighbors, the mix I'd dreamed of: longhaired carpenter guys and shorthaired carpenter gals. Friendly Southern black men whose grandchildren played double Dutch on the sidewalk. A coven of pagans who danced with flutes in their adjoining backyards. A couple of lesbian chiropractors, and never mind about the crack house up the block and the speed freaks across the street and the unemployed young man next door who rattled my house and my brain with pounding rap music all day while I sat at my computer trying to earn a living as a freelance journalist.

I slept with a crowbar next to my bed for the first few months and installed a burglar alarm in my house, but for the first time since I'd left the Haight-Ashbury in 1972 and embarked on a course that led me, eventually, to Marxism and ten years of factory organizing and living among white working-class people who'd never met a Jew, let alone a communist, and believed (correctly, based on their own empirical experience) that there was no difference between the two—I felt again that I was living among my people.

Five years later I sold the first house I'd ever lived in without parents or a man, the nest from which I'd launched my brave new life, for $185,000—an inadvertent beneficiary of the Bay area real estate boom—and bought a three-story Victorian a few blocks away, big enough so that after six years together my lover, Ann, and I could live under the same roof, and Peter and Jesse would each have his own door to shut.

Now I find myself poised for what must honestly be named white flight, bound to my urban life not by principles but by the geographic restrictions imposed by joint custody—and by profound ambivalence.

As my parents did, as I scorned my parents for doing, I find myself yearning for the good and safe old days, when the drugs being bought and sold on my block were pot and peyote, when the absence of children in my life kept my lofty child-rearing principles untested and unshakable, when I never leashed my dog, locked my car, hesitated to take a walk alone at night.

As my parents did, as I came of age swearing I would never do, I find myself worrying about who my children's role models and friends are, and why my children choose them, and what these strangers might teach or convince my children to do.

As my parents did, as I never could imagine myself doing, I find myself turning to money as the balm for my fears, and I resolve to earn or somehow acquire more of it: money to move into a neighborhood or, better yet, a town, in which beepers are worn by pediatricians, not twelve-year-olds; in which the silence of night is not shattered by gunfire or the rattling of shopping carts filled with rags and bottles being pushed down the street; in which bicycles are left unchained outside shops without cast-iron bars on their windows, and teenagers speak politely to each other's parents on the telephone.

As my parents did, twice each month I tell Peter and Jesse that tomorrow the housecleaner is coming, and I want them to clean their rooms, so she can clean their rooms. And, just as I did thirty years ago, my sons stall and argue and invoke their right to privacy and constitutional amendments not yet written, until I glower and growl and threaten to withhold their allowances and inevitably end the evening sulking in my room, blaming myself for spoiling these boys who will someday, I am certain, leave wet towels and underwear on the floors of their own houses, and will therefore be divorced by their feminist wives and separated from their own children—all because their mother, who could afford to hire a housecleaner, trained them to expect a woman to swab out their dirty toilets, change their flannel sheets, and pick up their smelly socks.

As my parents were, I am called to parent conferences three, six, eleven times in each school year, and confronted with relentless rows of F's in Citizenship, which causes me to bemoan my childhood, the sixties, my own and my children's laziness, everything that has caused me to fail so miserably as a disciplinarian. And yes, I have uttered aloud on several occasions the two words I swore I'd never say—"private school"—and my politically correct committment to "fighting to make the public schools work" has been replaced by the indignation of a property-tax payer at the failure of the schools to make their own damn selves work.

How have I come to these transgressions?

Is it that my kids have graduated from the safe if underfunded elementary school that I used to complain about having to drive them to and from every day, and they now take public transportation to a junior high school where young men twice my weight punch and kick the flesh of my flesh and steal the Chicago Bulls caps off their stylishly shorn heads?

Is it that life in the city—any city, but most certainly the one I live in, whose very name, to those who don't live here and many who do, evokes all that is terror-provoking in modern urban life—has simply gotten exponentially worse (along with my fear level) since I lived here happily eight years ago?

Is it that, despite all I'd sworn would never happen to me, the upper-middle-class values I ingested along with formula from sterilized bottles have curdled and congealed in my middle-aged soul?

And whatever the source of these twin fears—of the dangers in my life, and of a solution that contradicts all I've believed in—what can I do about it now?

What *should* I do about it now?

Would I be happier, would I feel like a better mother, would I *be* a better mother if I sent my kids off on mountain bikes to the very nearly all-white school I used to pass every morning on my way to work in Mill Valley, where the blond kids dress the way my kids dress, but without benefit of proximity to the people or the culture whose style they're emulating, whose overheard conversations once jolted me into a rare moment of perspective: Meredith, you'd be kicking yourself every day if you'd brought your kids up in a place like this.

Would my kids be happier?

Driving through a small California town one night on our way to a weekend at our cabin in the woods, I dreamily ask Peter and Jesse, "Wouldn't you love to move to the country? Where people are friendly and we wouldn't have to be afraid all the time?" "Yeah, right, Mom," answers Jesse, rolling his eyes in the rearview mirror. "Then we could hang out in the 7-Eleven parking lot every Friday night and smoke cigarettes. Sounds really great."

"But what's so much better about living where we live?" I persist. "What do you do on Friday nights that's so exciting?"

"I couldn't live without Telegraph," says Jesse of the Berkeley avenue on which the People's Park war was waged, where his father was shot while throwing tear gas grenades back at the National Guardsmen who'd fired them at him, where today homeless panhandlers extend their begging cups from sleeping bags stretched across the sidewalk, and Jesse is regularly threatened and occasionally robbed by the boys he beats at video games.

During a family trip to New York last summer, Peter overheard me muttering to myself that I could have chosen a worse place than Oakland to raise my kids. "I'm *glad* I grew up in Oakland, Mom," he said. "Now I'm prepared for anything. If I decide I want to live in New York someday, I know I'll be able to handle myself."

I'm anchored now in the city I chose, the life I chose all those years and decisions ago, because it's not just me, not just my lover and me, who live in it. This is the place and the life, the streets and the people, my children know and therefore is the place and the life they want to be in, and are old enough to say they don't want to be wrenched away from. Backed into a nineties corner by my sixties politics—and by my sons, whose childhoods and values reflect those politics—I am forced to confront the most difficult decision of all. Can I carry on the struggle to overcome what's wrong in the world, while keeping my children, my family, myself safe and sane within it?

I remember the night a year ago when Peter, at age twelve, requested (and was denied) the right to carry a knife, for self-protection, to junior high school. "I didn't raise you guys to believe in violence," I declared.

"Make up your mind, Mom," replied my clear-eyed son. "If you didn't want us to grow up this way, you shouldn't have raised us in this neighborhood."

Make up my mind, indeed.

WHAT IT'S LIKE
TO BE FAMILY NOW

Family Pictures

I pull into Richard's driveway, turn down the rap music that's blaring from the car radio, turn off the engine. Looking up at the house, I see that the miniblinds are shut tight, the front door is closed, the lights are off. It looks so . . . unwelcoming.

"Didn't Dad say he'd be home?" I ask, turning to face Peter and Jesse in the backseat.

"Prob'ly working in the basement," Peter mumbles, stuffing an errant pants leg into the huge plastic garbage bag of clothing in his lap.

"Oh," I say, swallowing a sudden gulp of protectiveness. It's noon, and the kids haven't eaten since bagels at nine. Will Richard take a break, make lunch for them, eat with them? They eat so differently when they're with him—according to their reports, anyway. Campbell's soup, frozen fried shrimp, roast beef sandwiches from the deli, store-bought cookies.

Get a grip, Mer, I tell myself. *After nine years you should be used to this, already.*

"Got everything, guys?" I ask, refocusing on the task at hand.

Peter nods. Of course he does. Hyperfunctional, hyperorganized, he gets through this midweek transfer from Mom's house to Dad's on autopilot.

Each Tuesday night, without being reminded, he stuffs three or four pairs of jeans, three or four T-shirts, a couple of pairs of boxers, and a basketball into the garbage bag he appropriated for this purpose months ago. When he leaves for school Wednesday mornings Peter carefully leans the bag against the front door so that Ann or I— whichever of us is doing the ten-minute crosstown schlep to Richard's house later that day—can't miss it. Then he accepts his lunch money and a hug from me, squats to give his beloved dog Joe a soulful kiss good-bye, and strolls in his rolling, rhythmic gait—his father's gait—to the BART station a block away.

Transitions have never come easily for Jesse, and the repetitiveness of this one has not made it any easier. Every Wednesday morning, five or ten minutes after he should have left for school, Jesse gallops up and down the stairs, tossing his prized possessions from his room onto a heap at the foot of the stairs: the art supplies he needs for the various media he's currently working in; the shirt he needs for the basketball team he's currently playing on; the tapes of the hip-hop groups he's currently listening to.

When the pile is complete (or when he can no longer stand listening to me yelling at him about how many "tardies" he had on his last report card), Jesse warbles "Bye, Joe" in the lilting soprano tones he saves for Joe alone, pushes Peter's bag out of the way, and hurtles himself out the door and down the block—late, more often than not, for the train.

Normally the twice-weekly relocation of my children is achieved seamlessly (if somewhat labor-intensively). Wednesday morning they take BART to school from our house. Wednesday afternoon they take the bus after school to Richard's house. The weekend transfer occurs either Saturday morning at nine A.M. (weekends the kids spend with Ann and me) or Sunday night at six (weekends they spend with Richard).

Once or twice during most weeks, Richard and I, or Ann and Richard, talk on the phone for the purpose of exchanging late-breaking updates: educational, financial, medical, and behavioral. Report cards and basketball team schedules are transmitted from the fax machine of the on-duty parent to the fax machine of the off-. Once every month or two, we hold all-parent meetings to discuss metatrends ("What's our line on pot?") and major decisions ("Can we afford braces?").

This week the kids are on spring break, so they've been hanging out with me until noon on Wednesday—the demarcation point that divides their life with their moms from their life with their dad. Since this bisection began nine years ago, it has been painfully clear that— necessary as it might be for their parents' well-being—living in two houses does not meet these children's needs.

In the backseat, Jesse's eyes are darting around wildly, as if he's just awakened from a deep sleep and discovered himself sitting inexplicably in his mother's car, parked in the driveway of his father's house.

"Mom—my paints!" he yelps.

"They're right here, Babe," I say, patting the pile on the front seat. "With your pads." Jesse doesn't seem soothed by this information. He gazes at me blankly.

"Do you have your wallet, your bus pass, your backpack, your basketball shirt . . . ?" I prompt him. Jesse considers my question for a minute or two. Then I see his eyes glaze over again. It's too much for him. This whole thing is just too much for him, I think. And my heart aches, that same old ache.

Peter slides across the seat, nods at me to open the car door for him. "Bye, Sweetie," I say, as he clambers out awkwardly. That bag of clothing is just about as tall as he is—which, this week, is just about as tall as I am. "I love you. Have a good break."

"Love you, Mom," Peter answers numbly, and slams the car door shut with his foot. I turn around and see Jesse still sitting in the backseat. "Jess?" I say. He shakes his head slightly and lets himself out of the car, starts to follow Peter through Richard's gate.

"Jesse—your stuff!" I call to him. He turns around, opens the passenger door, gathers up: three drawing pads in three different sizes and different weights of paper, the red plastic tackle box in which he transports his colored pencils, a dog-eared, color-splattered box of acrylic paints, and a few loose pieces of binder paper, each bearing the easily recognizable face of a sports star—Charles Barkley, Magic John- son, Larry Bird—sketched on it.

"I love you, Jess," I say, as Jesse backs away from the car. I see that he's carrying a couple of pencils between his teeth. "See you Sunday night." Jesse doesn't answer (how could he!) or make eye contact with me. He stumbles, head down, through the wisteria-draped gate and up the wooden steps.

I sit in my car watching Peter and Jesse waiting to be admitted to their other house. A familiar lump swells in my throat.

My beloved sons. The boys I promised *everything* to—all the years I tried to imagine them into existence, every day that they swam and somersaulted inside me, every day since they were pulled, pulpy and squalling, from my body.

My sons, who sat side by side on the plaid Herculon couch in our living room one March night in 1984—five-year-old Peter in his Superman pajamas, nearly-four-year-old Jesse in his He-Man Underoos, their faces clean and shining, the tendrils of their golden curls still damp from the bath I'd just given them. They sat very still, these baby boys, on the couch where their parents had assembled them to say the word that, even at their tender ages, they knew they didn't want to hear.

The instant that word "divorce" was said Peter exploded; his tiny wiry body became a whirling tornado of grief. He catapulted off the couch, threw himself around the room, sobbing and yelling, "No, Mommy! No! No, Daddy! Please! Please!" Inconsolable, untouchable until he collapsed, exhausted, onto the brand-new Marimekko train-and-truck sheets that I'd meticulously tucked tightly onto his bunk bed that very morning.

As his brother wept and wailed, Jesse sat perfectly still on the couch, watching the chaos in his living room as if from some great distance. And when at last he could be heard above his brother's din, when at last he answered his parents' distraught questions—"Jesse? How do *you* feel? Do you know Mommy and Daddy still love you?"— Jesse said calmly: "When Daddy's not with me, Mommy will be with me. When Mommy's not with me, Daddy will be with me. I'll be okay, because someone will be with me all the time."

My beloved sons who are standing side by side now on their

father's porch, surrounded by twine-bound stacks of recycling-bound newspapers. Standing on their father's porch like vagabond orphans, their arms and mouths clutching at their worldly possessions, ringing their father's doorbell with their elbows, banging on their father's door with their feet.

"Peter," I call. He turns to look at me just as Richard opens the door. The two of them—six-foot-four-inch father, five-foot-seven-inch son—regard me out of two sets of matching hazel eyes.

"I could buy you a suitcase . . . ," I say lamely, embarrassed.

Peter shrugs, turns to greet his father, disappears inside the dark house. Jesse dances away from Richard's welcoming hug, drops his armload of pads and paints on the threshold, bends to pet and coo at Lucy. "My cat at Dad's," he calls her. Just as he calls Joe "my dog at Mom's."

Richard waves hello and good-bye at me, follows the kids inside. The door slams shut behind them. Still I sit, staring through the blinds at the shadows of my sons as they move through their father's house.

It's not supposed to be like this, I think. A kid is supposed to be able to call his cat "my cat." Period.

Thus begins my descent into joint-custody hell. Even as I feel the flames of guilt licking at my jagged edges, I am amazed that after all these years, with all the available evidence that Peter and Jesse are robustly healthy children, that their father and I are far happier living apart, that they are well loved by both of their mothers and their one loving father, that a functional new family has arisen from the ashes of the old—I still can be scorched by these feelings of grief, loss, remorse.

And yet I relish my weekly respite from the marathon of mother-hood. I am grateful for the chance to recharge my maternal battery, to come back fresh and juiced up to these boys I adore.

Having three or four nights a week for adult-only activities (sitting at Zen Center, biking to therapy, wandering dreamily for hours through bookstores and libraries, having dates with friends and dates with Ann) makes me eager to devote my three or four family nights, happily and wholeheartedly, to Peter and Jesse (when they'll have me).

There's so much about joint custody that works that, in my more idealistic moments, I wonder how anyone does it that primitive, full-time way. How *I* ever did it that way.

Then there are the less idealistic moments, when I feel over-whelmed by the things that don't work. The endless schlepping, nego-tiating, scheduling. The inevitable surfboard or bicycle at Dad's house when Peter needs it at Mom's; the inevitable portfolio or comic book at Mom's house when Jesse needs it at Dad's.

The years of eating Thanksgiving and Christmas dinners at child-less tables, while my children sit at their father's table with their father's family, eating their father's turkey. The iron-clad parameters within which Richard and I now live our ostensibly divorced lives: where we live, how much money we spend, when we take our vacations, who hangs out at our houses—all of these decisions now more subject to each other's approval than they were when we were married.

And, there is the disappointment. The picture of how it was supposed to be; how we meant for it to be—and the reality of how it is.

This is not the picture I had of myself as a mother, when I was sixteen or twenty or twenty-four: passing my babies from breast to breast in a commune, running naked with my children through wild-flower fields, growing up with my children as we crisscrossed the country in our Volkswagen bus.

This wasn't the picture I had when I succumbed, finally, to the way it was supposed to be, and took the biggest risk of all: sharing my children with just one man, raising them in the dreaded isolation of a nuclear family. When Rich and I stood together in the apartment we shared, our friends and comrades surrounding us, and said to each other the world-changing wedding vows we'd written ourselves, I never imag-ined (who ever does?) that all my lofty visions would dead-end in this most banal of American failures: the ragged rending of my children's lives into two houses, two families, two sets of rules and expectations. My sons reduced, half the time, to shadowy figures who eat cookies I didn't bake at a kitchen table where I never sit.

MT. EDEN HOSPITAL: DECEMBER 6, 1978

"Meredith . . . Can you hear me? Mer?" I hear a voice . . . Rich's voice . . . pulling me up, slowly up from the thick, deep swamp of anesthesia. I try to speak to him but my tongue seems to fill my whole mouth. I concentrate instead on trying to look in his direction. When I move my head gingerly on the pillow a bolt of pain shoots through my skull.

"Meredith, look. It's your son!" I know Rich is trying to tell me something, but what? His words are irritating my ringing ears.

"Can you open your eyes? Look—he's perfect!"

My eyelids feel like my tongue: swollen, useless, out of my control. I struggle to lift one, then the other. In front of me is a large, blurry shape that I barely recognize as Rich. My eyes swim into focus and I see his face: clean-shaven, red-eyed, and . . . glowing.

Before my brain can function, my heart registers the emotion that radiates like a halo around my husband: *I've never seen him so happy.*

A dim thought: *baby*—pulls me, at last, into the room.

"He's fine, Meredith. He's *great*! Look!" Rich leans over me, shows me the tiny bundle he's cradling in his arms. At one end is a pointy head covered with copper-colored fuzz. *My baby*, I think. *My baby is alive.*

"Is he . . . ?" I mumble. Rich's head bobs emphatically. He leans closer, positions the baby just below my chin. "They've done all the tests. He's fine, Babe. Completely normal."

I close my eyes, flooded with relief. The last face I saw before Rich's was the anesthesiologist's—masked, kindly-looking—murmuring words of reassurance I was too far gone to hear. Before the drugs he'd injected into me had a chance to work, I'd felt tugging on my abdomen and then searing pain. "We've got to get this baby out *right now*," I heard my obstetrician bark as he sliced me open, sliced me open in a big hurry to save the life of my baby, whose heart had stopped beating moments before.

"What day is it?" I ask Rich.

A cloud crosses his face. "Wednesday," he says. "You were in labor from Sunday to Tuesday. The baby was born yesterday at noon. You've been asleep since then. There was a lot of bleeding. They had to give you a bunch of drugs . . ."

I remember now: the first contractions . . . Rich timing them studiously, both of us laughing and hugging each other in between, high on anticipation. Our first baby! The baby we'd spent four years, countless tears, and thousands of insurance dollars conceiving was soon to be born just as we'd planned it: in the brass bed of our local hospital's Alternative Birth Center. The ABC had English country wallpaper on the walls, rubber sheets beneath the Laura Ashley linens on the bed, a tasteful spray of dried flowers on the oak bedside table, a medical team that promised minimal intervention. My brother, Drew, sister-in-law, Roberta, and seven-month-old niece, Josie, would be with us from start to ecstatic, drug-free finish.

And the last: writhing in the narrow, sweat-soaked labor bed nearly thirty-six hours later. Screaming for mercy, struggling to break free from the probes stuck to and up inside me, spitting ice chips at the nurse who tried to rub them on my cracked, swollen lips, plotting my path to the fourth-floor window to finally put a stop to this endless, useless pain.

And then Rich yelling for the doctor, standing in the hall outside my room yelling for *someone* to come and check the monitor, check me, because the baby's heartbeat seemed to have stopped. The nurse's reproving voice as she came into my room: "We'll have to ask you to leave, sir, if you're going to get hysterical." And then Rich running alongside the gurney they threw me on as they rushed me to emergency surgery, Rich running along with his hand on the oxygen mask they'd clapped to my face to try to keep our dying baby alive . . .

This was not the labor I had planned. Nothing like the way it was supposed to be. I was supposed to be conscious and euphoric throughout this birth and after it. I was supposed to spend the hours and days following my baby's birth bonding with him, the process all the books described as necessary for a close mother-child relationship.

Now I'd missed the first day and a half of my baby's life. The carefully orchestrated birth that was supposed to cement me to my baby forever had separated us instead. Would I—would our relationship—ever recover from this loss?

"Let me . . ." I reach out to hold my son, feel a tug and see the IV tubing attached to my hand. Tears sting my weary eyes. Not the way it was supposed to be at all.

Rich moves the baby to my other, unfettered side. I touch him for the first time. Instantly my body is suffused with a glow that feels the way Richard's face looks. My nipples tingle; my womb clenches.

My baby opens his eyes and looks straight at me. I'm in love. Forever. Despite everything that didn't happen the way it was supposed to, I know that I'm feeling now exactly the way I'm supposed to feel.

"I'll call the nurse," Rich says. "She said when you woke up she'd help you start breast-feeding."

Rich moves to the bedside phone, the baby nestled in his arms. I can't take my eyes off my son; his wide-open eyes are still fixed on mine.

Now we're a family, I think, gazing at my towering six-foot-four-inch husband, tiny twenty-inch son. *The way it's supposed to be.*

Mundane Miracles

DECEMBER 4, 1992

The phone rings as I'm tying a magenta ribbon around the last of the recycled paper–wrapped presents piled on my bed.

"Mer—it's me," says my best friend, Wendy. The sadness in her voice tells me why she's calling. "I'm not pregnant," she says. "Again."

"Oh, Wendy." I sigh. What else can I say? What could anyone have said to me, all those years when getting my period felt like going to a funeral—month after empty month? "It's so unfair," I tell her. "No one deserves to be a mother more than you do."

Wendy starts to cry. "It *does* feel unfair," she says. "Everything else has been so hard—having cancer twice, being so sick for so long . . . I just keep thinking my body will recover from everything it's been through and do *one normal thing*." She is sobbing now. "I took it all like a trooper. But I can't take this. Mer—I really need this one thing to come through. I really need to be a mom."

"I know you do, sweetie," I say, my own eyes filling with tears. Wendy cries for a while into the phone. "I still think you'll be a mom someday, one way or another," I tell her. "It could still happen."

"I know." Wendy hiccups. "I still feel hopeful. I just know some-where in there there must be an egg . . ."

There is so painfully little I can do for my grieving best friend. If I could give her a fertile egg from my own body, I would. If someday she asks me to do that, I will. But for now all I can give her is what I wish I'd had during my own four agonizing years of endometrial biopsies and hysterosalpingograms and Clomid and DES and mucous analyses and temperature charts and robotic sex and relentlessly regular menses: unconditional, optimistic support to help her survive the screaming grief of an empty womb.

"I'm so sorry this is happening to you," I tell Wendy. "Listen: maybe you should take a break for a few months. Give yourself and Michael some time off from worrying about this."

"I can't, Mer," Wendy says. "I'm thirty-seven years old. What if we miss the one month I ovulate? I just can't take that chance. I've got to keep trying."

Of course she does. "I understand," I say. And I do. Even at twenty-five, I was driven by that desperation: *What if it* never *happens?* "Is sex still fun, at least?" I ask her. I'm relieved to hear her giggling through her tears. "Sex with Michael is great," she says. "That's one thing I don't have to worry about."

"Well, then, go fuck your brains out," I say. She laughs. "It always helps to talk to you," she says.

I promise to send fertility energy Wendy's way, blow a few fertility kisses into the phone, and flop down across my waterbed. God, those were awful years. I couldn't get through a trip to the supermarket without choking on tears, staring enviously at all the frazzled mothers, imagining a pair of stubby legs composed of my genetic material poking through the kiddie seat in the shopping cart. Oh, the longing, the blood; the crying, the blood; the fantasies of all the hurts that would be healed, the holes that would be filled—if only the blood wouldn't come.

And now, fourteen years after my own infertility battle was won, not just my best friend but several women I know are crying and planning and fucking and inseminating their own way through the fray.

It hasn't been unusual in the past couple of years to get upset phone calls from more than one of them on one day. Wendy: thirty-seven, living happily with her boyfriend, Michael, recovering from breast cancer, visualizing and acupuncturing and willing her body to defy the laws of chemotherapy and aging and produce an egg, already. Molly: forty-three, lesbian and single, searching for a woman to share a baby with and an HIV-negative gay man to make it possible, already. Liza, whose Dalkon Shield scarred her tubes and ovaries; Jane, who spent three years and many thousands of dollars inseminating, then aborted after she found out the fetus had Down's syndrome.

It's been strange, watching my friends devote themselves so energetically to getting pregnant just as Ann and I are settling into midlife exhaustion. When we refinanced our house this fall, our calculations were centered on launching the postparenting phase of our lives: our seven-year loan commits us to leaving this rambling Victorian and setting out for our cozy two-bedroom dream house in the country the year after Jesse graduates from high school.

The very thought of being pregnant, let alone mothering an infant—approaching the starting line *now* of the race I've been running all these years—is overwhelming to consider. I've wondered, in fact, where I'll find the time and energy to be the kind of loving aunt I want to be to my friends' babies, should they materialize. The kind of energy Wendy's been happily shoveling at Peter and Jesse since their infancies.

Wendy at forty-three when her dream baby toddles off to kindergarten?

Wendy at fifty-five when her dream baby graduates from high school?

Seems impossible. And yet . . .

I glance at my bedside photo of Peter and Jesse, ages three and two, wearing their I'm the Big Brother/I'm the Little Brother T-shirts, their pudgy arms wrapped around each other, their dancing eyes crinkled into matching magnetic grins.

My heart swells and I wonder, as I've wondered nearly every day for fourteen years, how I can love them so much, how my love for them can keep stretching my heart this way. How is there room in my chest cavity for a heart so enlarged?

Does Wendy know, do my other friends know, that this sweet ache is the pot of gold they're chasing?

And do they know, could I or anyone ever tell them how hard it is—not the diapers and diarrhea, the dismal report cards and adolescent anger—but the really hard part: the making of a healthy family?

I didn't know.

I worried about all the wrong things, all those years of longing.

In the first few euphoric weeks following Peter's difficult birth, I thought my worries were over. It was as though every tear I'd shed, every stab of anguish I'd suffered in four years of infertility had been returned to me, transformed into its opposite. I was simply ecstatic.

Even with an emergency cesarean incision that left me split and stapled from navel to pubis, a husband on graveyard shift and not much advice from anyone, I sailed through the incessant feedings, the up-and-down all-nighters, the sudden and complete confinement to the house, the room, the bed that became the desert island on which my miraculously perfect son and I were happily marooned.

The murkiness of normal life, normal emotion, cleared like a glass of water long left on the sill. Every impulse I felt, every move I made was triggered by pure maternal love. My enthusiasm for meeting Peter's needs seemed to spring from a well that was endlessly and mysteriously refilled, perhaps during the two or three hours at a time that we slept.

I was every good mother in history. It was not so hard, as my mother had always claimed it was, to be a good mother. I was succeeding as a mother. I was not my mother. It was easy not to be my mother. I loved my son; I took care of my son. The good in me, in him, in the world, triumphed over evil every time I looked lovingly upon him.

Until the day I hit the wall.

The December sky was dismal and heavy with rain; it had been a long and unusually fussy day for both of us. I brought Peter's rooting lips to my cracked, aching nipple for what seemed like the twentieth time in as many hours, practicing Lamaze breathing to make the pain bearable. Peter began to nurse halfheartedly, without his usual get-it-done gusto: rolling my nipple around in his mouth, sucking painfully, licking uninterestedly. Then suddenly he spit my nipple out as if (it felt to me) it—I—was repulsive to him.

I was instantly, totally enraged. I saw myself throwing him against the wall, watched him fall to the floor in a small flannel heap: lifeless, silent, finally undemanding—my problem solved, my breasts left to heal, my nights blessed with blissful undisturbed sleep.

The vision scared me back into the room, but not out of my anger. I could barely breathe through the fury. For an instant I tottered on the edge. For an instant I was my mother. I was worse than my mother. I was every abusive mother in history. *I simply could not put that child's needs before mine for one more instant.*

And then the still-reasoning part of me spoke firmly. It told me to do what I had to do without hurting my child. It told me that doing what was best for my child might not be possible in that moment, but that the best I could do would be good enough. It reminded me that the main thing was *not-to-hurt-my-child.*

Carefully—not violently—I detached Peter from my breast and laid him down firmly—not violently—in the center of the bed. Breathing deeply, I hoisted myself up, walked out of the bedroom, closed the door behind me. I put my face in the pillows of the couch and screamed until the towering glacier of my own craving for a mother who could put my needs before hers—day after day, year after year, at that very moment when I needed to be loved that way myself—melted to sobs.

And then I walked back into the bedroom, slid between the covers, and took my innocent son in my arms again.

Since that day I've parented my children knowing that asking myself to make a healthy family is like asking a blind-since-birth person to draw a cloud. Nothing in my experience taught me how to do what Peter's and Jesse's existences—and, for the last nine years, my relationship with Ann—demand. Nothing taught me how to build into my family of choice the things a healthy family needs—things I never felt or saw or knew in my family of origin.

Parents who take care of themselves, and therefore have care to willingly give. It wasn't my mother's fault, but it became her children's pain, that when the war ended the women were ordered back to their kitchens—that in marrying my father my mother divorced her budding nineteen-year-old self: gave up her name and her job, agreed to produce the unwanted but requisite two children, set the clock of her shrunken life by my father's arrivals and departures from *his* all-important life in the men's club of the world outside, from which my mother (and nearly all the mothers) were banished.

It wasn't my mother's fault, but it became her children's pain, that her own unloving parents retired to Florida, a thousand miles away, and she had no one—not the extended family of her mother's generation, nor the support network of her daughter's—to ask for help when, as she told me, "This baby—you—arrived and I had no idea what to do with it." So that when a hired nanny told my mother she would spoil me if she held me during feedings, my mother agreed (but where was her *heart?*) to prop the bottle on a pile of diapers in my crib, close the door behind her, and go about her business until the bottle was empty and the baby (*me!*) needed changing.

And it became his children's pain that my father concluded from this quintessential fifties setup that the purpose of his family was to propel him—with attractively presented meals, neatly ironed boxer shorts, and regularly administered ego strokes—upward through the ranks of one corporation and then another, while he (and therefore we) became increasingly if unsatisfyingly affluent, and his stack of screenplays-in-progress yellowed in a drawer, and his alienation from his wife, his children, and his once-passionate self became complete.

Parents who are in love with each other. Whose relationship is alive, honest, tender and sexual, yet stable enough to support its own dailiness. Whose relationship teaches children the possibilities and the benefits of this one form of romantic love.

This I could not have learned from my parents, who might have loved each other once, but certainly didn't during all the years of my life with them—who simmered in tight-lipped anger through endless indigestible dinners around a properly set table, and divorced each other, twenty years belatedly, approximately one nanosecond after their younger child left home.

Mutual respect. When Peter was twelve and delivering to me weekly lectures about my deficiencies as a parent, he once held forth on my failure to teach him "respect." "Most of the kids in my class would never talk to their parents or teachers the way Jesse and I do," he informed me.

"Their parents would whup them. You aren't strict enough—you didn't teach us to respect adults."

"Sorry, Babe—I'm not buying it," I replied, unsnowed, for once, by the usual avalanche of introspection and guilt. "If you didn't respect me you wouldn't be as honest with me as you're being right now. If you didn't respect yourself you wouldn't expect me to care what you think. Whatever I taught you about respect, it's working."

Respect was in short supply in the Manhattan apartments where I grew up. I felt little of it for my parents. Beyond the natural insolence of childhood, and, later, the generational imperative to distrust anyone over thirty (most of all one's parents), I found it hard to admire this man and this woman who—despite the seemingly limitless privileges and power afforded them by adulthood—seemed incapable of making themselves or their children happy for more than fleeting moments.

The feeling, or lack thereof, was mutual. My brother and I were reminded often that everything we said and did "reflected on" our parents. And indeed, I felt and still fight feeling that I barely existed except as a shadow figure in the mirror where my parents regarded themselves.

Love, and the joyful free flow of same. I knew my parents loved me, but loved wasn't what I felt. Hugs, kisses, nibbles, snuggles, beaming welcomes, corny endearments, fair fights—basic currency among Ann, Peter, Jesse, and me—were locked in the vault of my parents' own loveless childhoods, inaccessible to my brother and me. I remember wanting to be sick, yearning for the rare cool touch of my mother's lips against my forehead—and playing catch (until my mother delivered to him a child of more appropriate gender) for hours with my father, hoping to be rewarded for my efforts to please him with an admiring adjective or even an affectionate pat.

This is what I have found, what my friends, I suspect, will find to be the hardest part of making family: stepping through and around the deficits and debris of the past, building without emotional reserves or suitable models a structure that is purely love-based, purely love-driven, and is therefore healthy for children and all living things.

Required for this task is a heart that's no less than fully open.

Unluckily, an open heart is the hardest thing to have, coming from a family that hurt.

Luckily, my kids have opened my heart, tugging at it daily for the sustenance they need as effectively as once they tugged at my breasts. Another irony: the wounds of my childhood, effortlessly tended by my children.

I look around at the stack of presents on my bed. Gifts purchased joyfully for two young men who hide so little of themselves from me that it's easy for me to give them what they want. Inside the boxes: pieces of the puzzle that is my baby boy at twelve and a half; pieces of the puzzle that is my firstborn son on the eve of his fourteenth birthday.

For Jesse the sensualist: a soft flannel bathrobe he'll rub against his cheek, coo over, and look ravishingly handsome in. (If my secret plan succeeds, he will find the robe a pleasing substitute for the towels he wraps around his slender waist each morning for the postshower scramble to his room—thereby eliminating the pile of damp towels that accumulates there weekly.)

For Jesse the artist: a Wolverine comic book he'll spend hours poring over and then reinterpreting in a series of the awesome, professional-quality drawings he's been amazing all of us with since he could hold a pencil.

For Jesse the fashion slave: A pair of red Gap boxer shorts to match (matching is everything!) his beloved Cincinnati Reds baseball shirt and matching (matching!) red knit Air Jordan shorts.

For Peter the fashion slave: brightly patterned boxer shorts—the top four or five inches of which will protrude above the waistband of the grotesquely oversized jeans that Peter, Jesse, and their friends suspend precariously from their narrow boy hips. "Sagging," this style is called. (My one stab at some good-natured teasing was silenced by a meaningful look and the two words Peter utters whenever the need arises to disqualify his mother as a judge of teenage trends: "Bell-bottoms," he said.)

For Peter the gourmet: a gift certificate for five (5) bottles of fresh-squeezed orange juice, to be redeemed at the produce market near the BART station on his way to school in the mornings.

And for Peter the surfer boy: a subscription to a surfing magazine, and a representation of the wet suit I'll buy him the next time I take him surfing: a tiny shellacked cutout of a business suit, to be presented floating in a glass of water.

What a wondrous, unsettling time in my life: saying good-bye, at once, to myself as mother (my babies' shoes and jeans are now bigger than mine); and as daughter (forsaking, at last, the ancient longing for the parents of my dreams). Coming to know at last—after forty-one years of living, fourteen years of mothering, thirteen years of therapy, and nine years of being well and consistently loved—the joy that flows from the mundane, miraculous, everyday process of making a healthy family.

Earthquake

October 17, 1989

It's five o'clock on a warm October afternoon. Against all odds, I am suddenly aware of being on the verge of a rare moment of peace.

Leaning back from my computer, I push the keyboard away from me, put aside the freelance project I'm working on, and succumb to the rosy urge that's pulling me up and out of the seductive whirlpool of frantic productivity ("must keep working . . . must earn money . . . must earn more money") and smack into the present.

The rare thing is, I'm noticing the possibility and the signs of feeling good, and welcoming them—not deflecting contentment with remorse about past mistakes real or imagined, anxieties about apocryphal calamities to come.

In the past six weeks, peaceful moments have been especially rare. On August 28—six years after Ann and I became bicoastal lovers; five years after she moved to an apartment two miles away in Oakland and got a job at a hip publishing company in Berkeley; one year after we bought a weekend cabin together; and a week after Ann nursed me through two screaming days and nights of a botched root canal, nursed me *as if she was my life partner and I was hers*—Ann and I decided to live together.

On the morning of August 28 Ann and I woke up, looked at each other, and agreed that after a half decade of schlepping clothes and kids and ourselves from one house to the other; a half decade of fighting out and loving through the astonishing plethora of differences between us, we were ready to tighten the family ties that bound us to each other and to Peter and Jesse. We called Tina, a gay-friendly real estate agent, and listed for her the attributes our fantasy house would have: bleached pine floors, sunlight in every room, a separate yet connected living space for Ann, an office for me, plus three bedrooms, two bathrooms, and a North Oakland address (so the kids could still walk to school) as close as possible to Berkeley (where their father, and all the action, are). We figured we had at least a few weeks to mull over our big decision.

The next morning Tina called and told us to hurry over to a three-story Victorian two blocks from my house. Ann and I gazed into the sun-drenched rooms, at the bleached pine floors, the attic room connected yet separate, and shared a rare moment of complete agreement. "We want it," we breathed, holding hands and beaming at Tina like two brides standing enraptured at the altar. "We do."

But the honeymoon was brief: our decision to buy our dream house instantly plunged me (because I already owned one) into double escrow, and therefore: double meetings with realtors, double forms in triplicate, and the double jeopardy of double mortgage payments, should any of the precariously positioned pieces of this simultaneous-selling-and-buying puzzle be jiggled out of place.

I will also be required, two weeks from today, to give up my beloved cozy (too cozy) cottage, whose contents even now are stacked around me in labeled and taped cardboard boxes.

And just to make sure there's enough excitement in my life, tomorrow I start the first full-time job I've had in years.

But for this one moment, I allow myself to notice that the sky outside the leaded-glass window is a flawless mirror of turquoise, smoothing and deepening as the day beckons night. I remind myself that I can quit the job if I don't like it; that the new house has three times as much room as this one, stripped woodwork, and an inspiring garden; that a nice young couple has contracted to buy this one.

Life is good, I surprise myself by thinking, and I lean back in my ergonomically correct chair to celebrate.

A rivulet of sweat runs down my rib cage. October! I crow, commending myself for having had the good sense to move, twenty years ago, to Northern California, where summer spreads each year like spilled syrup, reaching back to sop up a hunk of spring, seeping forward into fall. The morning news reported snow flurries today on the East Coast, my place of birth.

Two rooms away I hear the opening strains of a poorly orchestrated "Star-Spangled Banner." In a minute or two Jesse will call me to come watch the World Series with him—more proof of the superiority of my chosen home! Not one but two local championship baseball teams, now about to begin the duel that will prove one of them the greatest in the land. An hour or so into the game, I'll leave Jesse transfixed before the screen and go pick up Peter at his soccer game a few blocks away.

I envy my children their Bay area childhoods. Even in the poor, increasingly crime-ridden neighborhood where we can afford to live on my freelance writer's income, there are glorious green soccer fields, fathers whose schedules allow them to coach three o'clock games, short-sleeved sunny October afternoons.

Neither of my sons has ever owned a truly warm jacket, a hat, a pair of mittens. Neither of them has spent the long muffled months of winter confined to stuffy, steam-heated rooms where even a child's imagination is dulled by endless views of nothing-but-socked-in-gray out the window.

And, here in North Oakland, either or both of my sons' lesbian moms can pick them up from school or child care or a soccer game without inflicting upon them social ostracism, or worse.

I can hear Jesse chirping happily to himself as the singing and speeches wind on. Earlier today, the director of his after-school center called me at my freelance job across the Bay to tell me Jesse was complaining of an upset stomach.

"Probably just excited about the game," she said, but that was the excuse I'd been searching for to leave work early on this, my last day as a freelancer—to beat the bridge traffic on a day when everyone on both sides of it was going to be hurrying to get from the side of it where their jobs were to the side of it where the game, or their TV's, were located.

I picked Jesse up by four-thirty, in time to duly honor his alleged stomachache by pouring him a normally forbidden glass of 7UP and settling him back against piles of pillows in my bed, where he's been happily sipping soda through a bendy straw and watching the pregame festivities ever since.

After I bring Peter home to shower the Indian summer sweat and grass stains off his perennially tanned ten-year-old body, I'll wrench us all away from the big game long enough to make the ten-block drive to my mother's house for dinner. As has become common during the past couple of years, only Peter and Jesse, not their mother, have been invited for dinner—unspoken acknowledgment of the deepening estrangement between my mother and me, the gaping schism of old hurts, hostility, and despair that fractures the landscape of our shared and painful history.

But today I took a leap across the chasm, called my mother from work and asked if I could come for dinner tonight along with the kids. Maybe it was the heat that, even at eleven in the morning, reminded me of the summers when I was exiled, heartbroken throughout every moment of the endless eight weeks, to summer camp in the Poconos, where I would beg my way into the head counselor's office, dial my parents' number, and sob into the phone, "I miss you, Mommy. I want to come home *now*."

What did I miss? What made me think I would find it waiting for me, if only I could sneak up on it in the middle of a summer?

Whatever it was, I was missing it this morning, and my mother, sounding pleased if nervous, accepted my self-invitation. So tonight I am going to invest a few more hours in my relationship with the woman who birthed me.

Ordinarily, knowing I'm going to see my mother—even for the few minutes it takes to deposit or receive from her my children—provokes anxiety and dread, guilt and self-hatred. But in this sultry moment of bonus summer, with my sweet little one tucked tidily into my bed and my number one son winning (I just know it! On a gorgeous day like this!) his first soccer game of the season, I am suffused instead with anticipation. She's a good cook, my mother, and I love being cooked for, and it happens so rarely—I'm the mom in my circle of friends, the one who owns her house and has children and buys trunkfuls of groceries ·and bakes chocolate-chip cookies from scratch and stocks her pantry as if in continual preparation for impending disaster.

I calculate the evening now: we'll watch the game and eat till seven; I'll start mentioning homework at seven-thirty. Even allowing for the unavoidable delays, the kids and I should be back in our own nest by eight. Two hours. Maybe just this once, I'll escape the usual consequence of looking forward to being fed by my mother: the familiar bloated fullness in my belly, easily outweighed by the ancient yawning emptiness in my chest. Just two hours, I reassure myself . . .

I hear the earthquake before I feel it. The windows rattle; the foundation groans. The boom resounds through my toes, travels up my torso, fills my head. Before my brain can say the word "earthquake," a primal terror seizes my heart. *Is this the one . . . the end of . . . ?*

Time slows. I have plenty of time to note that this is not the crashing single thump of the other earthquakes I've lived through—but a methodical, rhythmic undulating of things that weren't meant to ripple: the bookshelves, the walls, the telephone pole outside my leaded-glass window.

Jesse! I think, but when I try to call to my son my throat is sealed. There is plenty of time, too much time, to watch and to feel as the earthquake grabs my house and throttles it like an abusive parent whose child's teeth are rattling in its head.

I gasp for breath and watch the kerosene lantern on the hall table tip to one side, right itself, tip to the other side, then right itself incredibly again.

Gas, turn off the . . . fire . . . doorway . . . I jump up, stagger into the hall. Outside—I think it's still coming from outside, all the pieces of my own house still seem intact—I hear heavy crashing and glass shattering, dogs howling, car alarms shrieking.

"Jesse!" I yell. His eight-year-old face appears in my bedroom doorway. From ten yards away I can see the yellow pallor of his skin. His eyes and mouth are big open circles of terror.

I open my arms and he runs to me through the shuddering house. As if he's in a funhouse, but this is no funhouse; Jesse barely keeps his footing as he skids along the oscillating hardwood floor.

"C'mere, Babe," I say, hearing in my own voice, as if from a great distance, the determination to sound calm and in control—like a mother. I wrap my arms around my son, pull him against my quivering chest, and position us in the center of the doorway. *Didn't they say doorways?*

In the living room, the fireplace screen rocks, topples, clatters to the floor. An avalanche of creosote and crumbled mortar tumbles noisily onto the hearth. The chimney is swaying. *Bathrooms . . . because the plumbing in the walls makes them stronger?*

Peter! I picture the soccer field, try to remember: are there light poles? Telephone poles close enough to fall on my son? Is he lying crushed a few blocks away? Ann! Whose loft office two miles away is built on landfill . . . a half block from where my new job was supposed to begin tomorrow. *Is it the world, my whole world that's . . .*

"It's okay, Sweetie," I murmur to the shivering child at my breast. Somewhere a siren wails.

It stops. The floor steadies beneath my feet. I glance back at my desk. The cursor on the amber monitor is still blinking.

"It's okay, Babe," I say to Jesse. "It's over now."

Jesse looks up at me, his face shattered. "That was a big earthquake," he says—so quickly, so young, already he is struggling to make reasonable an event that is the antithesis of reason.

"Yes," I say, relaxing my clenched grip on his body a bit. "A very big earthquake." I can almost think now. Crouching under beds? Aftershocks? Bathroom doorways? *Peter? Ann?*

"Let's go stand in the bathroom for a few minutes," I say to Jesse, pulling him with me. "Just until the first few aftershocks are over."

The phone rings. The phone? I realize I don't know if this was . . . a big earthquake, or . . . *the* big earthquake. Where was the epicenter? What is destroyed? Who is dead?

Time is moving faster now. Now that I must act, I barely have time to think. I pick up the phone, carry it into the bathroom, put my arms around Jesse again.

"Mer—are you okay?" It's Ann. Ann is alive. "Yeah," I say, anxious to reassure her. "Are you?"

"The whole building shook," she says, her voice quavering. "I was under my desk and my desk was rolling from one side of my office to the other. It almost pinned my fingers to the wall. Mer: *where are the kids?*"

"Jesse's here with me. Peter's at soccer," I say. My heart freezes; my arms are icy. I want to slam the phone down, grab Jesse, get to Peter. "I'm gonna go get him."

Everything is about survival now. And now I know what I need to survive: my hands on my babies, my lover alive. Let the chimney crumble, the two houses I own fall down, the whole world collapse—I just need my hands on my babies, my lover alive.

"Mer—be careful driving. I don't know if the streets are okay," Ann says.

"Come here. Hurry," I tell her, and hang up.

The phone rings again. Richard. "Jesse's okay," I say. "I'm going to get Peter. I'll call you when I get back."

"I'm coming over," Richard says. Of course he is—they're his kids, too. "I'll meet you back here," I say. *With both of our sons in one piece, please, God,* I think.

Outside, my neighbors are emerging slowly from their houses. Buffalo looks dazed; Deborah is crying. I let Jesse sit next to me in the front seat of the car. For once I don't lecture him about seat belts. *Safety?*

Sirens fill the air now, and smoke—I see a plume of it rising from what looks like downtown Berkeley. And a clamoring cacophony of car alarms—I never knew there were so many car alarms in the world.

I drive the route that Peter would take if he was freaked out enough to leave the game, his friends, his coach, and run for the imagined safety of his home. I don't see him until I screech to a stop in front of the soccer field. There he is—unbelievably, playing soccer.

"Stay here," I tell Jesse, and leap from the car. Could they all be in shock? There's Jack, the coach, Peter's teammates in their yellow and black nylon shirts . . . playing soccer.

"Peter!" I yell. He looks up at me, puzzled for an instant, then annoyed. I race toward him across the field.

"Mom! The game's not over till six!" he says, waving me away.

Finally I reach him, nearly tackle him to the ground in my eagerness to touch him. "Peter! There's been a big earthquake. Didn't you feel it?"

"An earthquake? So what? There's always earthquakes," Peter says impatiently. He's used to being embarrassed, in one way or another, by my intensity. Now he peers at me to see if, for once, it might be justified.

"A big earthquake," I repeat, still holding him tightly.

The coach looks around; the other kids stop playing. They see the smoke, hear the sirens. "You'd better hang on to these kids," I tell Jack. "Their parents'll be frantic."

"How big?" Jack asks me.

"I haven't heard anything yet," I tell him. "I just wanted to get to Peter. But . . . big."

Peter gets in the car. I see that he believes me—or, at least, he believes the undeniable evidence around him: the fire trucks screaming through the empty streets, the blank-faced people on their porches, the odd stillness in the smoky hot air, the near-hysterical announcers on the car radio—when he doesn't challenge his brother's right to the prized front seat. Instead, he scrutinizes Jesse's face, as if the Richter scale reading might be etched there. As, in fact, it might as well be. Jesse is ashen, distant.

"Peter didn't feel it," I explain to Jesse, to keep him from feeling, as he so often does, that Peter's reaction is appropriate and his own hopelessly immature.

"Damn!" Peter exclaims. "I always miss the good stuff. I can't believe I didn't even feel it!"

Jesse gapes at his older brother, incredulous. "You're lucky you missed it," he says flatly. "It was the worst thing that's ever happened to me in my whole life."

Ann is waiting as we pull up to the house. She throws her arms around all three of us.

Our neighbors are standing in clusters now, holding each other in the fading twilight, looking around and pointing at things. I follow Deborah's outstretched finger and see that Robert's chimney has been sliced off at the roof line. A few feet away, Deborah and Buffalo's living room window looks as if a missile went through it.

"Buffalo was sitting on the couch," Deborah is saying. "I called to him to help me get dinner about two seconds before Robert's chimney fell in right where he was sitting."

Robert asks me if I know how to turn off the gas line to my house. I look at him helplessly. Will there be fires now, too? Will there be *more* to be afraid of?

I lied to Jesse: the fear is not over. Already I know: the fear is just now beginning. My phone rings; I run inside, glad for the distraction.

"Meredith?" says my mother. "Are the boys with you?"

Hearing her voice, my old hopes bubble up burningly, like bile. "They're here. We're okay. Mom, I was so scared . . ."

"My living room is a pile of rubble," she interrupts me.

I swallow it all back down: the bitter taste of longing like vomit redigested. An aftershock rumbles through the house. "Oh, my God!" my mother cries in my ear.

"It was an aftershock, Mom. Look, I've got to get my gas turned off. I'll call you later."

"I'm coming over," she says quickly. "I want to see Peter and Jesse. I'll . . . I'll bring dinner."

And she does—the very dinner I was looking forward to sitting down at her table and eating, maybe a hundred hours ago. I cook my mother's steak in the electric toaster oven, heat a can of green beans from my well-stocked pantry on a camp stove.

From the kitchen I hear the TV blaring news, not of strikeout pitches and home runs scored, but of overpasses collapsed and a bridge destroyed—the bridge I would have been crossing when it tossed a car into the Bay, had Jesse not complained of a stomachache this afternoon.

Halfway through dinner—which I cannot eat because the greatest terror I have ever felt (or remember feeling) has filled me so completely that there is no room for breath, let alone food, in my body, even if I could manage to put some in my mouth or chew some—my mother looks at her watch, announces: "Well, the danger of tsunami is probably past by now."

My children's dilated eyes grow rounder. "Tsunami?" Peter squeaks out in a tiny voice, looking from his grandmother to me.

"Never mind, Sweetie," I tell him, and start clearing the table, while inside me an even smaller voice, the voice that was already crying out for a way to understand this, a way to breathe through this, to contain this, asks over and over, *"Tsunami? Tsunami?"*

"I'm going to sleep outside," my mother announces, and she rolls out Peter's sleeping bag in the backyard, while Ann and I move beds around so we can all sleep with our heads away from the windows that might be shattered by aftershocks, already predicted to be nearly as big as the earthquake itself—while TV stations operating on batteries announce fires out of control in San Francisco, hundreds feared crushed to death in Oakland, adobe missions collapsed in Santa Cruz, hundreds of thousands without power, water mains exploded, bridges and freeways and streets closed, phone lines jammed.

Staring silently at the television, as indeed I had imagined we would spend this carefully planned evening doing, my lover, my children, my mother, and I watch until we cannot stand to watch any longer.

I realize that my chest aches from inhaling without releasing breath; I realize that I feel I am holding the world together with my not-breathing. Tucking my children into their rearranged beds, surrounded by the neatly stacked boxes of toys and books and clothes that fill their bedroom, I realize that even knowing this, I cannot let go of my breath.

My mother offers to read the kids to sleep. Grateful and relieved, needing to take my own mother's mask off if even for a moment, I agree. I ask Ann to come with me into my workroom, where hours or eons ago I breathed and smiled and reveled in a turquoise sky, now black.

Ann and I try and fail to comfort each other. Each of us is unreach-able, wild with fear and grief. I want her to hold me—no, I want a *man* to hold me: a big, strong, unafraid man. How can I go into the future with this woman, who feels and shows as much of her feeling as I do? Is this the beginning of our new life together?

In the next room I hear the hum of my mother's voice, the unusual silence of my normally hyperinteractive children. My mother comes out of their room, her face strained and rigid. "They want you," she tells me. "I'm going to sleep."

My sons' eyelids are puffy with exhaustion, but their small, lean bodies are stiff. "It'll be okay," I tell them, lying first on the top bunk with Peter, then on the bottom bed with Jesse. "I'll be right here to keep you safe."

I scratch Peter's back, then Jesse's, then Peter's again, until both of them are breathing deeply, their worried mouths slackened at last in sleep. I sit down to begin my mother's vigil, with my back to my children and my eyes scanning the world through the windows of their bedroom—daring the world to come crashing through those windows and hurt my babies; and knowing, as I have never known it before, the futility of my bravado.

Highway 101

"Okay, Jesse: you know the rules," I say sternly, catching Jesse's eye in the rearview mirror. Our car is at a near-standstill in afternoon rush-hour traffic on Highway 101, creeping north through Marin County. Three sets of eyes—Jesse's, Peter's, and Wendy's—stare back at me, startled by my solemn tone. From the passenger seat, Ann looks at me questioningly.

"You tell me every time you want some junk food," I instruct Jesse. "And I'll stop at the next place we see. If you want a specific kind—McDonald's, Jack-in-the-Box, Burger King, whatever—tell me, and I'll make sure that's what you get." The three faces in the mirror relax into grins, nodding at each other reassuringly and bouncing a bit in their seats.

"It's a big responsibility, Jess," I conclude, struggling to keep a straight face. "The fates of the five people in this car are completely in your hands. But now that you're *eleven*, I'm sure you can handle it."

"McDonald's first," Jesse says without hesitation. His big brown eyes are fastened on mine, ready to gauge my reaction.

"Yes *sir*," I bark. "McDonald's it is!"

I gesture at Ann, and she takes a piece of paper out of the glove box. Glancing at it, she reports, "The nearest McDonald's is in San Rafael—we should be there in ten minutes." Jesse looks slightly incredulous. I realize he didn't believe we'd go through with this plan.

"Chicken McNuggets," Jesse says. "And fries. Large fries," he adds, leaning forward, still watching me intently.

"Whatever you say," I reply promptly. "All the fast food you can eat, and then some. You're king for the day, Babe."

Jesse sits back, his eyes sparkling. Ann squeezes my thigh; we exchange surreptitious grins. The car ahead of me lurches forward, and I navigate ours into the carpool lane.

"Make way for the Junk Food Express!" I cry, as we pick up speed.

"Oh boy! McDonald's!" crows Wendy, who buys organic juice and low-salt tamari even when she's broke. "What a great idea for a birthday party, Jess."

This great idea was hatched just a few days ago, when finally, after weeks of failed attempts, Ann and I cornered Jesse and told him he *had* to decide what he wanted to do for his birthday.

"I want Wendy to come," he said immediately.

"Of course, Wendy'll be there," I answered. Wendy has occupied a special place in Jesse's heart, and in our family, since she and Jesse met at a union organizing meeting in San Jose in 1981. Jesse was six months old, crawling around at his father's feet; Wendy fell in love with him— and, shortly thereafter, with his brother, his parents—and, a few years later, with Ann. Now neither Jesse nor Peter can remember a time when they didn't know Wendy. After more than a decade of the closest friendship I've ever known, I have trouble remembering that time myself.

"So, Jess . . . ," Ann prodded him, after a long, unhappy silence. Planning has never been easy for my younger son, whose gift for living exclusively in the present has frustrated and inspired me since he began demonstrating it, eleven years ago today.

"You want Wendy to come. And what else?"

"Umm . . . could we eat at Jack-in-the-Box?" Jesse asked tentatively. I feel for Jesse at times like this, when he wants something he thinks he's not *supposed to* want—in this case, to eat Grilled Bacon

Sourdough Burgers for his birthday dinner. It doesn't make it any easier that his older brother is solidly positioned at the other end of the spectrum: Peter hosted his last birthday party—having asked me to make reservations two weeks in advance—at a trendy Berkeley cafe specializing in Chesapeake Bay soft-shell crabs.

I know I don't make it easy for him, either. Jesse's culinary choices often spark a struggle between us, and within me: As the main mom responsible—half the time anyway—for his nutritional intake (as well as the development of his food snobbery), I feel compelled to urge Jesse to push his gastronomic envelope, to open his taste buds to new experiences.

In her dual capacities as Jesse's fellow plain-food-lover and guardian angel, Ann has reminded me often that many adults (herself, for example) manage to live well-rounded, healthy lives without sharing my taste in—or, more to the point, my value judgments about—food. Her support for Jesse's remarkable knowledge of, and enthusiasm for, what he likes made a deep impression on Jesse early on.

When Jesse was seven, Peter broke his wrist—his third broken bone that year—playing football after school. It was past dinnertime when Jesse and I sat in the emergency room waiting for Peter to be X-rayed, so I called Ann to ask her to bring some sandwiches. She arrived within twenty minutes and handed Jesse his favorite: Creamy Skippy and Welch's grape jelly on Pepperidge Farm white bread—the combination that, as Jesse advised us at age five, "always calms me right up."

He took a bite and looked at Ann thoughtfully. "When Peter gets hurt," Jesse said, "he tells the teacher. And then the teacher calls Mom. And then Mom calls you. You're like the doctor of love. When anybody needs love they just call you and you bring some right away."

In this conversation, in the planning of Jesse's birthday, for once, I felt free of my usual ambivalence. On this occasion, at least, I was going to lavish upon my son what I always intend, but don't always manage, to give him—and what his Mom Two, Ann, is so good at giving him: nothing less than unadulterated, unconditional validation.

"Sure!" Ann said. "Jack-in-the-Box is fine."

"It *is*?" Jesse asked, stunned.

"Or, how about this . . . ," I mused, determined to make Jesse's birthday A Big Event (because, despite his reticence, I know he'll be—we'll *both be*—disappointed if I don't). "What if we go to the cabin for the weekend and we stop at *every* Jack-in-the-Box along the way? And you can have *anything you want?*"

Jesse thought that over for a moment, and then asked, "Could we go to Burger King too?"

"Anywhere you want!" I exclaimed, thrilled to see Jesse asking for what he wanted, thrilled to be able to give it to him.

Our plan was a good one for Jesse: it freed him from the onerous premeditating, preparing, prearranging that make his birthdays—now that he's too old to let me arrange them for him—troublesome.

And our plan was a good one for Jesse's mom, too: it gave me an excuse to do what I still need to do—even now that my sons are too old to let me arrange their birthdays for them: premeditate, prepare, and prearrange to my heart's content.

The day after Jesse, Ann, and I reached our decision I went happily to work, mapping out every detail of his spontaneous celebration. I got approval from all concerned (Peter began strategizing what he would eat at each stop; Wendy got right into the spirit of the event: "I haven't had a cheeseburger in *years!*").

I applied my journalistic skills to researching our trip, and produced a list of all the fast-food outlets between our departure point (Oakland) and our destination (Ukiah, the closest junk-food-worthy town to our cabin). I now enjoy the security of knowing that at any point on our journey, Jesse will be no more than twenty minutes away from the junk food of his choice.

And, unknown to Jesse, I baked a cake, as I have every year on his birthday—a cake so loaded down with various configurations of chocolate that it borders on the truly obscene, and is therefore guaranteed to make my chocaholic birthday boy happy.

We cruise into the San Rafael McDonald's right on schedule. "Drive-through or eat here?" I inquire of my commandant.

"Drive-through," Jesse answers promptly.

"Welcome to McDonald's," crackles the disembodied voice through the gaily decorated speaker. "May I take your order, please?"

Jesse sticks his head out the car window. "Six-piece Chicken McNuggets, large fry and medium Coke—no ice," he says authoritatively.

The other occupants of the car add their orders—a disappointingly reasonable amount of food.

"That's it?" I demand, twisting around to peer at Wendy, Jesse, Peter, and Ann. "C'mon, you guys can do better than *that!*"

"And a hot apple pie," Peter says into the speaker.

"A root beer," Ann chips in.

"I'll have a milk, too," says Wendy. Four sets of eyes regard her incredulously. "I guess this junk-food thing might take some getting used to," she apologizes.

I peel a few bills from the thick wad I've loaded into my wallet, hand them to the uniformed clerk at the window, accept several large white bags in return, and point the car back toward the freeway. As Ann divvies up the contents of the bags, the air is instantly saturated with the competing and yet somehow harmonious aromas of deep-fried potatoes, barbecue dipping sauce, grease-grilled meats, sour pickle chips, and ketchup.

"How is everything?" I ask, leaning over to accept a hand-fed french fry from Ann.

"Mmmf," answers an unidentifiable voice from the backseat.

Gradually the chomping sounds abate and only intermittent burping disturbs the companionable silence as we roll along through the bucolic countryside of Sonoma County.

"Mom?" Jesse says.

"Yeah?" I ask, knowing what's coming.

"Jack-in-the-Box," Jesse says.

"You got it," I reply.

"Maybe we'd better get rid of some of this garbage before we accumulate more," Wendy says, stuffing ketchup-splattered napkins and Special Sauce–laden wrappers into the empty McDonald's bags.

Ann chuckles mischievously. "Or . . . ," she says, "we could *recycle* our McDonald's trash."

The rest of us await her explanation. *"At Jack-in-the-Box,"* she says. We're all cracking up now.

"Then we can bring the Jack-in-the-Box garbage to the next place we stop!" Peter says.

We can barely contain ourselves as we shout, "Chicken Fajita!" "Grilled Bacon Sourdough Burger!" "Curly Fries!" "Orange Soda!" into the gaping plastic mouth of the laughing clown at the Petaluma Jack-in-the-Box. At the window I hand the clerk another wad of money and accept from her another set of white paper bags.

"Mom! Mom! Here!" Jesse passes me one and then another of the three McDonald's bags packed with McDonald's garbage. I, in turn, solemnly hand the bags to the clerk, who looks at me blankly.

"You don't mind getting rid of these for us, do you?" I ask politely. The clerk stares at me for a moment. Then she holds the McDonald's bags aloft disdainfully and says, "I'm afraid that'll cost you extra." All of us, including the clerk, burst out laughing. We bid her adieu, and drive on.

Several hours and a few more samplings of America's fastest fare later, we arrive at our home in the woods. We stumble over our pitch-black dog in the pitch-dark cabin, light candles and kerosene lamps, unload groceries and ice and sleeping bags and birthday presents and the final, unrecycled bag of Burger King garbage. Our chores completed, we convene around the kitchen table for the grand finale of Jesse's birthday celebration.

I unveil the cake. What birthday spirit my family has! I think proudly. Even with sugar screaming through their veins and grease congealing in their bloated stomachs, they all find it within themselves to ooh and aah over this year's version of Death by Chocolate, my annual Jesse's-birthday special. This time it's three flavors of chocolate chips (semisweet, milk, and white) melted into triple-chocolate-mocha cake, slathered with a full two inches of butter-fudge frosting. Bless their cholesterol-coated hearts: my loved ones all ask for seconds.

Jesse blows out the twelve candles and then, with frosting lining his mouth like punk lipstick and chocolate crumbs clinging to his cheeks, he opens his presents. From me: his own racquetball racquet, so he won't have to borrow one anymore when the four of us play at the Y on Tuesday nights. From Wendy: a new set of charcoal pencils—just what he wanted, but hadn't yet asked for—and the pads to go with them. From Peter: the Chicago Bulls T-shirt that Peter alone knew Jesse had been coveting. From Ann: a boom box for his room at our house, so he won't have to carry the one from his room at Dad's back and forth twice a week anymore.

Unbelievably (considering the contents of our digestive systems), we all agree that we're ready for bed. But the day can't end until its highlights have been duly recorded in our cabin journal—in which, over the past three years, Peter and Jesse have written and drawn about such landmark family events as The Night the Fox Scared Wendy and Peter to Death While They Were Using the Outhouse Together in the Dark; The Day We Hiked to Big Rock in the Snow While Making Up a Million Versions of the Diarrhea Song; and The Time Mom Wouldn't Slow the Car Down Even Though There Was a Poor Defenseless Jackrabbit Running Ahead of Us on the Road.

Jesse writes:

> It's my birthday and for dinner me, Mom, Peter, Wendy and Ann were on a mission: to annoy every drive in clerk in Ukiah, Petaluma, or any other place in America.
>   First stop: McDonalds drive thru.
>   Code name: McDonalds, food folks and farts.
>   We would have to bring the bag to annoy the clerk at the next stop.
>   Next stop: Jack in the Box.
>   Mission: Destroy all means of laughter from Jack in the Box drive thru clerk.

Yawning, Jesse hands the journal to Ann and crawls onto his futon. Ann expands on Jesse's entry.

> For Jesse's birthday we stopped at *any* fast food place in *any* town, *any* time, *any* meal he wanted . . . *all* the way up here. A grand total of 3 orders of fries, 32 chicken nuggets, 1 cheeseburger, 1 bacon sourdough burger, 2 chicken fajitas (one just with onion, one with everything), 2 root beers, 1 small coke, 1 medium coke (no ice), 2 small orange sodas, 1 milk and a McChicken sandwich later we all sat down to chocolate cake with 3 kinds of chocolate chips . . . Are we American or *what?* Then presents and now we'll start reading *The Return of the Indian.* Happy Birthday #11, Jesse. Love, Ann.

While Wendy and I crumple discarded gift wrap into the kindling box and brush our teeth by candlelight, Ann, Peter, and Jesse settle in for the ritual that brings to a soothing close every one of our nights in the cabin: Peter and Jesse zipped into their sleeping bags, Ann in the rocking chair reading to them by battery-powered Itty Bitty Book Light. Knowing that Ann's calm, even voice will read me to sleep, too, seconds after my head hits the pillow, I stop on my way to bed to kiss my kids and my Wendy good-night.

"Was it a good birthday, Jess?" I whisper.

"Shhh, Mom," he whispers back. "I'm trying to hear the story."

I know it's not just the french fries and chocolate cake that are making me feel so full as I tuck myself into the platform bed Ann and I share. Through the window, opened to the warm May night, a soft evening breeze carries the scent of madrone in bloom. In the silence of the deep woods my lover's voice rises and falls, interrupted periodically by the three-part harmony of my children's and my best friend's responses.

I am wholly satisfied because my mission (in addition to annoying every drive-in clerk in America, that is) has been accomplished. Our wonderful, if somewhat unconventional, family has had a wonderful, if somewhat unconventional, Jesse's birthday. Thanks to Jesse's determination to enjoy his birthday, not the way he was *supposed to* want to celebrate it—but the way he *wanted* to celebrate it, we all got to take a joy ride outside the city limits of the "should-be's" of nutrition and biological determinants and ceremony.

Our family has just had a day that will drift like a leaf onto that growing pile of days, months, years that make our family life what it is. Not perfect, not predictable, not the way I or anyone else might have planned it—but good and full and real. Just the way it is.

Throw Mom from the Train

August 1, 1992

Eight-thirty on a sunny midsummer Monday morning. Peter and I are driving down Martin Luther King, Jr. Way, on our way to the Amtrak station in West Oakland. Rap music blasts from the radio. Before turning the dial to his favorite station, Peter asked my permission to do so (this ritual the result of a lecture I delivered a few months ago—when my sons became devoted to radio stations specializing in misogynist odes to gang violence—on the subject of courtesy and boundaries and who paid for this car, anyway).

As usual, Peter and I have been jockeying for control of the volume knob since we got into the car.

As has also become customary in the past year or so, we have been mostly silent during the twenty-minute ride: Peter because (I must try to understand) it is his developmental task to separate from his mother, to whom he has always been extremely close, and with whom he shared, throughout the first eleven years of his life, countless hours daily of joyful chatter.

And I because it makes me feel like the kind of dweeby mother I swore I'd never be to keep hopefully chirping questions at this once-exuberant, now-taciturn son of mine.

This firstborn son of mine, who is about to board a train that will take him three hundred miles away from me, where he will live near his beloved ocean with his aunt and uncle and cousins, where I will not see him, for twenty-eight days.

"I didn't give you my phone number at work!" I cry into the silence. My heart is pounding. I knew it! It's simply not possible for him to go.

But Peter calmly opens the glove box, extracts a pen and a small blue spiral notebook—the notebook I've transferred from glove box to glove box in each of the four cars I've owned since he was two and beginning to talk—the notebook I kept with me everywhere I went with Peter, and then with Peter and Jesse, so I could record each word they invented and then babbled so earnestly from their sweaty vinyl car seats: "hangimer" for hamburger, "reald" for world, "hostibul," "pisgetti," "incited."

Peter flips past the pages of baby words scribbled in various colors of fading ink, rips out a clean sheet, writes down the phone number I give him, folds the sheet in half, and writes "DON'T THROW AWAY" on the side that faces out. How can this boy be so competent?

We pull into the Amtrak parking lot. I have vowed not to mention, again, how much I will miss him. Instead, I comment on the architecture of the station—"Even in the most modern cities, train stations are usually neat old buildings . . ." A year ago, or maybe last weekend when he wasn't endangered by connecting too deeply with me, Peter would have launched a conversation from my comment, asked me flattering questions, flashed his intelligence at me like bright morning sunlight in a mirror. Today the conversation dies in utero.

I park the car. Peter slings his bag over one shoulder, removes his bicycle from the trunk, and begins wheeling it toward the baggage area. I follow him.

Walking behind my son, I notice his width, his height, his confidence. The gray nylon suitcase sits lightly on his back; it bent me double when I lifted it into the car. I bought that bag when my children were in nursery school, during my journalist years, when I traveled often for work, stopping in airport gift shops and local malls to buy them presents

I'd pack carefully into that bag: Chicago Cubs pencils, Atlanta Braves caps, maple sugar candy from Vermont.

Now my suitcase is filled with Girbaud jeans and Stussy T-shirts that Peter wouldn't let me go with him to buy. His announcement, a few months ago, that henceforth he would shop without me was accompanied by only a flicker of acknowledgment that up until then, shopping had been one of the special things we loved to do together.

"Oh, really? And how do you think you'll pay for all those clothes?" I'd sputtered, for want of a more honest argument.

Peter's glance was sympathetic, slightly pitying. "Sorry, Mom. I know you like to go shopping with me. But that's what *you* like. *I* like to go shopping with my friends. Think about it: did you want to go shopping with your mom when *you* were thirteen?"

In the station's baggage room, a friendly gray-haired black man offers Peter a cardboard bicycle box, helps him roll the bike into it. Peter tapes the box shut efficiently and asks the man if he can borrow a marker, with which he writes his name in large black letters on each side of the box. It occurs to me that so far, with the exception of the chauffeur service I've provided (for which a city bus could easily, and less intrusively, have substituted), I have been an utterly superfluous accessory in this process of sending Peter away.

Peter and I join the line of perhaps fifty people waiting for Train 11 to Santa Barbara. Yesterday I asked him what he thought he'd do for ten hours on a train.

"First I'll cruise around looking for girls," he answered promptly. "If I don't find one, I'll go to sleep."

Not yet fully disabused of the delusion that there might still be some wisdom I could impart to my son, I advised him to buy a few magazines. "I mean really, Hon, what are the odds that you'll find a thirteen-year-old girl traveling alone to Santa Barbara?"

"Pretty good, Mom," Peter answered. "I'm a thirteen-year-old boy traveling alone to Santa Barbara."

I note now that about half of the people on the line for Train 11 appear to be between the ages of twelve and seventeen. At least two thirds of those teenagers are girls. How could he have known? I watch

Peter sorting the girls into categories of relative desirability. I guess we're still shopping buddies after all: I predict his choices—as I've done for a decade or so in toy stores, amusement parks, Chinese restaurants, clothing stores—and watch his eyes light on one girl I've imagined him choosing, then another.

Peter moves a few feet away from me, assumes a look and matching stance of studied boredom. My last few moments with my son, and now I see that the best way to prepare him for his trip is to pretend I'm not with him.

This letting go of Peter is nothing new. Despite the four years of infertility that preceded his conception, despite the thirty-six hours of labor that preceded his birth (and nearly killed both of us)—since this child was born—I've been preparing him to leave me, preparing myself to let him go. I was better at it when he was a baby.

I wanted him to feel differently in and about the world than I do. I wanted him to swallow with the milk from my breasts the conviction that people are to be trusted, that love is not scarce, that loving arms need not be his mother's. I handed him to people frequently so he could know this, until one day while loading Huggies into the trunk of my Volvo with one hand and pressing Peter against my shoulder with the other, I agreed to hand him, swaddled in his flowered cotton crib blanket, to a woman in the K Mart parking lot, a stranger who asked if she could hold the baby—a woman who, I realized when I stepped back and watched her holding my infant son, was mildly deranged, and likely to take off running with him in her arms—and so I snatched him back.

I wanted him to know that I birthed him, but did not own him, and so I told my fingers to open, to release him the first time Peter swam away from me, snuggled one moment against my chest in the warm blue pool, his tiny cold fingers grasping at my neck, and then suddenly pushing off against me, his three-year-old feet kicking at my ribs—as he used to, but, oddly, from the outside now—paddling furiously away on his own. All those goings away: wobbling away from me on his first two-wheeled bike ride, swaggering away from me on his first day of kinder-garten, and now rolling away from me on a silver train full of girls wearing braces and bras.

Peter knows this about me: that I am determined to let him go, and that in each instance when I am called upon to do it I find it nearly unbearable. Last night while he packed, refusing my offers of help, proudly showing me the beach shoes he'd nested together, wrapping his tube of Sassoon gel in a pair of striped Gap boxers, neatly folding shirts I'd never even seen, I wondered aloud whether I'd be able to get on board with him in the morning, to help him get settled.

"I know you, Mom," he said, grinning at me. "You'll get on the train with me and you'll ask the conductor for pillows and you'll make a little nest out of pillows and you'll say, 'Here, Sweetie, when you get tired you can take a little nap on these pillows . . .' "

But as he teased me in that new way of his, the way that makes me feel at once deeply known and shoved away, he watched my face attentively. And he giggled when I showed him I could make fun of myself, too:

"It'll be like the movie *Throw Momma from the Train*," I said. "They'll probably have to kick me off to get me to let go of you"—and later, when I bent over his nearly man-sized body, stretched the full length of his bed, to kiss him good-night for the next twenty-eight nights, Peter murmured a word I hadn't heard for years. "I love you, Mommy," he murmured.

The train arrives; the crowd tenses. I become wholly focused on an immediate and finite task: to ensure that my son gets a seat, a good seat, the best seat: a window seat on the ocean side of the train.

I push my way through the line. When the gate opens I gallop shamelessly toward the first open coach. I swing myself up into the train and speed-walk down the aisle. I find an empty seat and evaluate it quickly as passengers stream by me: it's on the right side of the train, but not a window. I drop my jacket onto it in case it's the best I can do.

Peter strides past me. "Stay here, Mom," he instructs me, continuing down the aisle. "I'll see if I can find something better."

And sure enough, moments later he gestures for me to come to where he is: a window seat at the rear of the next car, a truly primo location with extra leg room and privacy. I sink into the empty seat next to his. Just as I'm about to show him the lever that raises and lowers the back, Peter exclaims, "Look! I can put the seat all the way down! Cool!"

Suddenly, my son is more animated than I've seen him in years. His sweet freckled face is open, glowing; his hazel eyes sparkling and darting. He looks out the window, he looks up at the luggage rack, he looks at the people across the aisle, he looks out the window again. He bounces up and down in his seat—a sitting-down version of that exuberant, uniquely Peter, running-while-staying-in-one-place move he's made since he could stand up—the surest sign that he's at his happiest, his most "incited."

"Cool!" Peter declares again, and finally turns to look at me.

"It's gonna be fun, huh?" I say, and hug him. He hugs me back; then a shadow clouds his face. "Are you a little scared, Sweetie?" I ask him.

He considers this seriously for a moment. "No, not scared—it's just something new, something I've never done before." This time, he reaches out for me, pulls me close to him. "I love you, Mom," he says. "I love you, too, Peter," I answer.

Peter finds a place to stash the paper bag of snacks he agreed, after much cajoling, to let me pack for him. In it, unknown to him, is a yogurt, some dried apricots, a couple of See's candies I'd been saving (a mother's habit) for an occasion like this one, some carrot sticks, a toasted raisin bagel with cream cheese. Taped to the bagel's tinfoil wrapping is a love note, much like the hundreds of love notes I've written and slipped into Peter's and Jesse's lunch bags since they started carrying their lunches to school.

"Roses are red," the note begins, as each of the notes has begun. "The ocean is blue/have a great time, surfer dude/and remember: I love you."

"You better get off the train, Mom," Peter says now.

"Okay, Hon. Now remember: call me collect anytime. And if you're not happy you don't have to stay . . ."

"Okay, Mom, I know. You better go." We hug once more; I stand to go; Peter jumps to his feet and presses himself against me. "Bye, Mom. I love you."

I walk away from him, turn back to wave, and know there has to be a moment when I don't see him anymore. Tears burn my eyes.

I push against the door of the train. It doesn't open. I tell myself I must have come in through a different door, and walk farther down the aisle. The door there, too, is unmoving. And the next one.

I notice that people aren't milling around anymore. I ask a woman who's on line for the bathroom, "Where's the door to get off the train?" She looks at me quizzically. "You *don't* get off the train now," she says. "It's about to leave."

My heart racing—I have to be at work in half an hour! I can't go to Santa Barbara! I can't *really* go with Peter!—I pry open a window, stick my head out.

"Hey!" I yell at an Amtrak worker, who's waving at the conductor to go. "Hey! I need to get off the train!" He runs down the platform, slides to a stop in front of me. "What? Why do you need to get off? Are you a visitor?"

"A visitor?" I'm dumbfounded. What does he mean? The train begins to move. "I'm a . . . a . . . *mother!*" I yell back. He waves frantically at the conductor. The train slows and stops. He unlocks the door for me and I jump out. I glance back only once, to make sure Peter was too far away from the scene of this debacle to have witnessed it.

Throw Momma from the train, indeed, I think as the train pulls out of the station behind me. I'm surprised by my tears—how quickly they come, how strongly they erupt from me. I tell myself he'll be back in a month, that this isn't really what it feels like: my son leaving me for good. But it's closer, I think. Each time now it's closer.

At nine o'clock that night the phone rings. "Mom?" Peter says. My heart sings. He called me! On his first night away!

"How are you, Sweetie? How was the trip?"

He chuckles. "Great," he says meaningfully. Clearly, there's something here I'm supposed to get him to tell me.

"What did you do all that time?"

"Oh, I walked around," Peter says. I can hear his smile through his coy, measured words.

"For ten hours?" I prompt him.

". . . until I met some kids."

Now I'm getting warmer. "Some kids?"

"Someone. A girl," Peter says, sounding utterly smug, elated . . . incited.

"You met a *girl?*" I am incredulous. Thirteen years old, and he's better at getting what he wants than most adults I know. "Where does she live?"

"Santa Barbara!" he answers. How can this boy be so lucky?

This may be Peter's version of "I told you so," but it's great news to me. Peter called me to tell me he met a girl! He hasn't volunteered the names of his friends, let alone his girlfriends, for so long I've given up asking.

"Will you see her again?" I ask.

"Yeaahh," he drawls with great satisfaction.

"Well, I better go, Mom," he says now. "This is long distance."

Yes, it is. And the least distance I've felt between Peter and me in a long, long time. Is separation our new path to closeness?

"I love you, Sweetie," I say for perhaps the tenth time today. "Have a great time."

"Okay, Mom. You too," Peter answers and hangs up.

I replace the receiver, and grin idiotically at the phone. Disconnected, and as profoundly connected to Peter as ever—and always.

WHAT IT'S LIKE
TO LOVE NOW

First Date with Ann

I'm barely awake when the clenched fist in my abdomen sends me an unmistakable two-word message: bladder infection. "Fuck!" I swear aloud, naming at once my reaction, the cause of my condition, and the activity I'm afraid this condition will preclude.

I planned to become a lesbian today, and while I'm pretty sure lesbians don't call what they—*we*—do "fucking," it's what I've always called sex and will, until someone teaches me something better. Which is what I was hoping a semistranger named Ann would do, about five hours from now.

Sitting on the toilet dribbling pee and wincing at the all-too-familiar searing sensation that follows, I curse my ill-fated decision to give sex with Rich one last try. Was it two nights ago, or three? I can't remember . . . as usual. Which is one good reason that my ten-year, two-child, one-mortgage, two-car, one-checkbook marriage is ending. I'm counting on Ann to give me another one (good reason, not marriage. That fantasy will come later).

"Not bloody likely," I fret, noting the bright drops of blood in the toilet. Is that a smidgen of relief I feel at the thought that a medical restriction might come between me and my long-anticipated new sexual identity? I grab the bottle of sulfa pills out of the medicine cabinet, promising myself, as I've done each morning since my husband left our home six weeks ago, to scrub out the razor hairs and dried-on shaving cream blobs once and for all.

Before I can set off for my rendezvous with destiny, I've got to get the kids to nursery school. Tying their sneakers is so painful I'm wondering how I can possibly pull off a tryst. I explain to their teacher that Peter and Jesse's dad will be picking them up tonight, limp stiff-legged out to my car, and struggle to stand up straight—so to speak—long enough to pump a tankful of gas.

So far, I admit to myself as I head north out of San Jose, the big day isn't going terribly well.

By the time the San Francisco skyline comes into view, the drug has kicked in. So has the high anxiety. Ending a marriage is one thing. People do that every day. Becoming a lesbian is another. People only do that every day on *Donahue*.

I barely know this woman. We spent three days together, along with twenty thousand other people at a publishing convention in Dallas, eleven months and one marital separation ago. I thought she was a boy until I saw her name on the book she was at the convention to promote: *One Teenager in Ten: Writings by Gay and Lesbian Youth*. She thought I was a married straight woman until she caught the lusty look in my eye. Until she read the poem I sent her as soon as she got home to Boston and I got home to San Jose—ambiguous in intention, but undeniably horny in inspiration. We exchanged equally ambiguous letters and phone calls throughout the next year. When Ann called to say she was coming to visit her brother in California we began a series of awkward negotiations to determine the nature of our impending liaison.

"I'll stay with my friends in San Francisco. You and I could meet for lunch . . . if you have time," she offered.

"You could stay with Rich and me; we could all hang out together," I countered.

"I could just come meet the kids," Ann responded, beating a hasty retreat around the bush.

And then, six weeks before Ann's scheduled arrival, four years' worth of marriage counseling came to an end and Rich moved out. Days after his departure I called my one lesbian friend, a therapist, and asked her where someone would go if someone wanted to have an affair with someone of the same gender who was coming for a visit from an unnamed East Coast city. And someone's house wasn't a possibility because it was where someone's husband would stay with someone's children while someone went off for the weekend to have sex with someone she'd never had sex with before (who happened to be a woman).

"It's about time," applauded my advisor, who'd had not-entirely-covert designs on me herself. "Go to a gay resort on the Russian River. Try Fife's or The Woods. And tell *someone* I hope everything . . . *everyone* comes out great." She was still chuckling as I hung up the phone.

I called Fife's. "I'd like to reserve a room for two . . ." So far, so good. I was pretty sure the guy on the other end couldn't tell I wasn't really gay. Yet. ". . . with twin beds."

Long silence. "Twin beds?" he repeated, incredulously. Clearly, this wasn't a request he got often. "All we've got are queens," he'd answered imperiously, sounding very much like one, even to my uninitiated ears.

"Well, it's for me and a *friend*," I stammered, "and we don't really want to sleep in one bed . . ."

"Hold a sec," my tormentor snapped. I heard his muffled voice, then another man's. Then laughter.

"Turns out we have a couple of twins we can roll into a cabin," he said. I hoped fleetingly that he meant twin *beds*, and that I wouldn't be charged extra for a ménage-à-twins. This was going to be enough of a challenge with just Ann and me in the room.

"I'll take it. Thanks," I said, and promptly broke into a full body sweat.

But all that was weeks ago. Before I'd prepared my still-husband, my best friend, my uncomprehending two- and three-year-old sons, and my journal for my upcoming journey to The Other Side. And before I'd managed to get this goddamn bladder infection.

And now, bladder infection and last-minute terrors notwithstanding, I'm on my way. Slowly. I'm having to stop every few minutes to pee, and the truth is, heterosexual marriage—especially the kind I had, in which sexual encounters were easily prevented by bladder infections, nonspecific apathy, or imperceptible shifts in the atmospheric pressure—is looking pretty appealing. I'm not sure what's *less* appealing right now: the thought of letting the seam of my jeans, let alone a new lover, touch my lower chakra—or the thought of embarking on yet another new phase of my thirty-four-year-old life.

I pull up in front of the house where I'm to meet Ann, and practice my Lamaze breathing. It doesn't do a bit more for me now than it did when I was screaming for mercy in labor. I knock on the door, and the woman I've imagined myself in bed with for the past eleven months answers it.

She's very small. She's smiling. I think of a photo of herself she'd sent me, ten years old, with braids down to her waist. I wish she still had those braids. I wish *I* had those braids. We hug stiffly, unembracingly. I realize she is exactly the same size as I am. My bladder aches, my heart pounds, my brain's taken the last train out of town. "Hi," we both say. "So you were really there all that time," I say. She nods and smiles again. When she's not touching me, she seems so small.

Ann slings her knapsack over her shoulder and we get in the car. "I've never been to the Russian River," she says. Having spent seventeen years as a heterosexual woman grappling with the ethics and feasibility of faking orgasms, I am faced—and so early in my career as a lesbian— with deciding whether or not to fake previous homosexual experience. "Me neither," I say.

Fortunately, Ann initiates small talk as we head across San Francisco. I, meanwhile, have been overcome by acute respiratory distress. My lungs seem to have collapsed, and I'm desperately trying to suck some air without making my condition—this new condition—apparent to my unsuspecting suitor . . . suitress?

The next words I speak are to an Alhambra Water delivery truck driver, twenty minutes later, when I finally get enough oxygen to my brain to realize that somehow the car I'm driving is heading south— back to San Jose, and away from the Russian River.

"How do I get to the Golden Gate Bridge?" I manage to squeak out.

The truck driver glances at my license plates; he seems surprised to see that the car isn't a rental. "Do you have a map?" he asks. I glance at Ann to see if the weekend is over yet. She seems quite unconcerned. I realize then that she and I are very much unalike. By this time, I would've asked, snidely, just how long she'd lived in the Bay area (twenty years, in my case). I would've asked, ever so patiently, if she wanted me to drive. I would've told her to let me off at the nearest lesbian bar so I could find myself some competent, *real* lesbian worth spending a weekend with.

"I'm getting to see more of the city than I'd thought I would," Ann says, with no detectable sarcasm. I apologize, she shakes her head and smiles, and we fall silent. Once we've left the city and are zooming up the right freeway in the right direction, I steal a surreptitious peek at her chest. Pay dirt! Her pale blue button-down shirt is gapped between the middle two buttons, providing me a clear view of her braless, petite, but undeniably female breasts. I allow myself a moment of disappointment—they're not quite the voluptuous kind I'd dreamed of—before acknowledging that, like her body, her breasts are about the same size as mine.

We arrive at Fife's. I park the car. Together, silently, we approach the registration desk. It is not just my heart and bladder that are pounding now. My fingernails are pounding. My eyelashes are pounding. I say my name to the man behind the desk.

"Ah, yes!" he exclaims loudly enough for all the real gay people in the fifty-acre resort to hear. "The ladies with the *twin beds!*"

Without looking at Ann, I snatch the keys from his hand and slink back to the car.

"I just thought . . . ," I mutter in Ann's direction as we approach Cabin 7. "It's okay, Meredith," she says, her smile a bit stretched now. "Whatever you want to do is fine."

What I want to do, I realize as we let ourselves into Cabin 7, is lie down. With Ann. I don't care about the food I've left to spoil in the car or what my husband will think or all the years I've spent longing for sex with a woman, or even the resounding pain in my bladder. I don't know what I want to do, once we're lying down together. I just want to do it. Just like I wanted to with John Melnikoff in fourth grade. Just like I wanted to with Paul when I first saw him hawking his underground newspapers outside our high school. Just like I wanted to, at one time, with my clearly soon-to-be-ex-husband.

The most unexpected thing about this feeling is that it's so utterly familiar. I always thought lust would feel different when it wasn't heterosexual.

I really do want to have sex with this person, I realize to my own great surprise. I really do want to have sex with this *woman*.

But not just yet. Before I can cross the line that I have approached and avoided for thirty years or so, I must avoid it awhile longer. I say I need a nap. Ann says she'll go for a walk. I declare that I'm not really tired. I jump up and suggest a walk together. Ann and I walk along the narrow sandy path to the river, and there, on the rocky riverbank, I am overwhelmed again by the magnetic pull of gravity, or lust. So I do. Lie down. On my back, with my too-small breasts and my fantasies pointed at the sky. Because I simply cannot stand up when I am this close to Ann, this close to my dream.

She stands with her left foot brushing my right thigh, skipping flat rocks across the slow-moving muddy river. She places three sun-warmed stones carefully on my stomach. She might as well have reached down and caressed my clit. I'm sure she can hear the gathering and dripping of juices between my legs. I wonder if this is lesbian flirting. If she feels what I feel. If she would believe that I feel what she feels.

We go to a restaurant for dinner. She eats a burger; I toy with my tortellini. "I thought most lesbians were vegetarians," I comment. She winces but says patiently, "I'm not."

It's getting dark out. Ann orders a beer. "Are you an alcoholic?" I ask. (I restrain myself from confiding that I've read that many gay people are.) She asks why I'm asking. I ask how old she was when her father died. She asks if I'm nervous about going back to our cabin, about going to bed. I nod. She says, again, "Meredith, we don't have to do anything you don't want to do." We go to the cabin. What *do* I want to do?

I unpack the nightgown I've purchased for this occasion—a flannel one, to prove my intimate knowledge of lesbians' affinity for flannel. I go into the bathroom to put it on, peeling the sopping, sticky underpants off my inflamed genitals. When I come out Ann is in one of the twin beds, wearing a white cotton T-shirt. I wonder if that means I won't get any points for the flannel. I wonder what else, if anything, she's wearing.

I climb into the empty twin bed. I'm shaking; my teeth are chattering. I think of my husband, my children. I close my eyes and see a movie of me getting up, getting into bed with Ann, her arms folding around me, her fingers doing things between my legs no man could ever know to do, my hands squeezing her breasts, her nipples against my nipples. If I ever had a bladder infection, I can't remember it now. If I ever thought I was kidding about this lesbian thing, I was wrong.

I kick the blanket off my legs, leap up, and slide into bed with Ann. She puts her arms around me and breathes deeply. I am quaking inside and outside. She says, even now, "It's okay, Meredith. We can just hold each other."

My body has a need that's burning a hole through the mattress. My brain is hanging on for dear life to what remains of my heterosexuality. Ann strokes my arms with her soft, small, hairless hands. I think of the night, just a few short weeks ago, when Rich and I told our sons we were separating. I think of how Peter asks every day when Daddy and I are going to live together again. Ann's hand brushes past my breast. My cunt clutches. I pull away slightly.

Eventually Ann falls asleep. I listen to her kitty snores and think of the nights I've spent kicking Rich so he'll stop snoring, snores that shook the bed and made sleeping together intolerable and finally impossible. Snores that made me wake up angrier even than I'd fallen asleep.

Ann's digital watch beeps on the hour. After the fourth beep I slip out from between her arms, pull on my clothes, and walk into the dark night. The air is scented with jasmine, like the jasmine Rich planted along the fence of our home in San Jose. There's a phone booth outside the hotel office, with a night light that guides me to it. I dial my home number, where my husband and children sleep.

Before it rings, I hang up. What will I say? "This is your last chance to save me from this," I imagine myself saying to Rich. "Please . . . save me from this."

I know he can't. I know I can't. I know that "lesbian" isn't really the right word, that my need to separate my life from Rich's and my need to feel Ann's hands and mouth on me are two different needs with two different sources. I know that I have lusted after men, and that I now lust after a woman who sleeps just a few yards from where I stand. I go to where she is.

Crossing the Line

APRIL 24, 1993

Ann and I are facing each other, holding hands and looking deeply into each other's eyes, as Reverend Perry has instructed us to do.

"Now each of you in turn," the Reverend tells us, "say what it is that you love about your partner. Then, say why this ceremony is so important to you."

As Ann leans forward to whisper in my ear, the air hums with the sound of fifteen hundred other brides and grooms doing the same thing. In front of us, two gorgeous young men in matching tuxes are wrapped around each other, tears coursing down their tanned, smooth-shaven faces. Next to us our friends Catherine and Barbara are renewing the commitment they first made ten years ago.

"We gather together here today," Reverend Perry declares, his raspy Southern voice booming from the huge speakers on the steps of the IRS building, "to stand before our friends, the larger society, and the United States Government to proclaim our right to love each other. We stand here in the light with glad hearts, knowing that, despite the lies that have been perpetrated against us, love makes a family—nothing else, nothing less!

"Now, participants, turn to your beloveds and repeat after me: 'I pledge myself to recognize your needs, and to encourage your full potential, and to love you even as I love myself.' "

"Better," Ann and I mouth to each other at the same instant. We dissolve into weepy giggles.

" 'We proclaim together our rights as couples,' " Reverend Perry concludes, " 'in hope that the day will come when not only our own community will recognize our relationships, but the laws of our country will also.'

"Couples, you may kiss. Congratulations to one and all!"

All around us men and men, women and women, women and men are hugging, laughing, kissing, crying.

I feel a hand on my shoulder and turn to see the man who has touched me. My heart clutches. He has the ghost look—the look of the people in the death camps, the look of humans aged savagely not by time, but by inhuman forces: emaciated, balding, hollow-cheeked and sallow-skinned. Standing arm in arm with him is another gaunt man, his face stained with the purple bruises of Kaposi's sarcoma and a pink carnation pinned to his lapel. I notice that they are wearing matching gold wedding bands.

"Here, ladies . . ." The man holds out a single long-stemmed red rose, wrapped in lavender tissue and resting on a bed of ferns.

"This is for you girls," he says, ". . . *from Oregon.*"

The man looks at Ann and then at me, searching our eyes to see if we understand the significance of his words, and his deed. Of course we do: gay people in Oregon are under siege.

In the last election the Oregon voters rejected—too narrowly for comfort—one of the many insidious antigay ordinances that have been worming their way onto ballots all over the country. Already the right-wingers in Oregon are organizing to try again. Not long ago in Salem, a lesbian activist and the gay man who shared her home were incinerated, firebombed in their beds as they slept.

"Thank you," I say, taking the rose, my eyes brimming once again.

The two men and Ann and I fall into each other's arms.

"Congratulations, girls," the man's lover says to us.

"Congratulations, boys," we say to the two of them.

Hugging these spindly, wasted men's bodies reminds me of the last time I hugged my dying best man friend, Peter Babcock. He was here with me six years ago, the last time we came to Washington to march for gay rights. There's a snapshot in my head of Peter: backlit by the sinking sun at day's end, grinning his lopsided grin as I took his picture with half a million marchers, the Washington Monument, and the AIDS quilt behind him. It was Peter who pushed me, as he so often did, to go to the '87 march. "You know you'll want to write about it," he said. And then he gave me a place to publish what I wrote: Volume One, Issue One of *Out/ Look*, the magazine we worked on together for years.

Tomorrow when the new squares are added to the quilt, Peter's will be among them. I have a vision, suddenly, of Peter back here with me—and then, of all the men back here with us. *How many of us would there be, if we hadn't lost nearly half of the men? How many who are here today won't be here for the next one?*

The ceremony completed, speakers take the stage. A man who, with his lover, is suing the District of Columbia for a marriage license says angrily, "Seven million gays and lesbians voted for Clinton in November. A million of us will be here tomorrow, marching for our civil rights, and Clinton has fled the city. He should be here. He should witness this."

The crowd explodes in applause, clapping in time to the chant: "*Where's Bill? Where's Bill? Where's Bill?*"

"Where's Hillary?" yells a bridegroom standing near me. "I wanna do her hair!"

I love these people, I think, standing there in the capital of my country with the sun in my eyes, my arms around Ann, and an ear-to-ear grin on my face.

I love the emotional roller-coaster ride of being in this emotion-driven movement. (It's not for the faint of heart—nor the inflexible of temperament—this business of fighting for laughter and love while facing down a tidal wave of bigotry and death.)

I love the wit and the soul and the resilience of this gay and lesbian culture.

As the crowd begins to disperse, I look down and see that the asphalt beneath our feet is covered with hundreds of pink, green, yellow, and lavender hearts drawn in chalk. Inside each one is a scribbled declaration of love.

"Tim and JD—8 years and forever"; "Sue Loves Sue"; "Aaron and Derrick, Married 4/24/93."

Some of the wedding participants crouch on the ground now, squeezing their own messages into the small spaces left between the others.

Catherine and Barbara come close for postnuptial hugs. "I hope it doesn't rain for a few days," Catherine says, nodding at the colorful chalk hearts we've left behind on the gray pavement like confetti strewn on the steps of a church. Arms linked, the four of us stroll across the street for some honeymoon people-watching.

A couple of brides wearing T-shirts, vests, and jeans have spread an elaborate picnic—replete with damask tablecloth and napkins, gleaming silver flatware, and crystal champagne goblets—on the lawn that rings the U.S. Treasury building. A couple of grooms are offering hunks of chocolate wedding cake to their fellow newlyweds.

Two older women, both wearing trailing white lace gowns and tiaras on their matching crew cuts, are toasting each other with bottles of Perrier and posing for photographs. One bare-chested man carries another over the "threshold" (the curb in front of the IRS building); they kiss deeply amid hoots and cheers from the people around them.

I love these people.

I loved arriving at Dulles airport last night, exchanging knowing grins with the throngs of men and women with rainbow flags in their hands, pink triangles on their duffel bags, determination in their eyes, and their politics on their T-shirts.

But Mom, he *is* the right girl.

Nobody knows I'm a lesbian.

I can't even THINK straight.
(Worn by as many men as women.)

And then there was the T-shirt I saw on a burly unsmiling man in a black leather vest—the slogan that grabbed my heart and froze the smile on my face:

<blockquote>
All I Want:
the cure,
and my friends back.
</blockquote>

I loved being on airplanes full of demonstrators yesterday . . . every conversation becoming a group discussion.

One woman to another: "Your mother's fine with you being a lesbian? My mother can't even *pronounce* the word 'lesbian'!"

Woman's voice, from several rows away: "Mine, either . . . she can manage 'gay' but she can't spit out the L-word."

Man's voice from the bathroom line: "Listen, girls, my mother can't even say 'gay.' Do you think a million of us in the streets might add a few words to our moms' vocabularies?"

Whoever's writing all those books about the crisis between men and women, I thought, listening to the happy intragender chatter issuing forth from all corners of this intergender group—those books about men and women living on two separate planets—hasn't been to Planet Queer lately.

I loved the gay flight attendant wearing "Lift the Ban" dog tags on his United Airlines uniform, who fraternized happily with us throughout the flight and then announced over the plane's sound system as we touched down, "Welcome to Washington. Thank you for flying the friendly skies of United. Enjoy your stay. And—march with pride." (Raucous applause.)

I love being surrounded by queeny gay men who unleash the not-so-closeted queeny gay man in me.

"Only the color scheme has changed," sighed the man wearing Freedom Rings in his ears as a planeload of San Francisco marchers filed onto our second plane of the morning, a connecting flight from Chicago.

"Do you think there's even a *smidge* of a chance they'll feed us something *edible* this time?" Twenty minutes later, he and I were still dishing the dishes they serve on airplanes these days, designing *fabulous* gourmet meals that could easily, we were certain, be nutritiously prepared and attractively presented even under the *tackiest* of kitchen conditions.

"Oh boy, here we go," said Ann, rolling her eyes at me affectionately, her hand on my thigh. (It's okay to put your hand on your same-sex lover's thigh on an airplane when the whole plane, and all the planes on all the airlines for several days running, are full of gay folks on their way to our nation's capital to change the world so that someday, it will be okay to put your hand on your same-sex lover's thigh, on an airplane or anywhere else, *any*time.)

"Queen Mer rides again," Ann proclaimed. "You get right into your New York mode, don't you: talking to everyone, getting everyone's opinion on everything. You're really in your element with these boys, aren't you, Babe?"

Indeed I am. In my element with these boys (my bond with my friend Tod: he's a process-everything lesbian trapped in a gay man's body; I'm a dish-'n'-brunch gay man trapped in a lesbian's body. We understand each other completely).

And in my element with these girls—my sisters—too.

Not since the sixties have I felt so at one with a movement. It's like coming home: coming back to Washington to demonstrate with several hundred thousand of my closest friends.

(I remember the first time, twenty-six years ago. My boyfriend, Paul, and I chartered a bus to take fifty Bronx High School of Science students to Exorcise the Pentagon. On the way to Washington we practiced going limp, waved at the cars full of fellow demonstrators on the New Jersey Turnpike, sang Jefferson Airplane and Country Joe and the Fish songs. I wore my best outfit: a thigh-high knit minidress with peace signs woven into the fabric and knee-high suede Capezio boots.

Twelve hours later we rode home in silence. Slumped against each other, our clothing torn and stained, knees scraped raw, faces streaked with tears. Maced, chased through the mud, and beaten bloody by baby-faced National Guardsmen, we were no longer children, no longer innocent: sobered and transformed in a day from peaceniks to revolutionaries.)

Not since the sixties have I had such a sense of being right where I want to be—in the center of history—in just the right place at just the right time. And—a miracle!—with just the right sexual orientation, no less.

How did I get so lucky? I have marveled at my good fortune a thousand times since I woke up in a gay resort with my arms around Ann nine years ago.

How did I get lucky enough to be gay right now—at the best time in history to be gay, at the best time in my life to be gay, in the best place on earth to be gay?

I've lived every day of my lesbian life grateful to be living it in the San Francisco Bay area, world headquarters of gay liberation, and grateful to have had (for the most part) welcoming arms to come out into—in my personal and in my professional life.

My career as a freelance journalist was scarcely affected by my transition, in 1984, from married suburban wife to unmarried urban lesbian. The mostly male magazine editors I wrote for accepted—some with admirable grace, some with unprecedented, transparent sexual titillation—the changes in my byline that paralleled the shift in my sexual identity. And so in that year I went, in print, from "Meredith Graham" to "Meredith Maran Graham," and finally, on my first "gay story," to "Meredith Maran."

In 1987, hired into a company the gayvine warned me was dangerously homophobic, I served a brief and utterly miserable stint in the closet. There I learned what it's like for most people to be gay: changing pronouns, concealing details, avoiding Monday-morning questions about my weekends, and maintaining the chilling distance (toxic for a relationship junkie like me, whose drug of choice is people) required to keep a fundamental fact of my life hidden from my coworkers.

The '87 gay march ended my emotional exile. I returned from Washington euphoric, unwilling to keep what I'd found there to myself. I shared my march photos and my tears with my boss, who hugged me and said she'd known I was a lesbian when she hired me; and with the people on my staff, who, it turned out, had been waiting for me to open up and give them a chance to be close to me; and (in the women's bathroom) with a closeted lesbian coworker, who started easing out of secrecy soon thereafter. Ruing the wasted months of isolation, I resolved to go into the future assuming the best of everyone—and choosing my surroundings carefully so that the assumption would cause me no harm.

Ann's picture has been on my desk in each of the three socially responsible businesses I've worked for since then. Gratefully (if somewhat cynically) I have come to see that being a joyously visible lesbian has enhanced my value in the marketplace. It's been good for my career because, for companies that sell progressive politics along with their products, employing a highly placed lesbian is good for business.

With one painful exception, my transition was readily accepted by friends and family, too. I've never concealed my bisexual longings, and I've always chosen friends who understand—or, in many cases, share them. So when Rich moved out and Ann moved from Boston to be with me, my closest friends' situations were not so different from mine. Wendy had just left a woman for a man; Joanne was leaving her husband for a woman, and Sue was soon to become lovers with a woman friend.

(Until they were nine or ten, Peter and Jesse thought all women were bisexual and all men were straight. There was little in their experience to contradict this theory.)

My brother, recalling all the girls and women he'd watched me panting over all my life, said simply, "It's about time." My sister-in-law was intrigued and slightly envious, imagining (not entirely inaccurately) limitless feasts of oral sex. My mother, whose Berkeley friendship circle included several gray-haired lesbians, was unruffled. And, in one of our more harmonious postdivorce conversations, my joint-custodial ex-husband acknowledged he'd "gotten off easy."

"If you were with a man now," Rich said, "I'd have to share my kids with another father. Another mother is much less threatening."

Painfully but not unexpectedly, my wide-open heart was wounded in a most familiar way by my father. He responded to my news by informing me that being with a woman was just my latest attempt to "do the most dramatic thing, take up every fad, get attention any way you can, as usual."

Two years later, finding me still engaged in the "fad" of my relationship with Ann, my father told me he had "evidence" that my lesbianism was damaging Peter and Jesse (whom he'd seen maybe fifteen times in their six- and seven-year-old lives). Prohibited from enforcing his disapproval as he did throughout my adolescence—by forbidding me to see every boyfriend I ever had—he instead forbade Ann to see him.

The day before a holiday dinner he hosted with his third wife, my father (whom my kids called "Sid") called to tell me that Ann (whom my kids called "Mom Two") was not "family." Therefore, he said, she was not invited to his home for our Jewish family's Christmas celebration.

"Two years or twenty-five years, it makes no difference," my father told me in our last conversation, the conversation that—despite his belated attempts to retract it—estranged him not only from his unwanted lesbian daughter-in-law, but from his daughter and his grandsons as well. "A homosexual relationship will never be legitimate, and Ann will never be a member of this family."

Separating myself from my father devastated and relieved me. Even as I struggled to construct an interior wall that would shield me, at last, from his judgments, I learned that Peter *was* being hurt—not, as my father claimed, within our family—but by Peter's third-grade classmates who shared my father's views of homosexuality.

Unknown to Ann and me, Peter had gone to school one day and announced to his classmates that his moms were gay. And unknown to us, he'd been, for weeks, the target of their taunting. Finally Peter confided in a teacher who he sensed was "on our side." She called me, came out to me, and suggested that we meet with the other gay parents and teachers she knew of at our school. The meetings that resulted from Peter's disclosure in turn resulted in mandatory antihomophobia training for the staff and students, and a school that was safer for kids in all kinds of nontraditional families.

Peter and Jesse learned from this experience a seemingly contradictory lesson that has guided their behavior ever since: Be careful whom you tell; and, good things can happen even when you tell the wrong people.

Throughout Peter's and Jesse's remaining years in elementary school, their same-sex parental unit was a nonissue. When their friends spent the night at our house, we'd all have waffles together in the morning. When their friends spent weekends with us in our one-room cabin, Ann and I would zip a roomful of tousled boys (and their teddy bears) into sleeping bags and retire to our conjugal bed.

Then junior high school and adolescence came upon us. Peter and Jesse left behind their teddy bears and most of the kids they'd hung out with since kindergarten—and started entertaining their new friends at their father's house only. After two years of eerily quiet weekends, Ann and I asked if it was their father's heterosexuality that was making his house so popular.

"It's just 'cause we're at Dad's on Friday nights—that's when everyone gets together," Peter said. "Dad has Sega Genesis," Jesse said, "and he lets us mess up his house, not like *you* guys."

The truth came out, so to speak, when I did—in a full-page article about lesbian mothers in *The San Francisco Examiner*. Before the piece appeared, I told the kids I'd use a pseudonym if they were worried about their friends finding out I was gay.

Without a moment's hesitation, Jesse said, "Of course you should use your real name, Mom. Otherwise, what's the point?" Peter asked for some time to think about it. The next day he came to me while I was washing the dishes and told me he'd made a decision.

"I'm going to call everyone I'm close to," my fourteen-year-old son told me, "and tell them you're gay. Today. Then I won't have to worry anymore about my friends coming over here and seeing the pictures of you and Ann. If they can't handle it, that's their problem."

This time around, Peter's disclosure had better results. His best friend, Carlos, said, "God, Peter, I've known about your mom and Ann since we were five years old." His new girlfriend, Sara, asked, "How could you even *think* I'd have a problem with that?"

Meanwhile I grapple with *my* problem: that old mother's problem, guilt. "If I could have stayed married to their dad, if I wasn't gay, if I wasn't so out about it . . . ," the tape runs, in a voice sounding very much like my father's. "They love Ann, they have a happy mother, they're learning up close about tolerance and justice . . . ," my own voice answers—most of the time.

How did I get lucky enough—brave enough—to finally cross the line? The line I'd approached and avoided since the day I screwed up my courage and nibbled on Gail Rosensweig's ear in the coat closet of Mrs. Fink's first-grade classroom. (I told Gail I wanted to see if her ear tasted or just looked like an apricot. I lied.)

The line I teetered on, all those years of knowing I wanted something the other girls didn't want. Falling madly in love with Alan and Amy at exactly the same time in exactly the same way (age ten). Being in love with Paul, and sleeping on my hands to keep them from Cathy's body when I lay tremblingly near to her at pajama parties (age fifteen).

Following Judy home from Berkeley Women's Health Collective meetings like the lovesick puppy I was, and having my beloved boyfriend of two years pack up and leave me the day I confessed my unrequited—"disgusting," he called it—lust for her (age twenty-one).

Getting married to a nice man, a reliable man, a comrade if not a passion-mate, in hopes of satisfying the insatiable me who had felt, since birth, *wrong* for wanting what I wanted: attention, tenderness, orgasms, girls, boys; everything from everyone, all the time (age twenty-three).

Avoiding, and then, near the end of the married years, approaching . . .

Devouring lesbian novels on the train home to San Jose from my six-dollar-an-hour job at Good Vibrations, San Francisco's woman-friendly sex-toy store. Renting porn movies of women making love to women, then coming suddenly alive in my moribund marital bed (intended for the pleasure of men, these grade-Z movies worked wonders on me). Meeting real live lesbians. (The job in the vibrator store helped.) Artlessly grilling the lesbians I met. ("Who puts whose arm around who at the movies? Don't you like fucking? Do you fight about housework?")

And finally, sitting in the family room of our tract house in San Jose, at the desk my husband built for me, writing a lusty poem to a woman I'd met at a publishing conference in Dallas: a real live lifelong lesbian named Ann who lived (safely and permanently, I thought) three thousand miles away.

How did I get lucky enough to be gay with Ann?

(When he was four years old and struggling to grasp the concept, Jesse asked, over and over: "Daddy's the one you're straight with, and Ann's the one you're gay with. Right, Mommy?")

How did I get lucky enough to find, in my first woman lover, everything I'd wanted since I first realized such a thing was possible? In one small package I got a best friend; someone to borrow Jockey bikinis from in emergencies; a twenty-four-hour sexual supermarket (always open, always offering the good stuff I'm hungry for). I got another mother to mother with, another mother to mother me. A girl as unlike me as any girl could be: soft-spoken, androgynous, independent. A girl just like me, who writes down her dreams and lives from her heart and cares about nothing more than she cares about loving, and loving well.

Striding out into the full-spectrum sunlight of my sexuality summoned up parts of me long buried in shadow. Not just lesbian me, but femme me (freed at last to wear ribbons in my hair and garden and bake without fear of being "too much of a woman"). And butchy me (happily dressed in suits and ties, supremely confident in my womanness). And, unexpectedly, bisexual me (*men,* now, are the exotic creatures!).

With Ann I have felt more safe, and more insecure than ever before. She gives me good loving—wholehearted, knowing, passionate, and steady—and, her devotion evokes my deepest ancient ache: the unfulfilled fantasy of the perfect, all-forgiving mom.

I bloom in the softness of her arms, the protectiveness of her embrace, the enveloping sense of being *always loved.* And, I quake with terror when I walk down a dark city street with my five-foot-six, 110-pound woman lover who cannot shield me, as my six-foot-four, 210-pound husband did, from a world unsafe for women. I turn away from her laser attention sometimes—I feel suffocated and overwhelmed by all that intensity, sometimes. And, I cling to her when she turns away from me, when she draws the line and says: I'm here; you're there.

Ann's unwillingness to scale the perilous sheer wall of my motherlove fantasy; to compromise the boundaries that keep our passion throbbing; to soothe me with promises borrowed from the kind of straight marriage I ran to her to escape, kept me unbalanced and captivated and grasping throughout our first many years together.

Three months after we'd become lovers, four months before her eagerly anticipated move to California, Ann and I were walking hand in hand through a Vermont wildflower meadow when I was suddenly struck by the implications of my "lifestyle change."

"You're never going to marry me!" I cried.

"True," she agreed, smiling and squeezing my hand.

"But how will we stay together?" I demanded.

"We'll wake up every day and see if we're still in love," Ann answered unhesitatingly. "If we are, we'll stay together. If we're not, why would we want to?"

In love? After ten years in a hopelessly merged marriage, I found Ann's criterion—and her soon-to-be revealed insistence on separate checkbooks, separate domiciles, separate friendships, and three nights each week spent separately—unthinkable and destined to divide us. If this was what it meant to be a lesbian, I wasn't sure I had it in me, after all.

We'd been together ten months when Ann announced her plan to go on a two-week vacation with Ellen, her first lover (twenty years ago) and best friend (since then). I wept, I wailed, I threatened, I whined every day and night for a month. When all else failed I tried reasoning with her.

"How would you feel if I went away with Rich, or Paul, or Danny?" I asked, attempting my first imitation of an adult since Ann announced her plan to desert me.

"Horrible," she answered. "But it's different with women. With lesbians. Ellen's my best friend. Anyway, Mer," she added, "you know you'd feel this way even if Ellen had never been my lover. You just don't want me to leave you, ever. You feel abandoned every time I try to have my own life."

I cajoled and argued and cried until the day Ann left and through all the bone-achingly lonely days she was gone. But I knew she was right.

A million hurt feelings later, celebrating our first anniversary at the

Ukiah Motel 6, I toasted Ann with lukewarm champagne in motel-issue plastic cups and made an afterglow-inspired, slightly drunken proposal.

"If we're still together after ten years," I said, "let's get married."

Ann looked at me intently for a moment. I looked intently back at her. And then we collapsed on the disheveled floral polyester bedspread, laughing hysterically. Never mind the legal sanctions against marriage between two women. It was the reality of how badly we fought, how often we fought, the differences between us—WASP versus Jew, lifelong lesbian versus blossoming bisexual, type B versus type A—that made our one year together amazing; ten years, surely, impossible.

At the end of this decade together, as when it began, Ann and I regard each other, and what courses between us, with wonder verging on disbelief. As is true in the community and the movement of which we are so much a part—nothing is assumed, sanctioned, or guaranteed. Everything is invented as we go. Joy flips suddenly into grief; grief into rage; rage into healing; healing into openhearted love.

And love—isn't love the engine that drives us all? The glue that brings together one with another, the many within each one? Good strong love that welcomes all the parts, shines light into the dark corners, makes us safe enough to suffer and to relax, to march and to moan, to finally be fully who we are.

One Friendship

JULY 22, 1993/5 P.M. PST

I've known Zoe so long and I know her so well that I can tell what kind of conversation we're going to have as soon as I hear her voice on my answering machine.

Most of the time she's calling to check in and catch up. "Hi, Mer. It's me. How *are* you? Call me."

Maybe we've exceeded the month or two we normally go between phone calls. Maybe she's just had some therapeutic insight about her own childhood, or mine; or she's just met or said good-bye to a particularly promising or disappointing man; or her building is going co-op and she's deciding whether to buy her apartment, or move to another rental—maybe a loft in TriBeCa.

When I get that kind of message from Zoe I wait until one of the rare moments when we're both awake, and the long-distance rates are cheap, and I have a guaranteed hour of solitude ahead of me, and I can stretch out in a hot bath or in bed and spend some uninterrupted time in the longest friendship I'm likely to know in my lifetime.

Some of Zoe's messages are news bulletins: tantalizing, mischievous, designed to provoke my curiosity and, thereby, a speedier response. "Me-e-r, it's me. I have something to tell you, and you're really going to want to hear it . . ."

When I leave Zoe a message like that, it's usually to report one of the major milestones I've shared with her over the years: when I was moving out of my parents' house, moving to New Mexico, to London, to San Francisco; when I was breaking up with Paul, moving in with Danny, marrying Rich; pregnant at last; sleeping with Ann; buying a house; exchanging one job for another.

But Zoe's life markers are more internal, less reducible to headlines than mine. She's always lived in New York, has never been married, does not have or want children, did in fact decide to stay in her apartment, and doesn't talk much about her highly successful career as a set designer.

Once in a while Zoe's calls are sparked by an encounter with some New York character from our girlhoods. Two years ago, for instance, she bumped into Mr. Hrbeck, our seventh-grade social studies teacher and shared love object. Mr. Hrbeck had been, in the first year of our friendship, the unknowing beneficiary of the greatest passion Zoe and I—or womankind, we were certain—had ever known. We fed our precious obsession a rich diet: on weekends, multiple viewings of *The World of Henry Orient;* on school days, covert love-missions which entailed ducking in and out of doorways along Second Avenue while furtively following the man of our dreams home to his pregnant wife.

"I introduced myself, but of course he had no idea who I was," Zoe sputtered between giggles. "Mer," she added, "he's still so *sexy!*"—a revelation that provoked a side-splitting bout of long-distance hysterical laughter.

Or Zoe's messages might involve the sometimes psychic, often inexplicable and always remarkable overlap between our seemingly noncontiguous lives—like the one she left me the day after Thanksgiving last year.

"Guess what, Mer," said her disembodied voice on my machine. "We really *are* related! Call me if you want to hear more . . ."

Of course, I called her immediately—before I put down my keys, listened to my other messages, or even stopped to consider the cost of the midday call. Interrupted periodically by my excited little screams, she told me that the woman sitting next to her at her family's Thanksgiving dinner had turned out to be distantly related, by marriage, to Zoe—and a second cousin of mine. Thus was proven the theory of our connectedness that Zoe and I had conceived when we were thirteen years old.

From the day we met—while she was waiting on the corner of Eighty-second and Lex to walk to Robert F. Wagner Junior High School with her soon-to-be-supplanted best friend, the chronically tardy and (as I repeatedly reminded Zoe) glamorous but superficial Gigi Monroe—Zoe and I knew that something deeper than mere friendship bound us. Nothing less than family ties, possibly going back several generations to our ancestors in Kiev, could explain the multitude of coincidences that proved our friendship was cosmically destined to be.

For example, both Zoe and I—*even before we knew each other!*—slept with our hair painfully wrapped around rollers the size of soup cans, an attempt to straighten the kinky curls that we both concealed under scarves we tied tightly around our heads on especially humid days. And: Zoe's cousin and my brother were both named Drew—not the usual Andrew, but *Drew*! And: Zoe's brother and my brother (who also became best friends, though briefly) *were both born on Valentine's Day 1956,* with the same birthmark on the same spot on the tips of their identically shaped noses!

Finally, all these years later, our theory had been confirmed. And with unexpected benefits: not only did I get to be Zoe's cousin—but, thanks to Zoe, I also got to know my blood cousin Ellie, who turned out to be the most kindred spirit in my family of origin.

There's one kind of message that I dread getting from Zoe. My heart sinks when I hear her voice on my machine sounding uncharacteristically humorless, her words ominous: "Meredith, I need to talk to you. Call me as soon as you can."

Zoe left a message like that nineteen years ago, when her first serious relationship broke up. And sixteen years ago, when she called to tell me that her mother was dead. And five years ago, when her aunt was diagnosed with cancer. And nine years ago, the time she was mad at me for not being supportive enough when she had thyroid surgery.

And today.

I knew when I heard Zoe's message that she must have been distressed when she left it. Her voice was tightly strung, devoid of its usual laughter-on-the-verge-of-eruption lilt. But the real giveaway was that she left me instructions I certainly didn't need: "Call me back between noon and midnight."

Why would Zoe remind me of the hours she keeps? I know her schedule as well as I've known each of her phone numbers since 1963. The opposition between Zoe's night-owl biorhythm and my proclivity to function only between dawn and dusk is one of the most glaring differences between us—and it's the difference that nearly ruined our friendship in its early days.

Thrilled with my wonderful new best friend, I spent every Saturday and Sunday morning pacing my parents' apartment, glaring across Lexington Avenue at the drawn drapes that blocked my view into Zoe's mother's living room, stopping every twenty minutes or so to beseech Zoe, via the baby-blue light-up Princess phone beside her bed, to wake up and help me plan our adventures for the day. Which was half gone, according to my timetable, by the time Zoe was roused and ready to see me at noon.

Finally Zoe—always the mature one, the boundaried one, even at age thirteen—instituted the routine that saved our relationship. She informed me that I would henceforth be forbidden to call her before ten-thirty on weekend mornings. To reward my restraint, Zoe promised to cheerfully receive me at eleven.

Even since I moved to California twenty years ago (thereby establishing a three-hour time difference in our favor), communicating with Zoe still requires massive mathematical forethought. Just as when we were adolescents, I still have to wait a few hours after I get up to avoid waking Zoe before her designated daybreak (now noon). The only time we're in sync each day is at two A.M. Eastern Standard time; eleven P.M. Pacific—just before we both go to sleep.

When I heard Zoe's message today I knew there were only two

possible explanations for its tone and content. Either she needed to tell me about something really bad that had happened to her, or she was really angry at me.

In either case, I couldn't afford to wait for the rates to go down. I called and got her outgoing message: a most professional-sounding Zoe issuing sharply enunciated directions—intended for the directors who call her to meetings at a moment's notice—for reaching her via beeper.

We are so different, I thought, as I often do. My answering machine is currently broadcasting the latest in a series of my highly unprofessional and, in the unsolicited opinion of many callers, obnoxious rhyming rap messages.

And so much the same. There's never been anyone else I can talk to the way I can talk to Zoe. No other friend who was in my childhood with me, who actually knows my parents. And no one else I laugh with until she's peeing in her pants and I'm rolling on the floor, convulsed and gasping, the way we used to do when we were thirteen and still do now, on the rare occasions when we find ourselves in the same place at the same time.

July 23, 1993/9:30 P.M. PST

I'm just easing myself into a steaming bubble bath when Zoe calls me back. "It was funny to hear your voice yesterday," I tell her, although, of course, it wasn't. "I was thinking about you before I got your message. Maybe because I knew I'd be having dinner with Toni, my editor—she's out here visiting from New York."

After a brief silence Zoe asks, "What *time* last night were you having dinner with Toni?"

"Six-thirty my time," I answer.

"Wow," Zoe says. "At nine-thirty last night I was having dinner with Mara. She'd just read a Bantam book that Toni edited; we ended up having this whole conversation about you and Toni—while you and Toni were having dinner together in Oakland."

"Weird," I say, although this kind of thing happens between Zoe and me all the time. But I'm too nervous to get into the Twilight Zone with her right now. I take a deep breath.

"So Zoe: you sounded upset yesterday. What's up?"

"I need to talk to you about your last visit to New York," she says. She sounds as strained and anxious as I feel. "I've been angry at you since then. I need to tell you about it so I can start really talking to you again."

I hate this, I think. I feel myself going under, losing oxygen, being sucked into the familiar undertow of despair and self-loathing. *What did I do to hurt Zoe?*

Struggling to stay afloat, I remind myself: Zoe and I have loved each other for a long, long time. I probably won't die from this.

"I want you to," I say. "I want you to tell me."

And so she does. She tells me that during my five-day visit to New York last winter—when I was meeting with publishers who wanted to buy my book, doing New York things with Zoe and a couple of other friends, taking my hometown by storm—she felt I wasn't paying attention to her. That I was self-absorbed and insensitive. She gives me several examples to illustrate each point. She says she didn't feel heard by me.

"H-u-r-t?" I ask, hopefully.

"H-e-a-r-d," she says. "Like that night when we were on the bus going uptown. I was telling you something really important about my family and you interrupted me to get the shirt you'd bought out of my bag. Do you remember that?"

Of course I do. It's my curse and my salvation that I remember every goddamn thing that anyone ever says, eats, wears, or does in my presence. From my own vantage point, of course.

That night on the Broadway bus: I remember that one minute Zoe was talking about food issues in her family, and the next minute I was telling her more than I'd ever told anyone about my own distress about food and weight. I remember that when it was time for me to get off the bus, two stops before Zoe's, I felt too opened up to end the conversation and too vulnerable to continue it. So I walked the four blocks from the bus stop to my hotel feeling raw and unfinished and lonely, crying and shivering as I plodded in my California "winter coat" through the crusty gray slush.

I tell Zoe all of this now. And then I wonder aloud, "How did the focus of that conversation shift from you to me?"

"Exactly," she says.

I'm swimming against the current now in shark-infested waters. *Selfish bitch,* I hear my mother, my father, my own angry self snapping. *No wonder you're having so much trouble with your friends. Who could stand you?*

Who could? In the past few months I've had difficult, teary conversations very much like this one with each of my three closest friends. The details and the roles vary—we wrangle about money differences and age differences and lifestyle differences; about who listens, who dominates, who nurtures, and who withholds; about who pays, who drives, who wants more contact, and who is unavailable; about who is willing to work all of this out, and how.

But the unspoken, underlying questions are always the same: Do you love me as much as I love you? If I risk really being there for you, will you really be there for me? *Are you like my mother, or is it safe for me to get close to you?*

More than anything or anyone—more even than work or children or lovers—it's always been my friendships that have bound me to my life. My friends who have given me perspective, solace, safe haven, fun—and the redeeming assurance that I am lovable over time.

When I was a child in elementary school, a hippie on a mountain in New Mexico, a frustrated housewife stranded in suburban San Jose, a creative director toiling in the cement canyons of San Francisco—the thing I looked forward to most in any day or week was the time I spent with friends. Going home with Helaine after school, sharing an after-dinner joint or two with Trippy and Lee, sitting in front of the fire with Wendy, listening to a lecture at Zen Center with Diana.

I've spent many of my favorite moments flopped across one girlfriend's bed or another's, talking and giggling and crying about boys and parents and clothes and jobs and illnesses and relationships and therapy. But somehow, these days, I find that my friendships aren't as effortless or as joyful as they used to be. These days, my closest friendships seem to require more processing, more pushing and pulling, more *work* than ever. And I wonder why this is true.

Have I sought out friends who, like me, are operating at an emotional deficit, running on the emptiness of an unloving childhood? Is the difficulty my friends and I have in trusting each other deeply, reeling each other in and out freely, the inevitable contest of un-mothered adults struggling to love one another as we ourselves were never loved?

Has my life—have I—been changing too fast and too much for my friendships to keep up?

Is it a generational thing? Last week I sent my brother a postcard: two lone people sitting in a huge empty auditorium beneath a banner that reads "Annual Convention, Adult Children of Normal Parents." Are my friends and I trying vainly to wrest from each other the sense of wholeness and rootedness that other generations absorbed organically from family, from ritual, from community?

Or is it just too damn scary nowadays to love a friend enough to last a lifetime? Because friends don't stay in the village anymore. Wives, husbands, lovers might be convinced or contracted with to stay, but friends go.

Friends get jobs that take them to other cities and jobs that take all their time. They fall in love with people who live far away, or get divorced and go somewhere far away to start over. When their kids leave home (or never appear), friends do too; roaming restlessly from this solo vacation to that three-month retreat. Friends make new friends and—as we've all been trained by our disposable cars and pens and answering machines to do—they don't assume it's worth the trouble to keep the old.

Friends get cancer and AIDS and die much too young.

Sometimes I can focus on the good stuff about my friendships and sail past the disappointments. Sometimes I feel grateful to be held in the wide, gentle web of the people who love me. I notice that two or three or sometimes five friends call me in a day. That I am woven into the lives of some remarkable people, closely and then loosely and then closely again, as these remarkable people are woven into mine. That we tell each other when we have our best or worst sex ever; when our articles and job applications are accepted or rejected; when our parents appear in the flesh, or otherwise; when we're sick or love-struck or broke or happy. That our lives are better daily because we know each other.

Sometimes, though, I watch *thirtysomething* reruns and wonder why my friendships aren't like theirs. Why my friendship "circle" is actually a disparate, disassembled constellation of connections: Zoe in New York; Wendy in Santa Cruz; Alan in Vermont; Sue in India; Paul and Lee and Sharrett still in New Mexico; Mariah in Virginia; Catherine in Washington. Even my Bay area friends are scattered across bridges and freeways; most of them don't know each other and few of them have relationships with my children.

In the absence of community, I invest heavily in continuity. With each birthday I am more aware of how difficult it is to make the kind of new friends who will someday be old friends. As my past becomes the greater portion of my life, it becomes increasingly important to me to have friends who have lived at least some of it with me. No new friend will have known my children as children, the way Wendy and Molly did. And a lifelong friendship begun tomorrow could only last half as long as my lifelong friendship with Zoe.

And so we do the hard work required to keep the old: stare down the demons, send our mothers out of the room, and slog through the sludge so we can finally get on with loving each other.

"I felt really judged by you, too," Zoe is saying. "Every time I told you about some situation or relationship I was trying to work through, you said, 'Just get over it already—here's how I did it.' "

"I didn't mean to judge you," I say. "I was trying to be helpful."

"It's not *helpful* to assume that you're the standard by which we should all be judged," Zoe says angrily. "My style is really different from yours, Merry. Our trains are on different schedules. You've eaten a piece of bread and swallowed half your water before I sit down at the table. Quick dramatic solutions don't work for me. And I didn't like being told that your pace is superior to mine."

I hate this. "Well, I don't like knowing that every time I come to New York you're squeezing me in around your jobs," I snap. "Like two summers ago when you couldn't go to the Yankees game with Ann and the kids and me . . ."

". . . And I apologized a thousand times and you still wouldn't look at me the rest of the time you were here," Zoe says. "That really hurt me. You *knew* I had to go to that meeting."

"Well I guess it's not just our pace that's different," I say haughtily. "It's our priorities, too. I would *never* do that to you."

"Never do what to me?" Zoe asks, sounding genuinely mystified.

"Prioritize work over our relationship," I answer.

"Merry," Zoe says wearily, "you make this choice—to see things I *have* to do as things I decide to do instead of being with you. I don't know why you do that to yourself."

"That's like saying people choose their parents," I snap. The echo of Ann's voice saying exactly what Zoe has just said to me intensifies my anger. "I don't *choose* to be less important to you than your career is."

I sink back against the warm porcelain of the tub. Hot tears splash onto the scented bubbles clinging to my body. "It's not just your career, either," I say, my voice catching on the words. "I've felt this way since we were thirteen years old. I'm always waiting for you, always wanting to be with you. And you're always doing something else."

Zoe answers gently, as if she's speaking to the lonely thirteen-year-old, not the petulant forty-one-year-old who's trying to make the loneliness of then sound reasonable now.

"Mer," she says, "I had a great time with you and the kids and Ann in New York that summer. I thought you did, too."

JUNE 1991: NEW YORK CITY

Of course I did. Except for the hours I spent sulking because Zoe was at the theater or shopping for props in SoHo, I had the best time I'd had there since Zoe and I were teenagers running amok through Manhattan. Better, maybe, because this time around Zoe and I had willing accomplices: my lover, and my sons—who were just the ages Zoe and I were when we first did the things we were doing now with them.

Zoe took us to the Carnegie Deli, where Peter's and Jesse's jaws dropped—but not wide enough—at the sight of the five-inch-tall corned beef sandwiches and two-pound hunks of chocolate cheesecake. She took us to the pizzeria near Robert F. Wagner Junior High, where she and I used to buy slices for fifteen cents; and the Canal Street knisherias where our grandfathers bought a shtikl of a pickle for a nickel.

And on our last night in New York, Zoe taught Peter and Jesse the trick she and I had mastered when we were their ages: how to gain admittance to the exclusive stores and hotels Zoe and I loved to scheme our way into simply because they wanted to keep us out.

"Remember," Zoe instructed my sons, as we stood outside the Plaza Hotel in our pizza-stained T-shirts and cutoff jeans, "lots of celebrities walk into this hotel looking grungier than you do. Just keep your nose in the air, walk as though you belong here, and whatever you do— don't start laughing till we're back outside. Ready? Let's go!"

Like earnest ducks and ducklings the five of us marched through the Plaza lobby. By keeping our jaws clenched and avoiding each other's eyes, we almost managed to complete our circuit through the hotel's restaurants, bars, and bathrooms before our laughter exploded. Then, as Zoe and I had done thirty years earlier, Peter, Jesse, Ann, Zoe, and I ran gasping and guffawing past the disapproving guests and concierges and doormen, and collapsed in hysterics around the hotel fountain.

"You got punished when your mother found out we did this, remember, Mer?" Zoe asked me, when we were all breathing normally again.

"Did what, Mom?" Peter asked. I turned to Zoe. She's often better at remembering events from my childhood than I am.

"What we just did," Zoe answered.

Peter and Jesse stared at me, disbelieving. "How'd your mother— how'd Rita find out?" Peter asked me.

Zoe laughed. "How good is your mother at keeping secrets?" she asked my sons. They rolled their eyes and shook their heads.

"She wasn't any better at it when she was a kid," Zoe said.

JULY 23, 1993/8:15 P.M. PST

"Mer?" Zoe says now. I feel my anger evaporating in the face of all those memories, all that history, ancient and modern.

"I think maybe you're right," I say quietly. Zoe says nothing. Now, for once, she's waiting for me. Or maybe, I think, she's been waiting for me longer and more often than I know.

"I mean about choosing to feel like I'm competing for your attention," I explain. "I have that problem in all my relationships. With Ann, and with my other friends.

"I think that's why I have a hard time giving you my full attention. I'm always competing—always trying to make sure I don't get taken advantage of. Not giving too much in case I don't get as much back. I'm sorry, Zoe. I know you love me. It's just that old mother thing . . ."

Once again, there is silence on the line. Finally Zoe says, "I'm impressed, Merry. With your lack of defensiveness. And with how quickly you could figure all that out."

"I'm impressed with you, too," I say, my voice quavering again. "I'm so glad you cared enough about our friendship to talk to me."

"I do care, Mer," Zoe says. "You know I love you. Our relationship means so much to me."

"Me too," I say. "But I never have the nerve to bring hard stuff up when I'm mad at someone. I can't believe anyone will stick around till the end of the conversation. God, Zoe—given your childhood, I'm surprised you don't have that problem too. You're so brave."

She laughs hollowly. "I never even entertain the notion that anyone will stick around at all," she says. "So I guess with me it's a case of nothing to lose."

My doorbell rings. Downstairs, Joe howls. "What time is it?" I ask Zoe.

"Eleven-fifteen here, eight-fifteen there. Why?" she answers.

"Shit—I gotta go. My friend Kathryn's here, and I'm in the bath-tub," I say.

"Be right there!" I yell in the direction of the front door, hoping to be heard above the barking.

"Who's Kathryn?" Zoe asks.

"A new friend," I answer. "A writer. I like her a lot. We're doing a little writing group together on Thursday nights. Listen: can I call you back in a couple of days, see how you're feeling after all this sinks in?"

"Okay," Zoe says.

"Oh, and Zoe—I know most of these calls end up on your bill. I seem to get your machine every time I call you . . ."

I hear Zoe inhale sharply. *Did that sound like a judgment?* I worry.

Quickly I add, "So if you get a message from me, call me when you get home and I'll call you right back on my dime. Okay?"

"Great," Zoe says. *She sounds okay,* I think, relieved.

"I love you," I say.

"I love you, too, Mer," Zoe says. "Talk to you soon."

I leap out of the tub, wrap myself in a towel, and gallop down the stairs. I don't want to keep my new friend Kathryn waiting.

After Zen

I'm driving home to Oakland from a four-day retreat at Sonoma Mountain Zen Center. I'm listening to a Thich Nhat Hanh tape, "Being Peace," and thinking about my lover. I'm chuckling because I'm watching myself listening to a self-improvement tape while earnestly fantasizing about improving someone else (Ann).

Pulling into the driveway of our house in Oakland, I realize that the four days of meditating, weed-pulling, and silence have had some effect. The jasmine that spills over our redwood fence fills my eyes, my nose, and I'm smiling. Its leaves have never looked so deeply green, its flowers so delicately pink, its perfume so pungent. Normally I scowl at the jasmine because it needs pruning. Now I'm smiling at it and remembering the very first time I smoked pot, the very first time I took acid. How everything was suddenly so . . . 3-D, and so perfect. How my taste buds would purr at greasy fried shrimp at three A.M. How I once took an afternoon to drink a glass of ginger ale because it took that long to have a conversation with every bubble. So it's true what the new age prophets promise: spiritual practice is a suitable substitute for drugs. Just say *zendo*?

In the kitchen, putting away the food I brought and didn't eat, I'm suddenly feeling nervous about the next time I'll see Ann. Tonight, after she comes home from karate class. I'm wishing I was back in the Zen Center kitchen, where people are silent and self-contained, where the outline of every utensil is drawn neatly at its place on the wall, where after every meal the leftovers are neatly labeled and dated and put away with the oldest food closest to the front of the refrigerator and the label facing out. After eight years, our relationship has come to a junction. Arrows point in every direction; no destination has been agreed upon. Any place of peace seems too far away to go.

Living together has been hard for Ann and me—harder, even, than we had imagined, all the years we contemplated and postponed it. Moving day was two weeks after the earthquake. On that day, Peter broke his wrist at school; the couple who'd agreed to buy my house backed out of the deal, leaving me with two $950 mortgages to pay; and the transmission fell out of Ann's Volkswagen bus. The whole first year was like that first day. One aftershock after another. The earthquake damaged our dream house—not irreparably, but up-settingly—and the earthquake damaged me. I couldn't breathe, couldn't rest, wouldn't drive on a bridge or a freeway, couldn't trust the earth or our new house or Ann or anything or anyone to stay still and hold me.

Like me, Ann needed comfort, and safety, and reassurance; what she had on her hands—and in her kitchen, in her bed, and next to her name on a deed of trust—was a leaky vessel. I was teetering toward collapse, alternately grasping and enraged, needy, terrified, self-absorbed—just as Ann's mother had been throughout her childhood. In reaction to her mother, then, and me, now, Ann withdrew and lashed out, came close and went away. Deeds of trust have been few and far between for us, these past two years; we have fought about everything, about nothing: about whose toothbrush is whose, about who is Mom and what constitutes motherhood, about couches versus futons and how many nights a week we should sleep together and about whether we have made a terrible mistake, choosing each other.

And yet—on weekends at our cabin, chopping wood together and making morning coffee for each other; and on Tuesday nights with Peter and Jesse, eating spaghetti and laughing at stupid family jokes and exchanging looks above the heads of the boys we both love better, most of the time, than we are able to love each other or ourselves—we have somehow found our way back to each other. Our way back . . . home to each other.

In my suitcase is a letter I've written to Ann. In it I vow to turn my focus inward, to interpret my anger as a clue to some buried hurt, to stop using it as a blunt scattershot weapon against her. I tell her I want to go on being lovers with her, that this desire is second only to my desire to learn to know and tell the truth about myself. I think I can do both. Between each glorious line of insightful self-reflection is scribbled the invisible ink of my persistent, unrepentant hope: that she will change and I won't have to.

The front door opens. Who's coming home at noon? Joe runs into the kitchen with Ann close behind. She looks radiantly beautiful to me, like the jasmine, glowing, pink-cheeked and vibrant. Her face is a face I love. Her face is smiling at me with love. I put down my bag of dried apricots—the apricots Ann sneaked into my suitcase, although in my leaving we were so uncertain. We hold each other. Lust beats between us like a trapped butterfly. Joe whines and scrabbles at our intertwined ankles. "I took him to the vet on my lunch hour," Ann says. "I didn't expect you home till tonight. How was it?"

I'm happy to have nothing to say. I just want to look at her face, to feel the love that suddenly seems miraculous. She's peering at me to see if I've decided to break up with her while I was away, although we promised each other not to do that. She seems to see that I love her, too. She tells me this story:

The second night I was away Ann took Peter and Jesse out to dinner. She told them what I've been wishing she would tell them for several years: that she was physically and sexually abused in her family from a very young age and that this history makes it hard for her to feel safe in the world and in our family.

My twelve- and thirteen-year-old sons responded to this information more lovingly, sensitively, and insightfully than any of the few adults—including their mother—Ann has shared it with.

Jesse leaned up against her, rubbed his cheek against her shoulder, acknowledged that despite his many complaints over the years, he guessed it was a good thing after all that Child Abuse Prevention does presentations in their school every year. He said he wished Ann's school had had a CAP program, too.

Peter asked if that was the reason Ann didn't want us to visit her family when we were in Boston last summer.

Both of them looked into her eyes and told her they were sorry such terrible things had happened to her.

Ann, Peter, and Jesse talked for two hours in the restaurant. When Ann went to pay, the cashier said, "Those are two sweet, sweet boys you've got there." Ann was so ecstatic about what was happening between her and the children she'd helped raise for the past eight years that she didn't even feel embarrassed to know their conversation had been overheard.

The words come out of Ann's mouth and land directly in my heart. In my absence—an absence I'd felt guilty about, as I'd felt guilty about every separation from my children in the past thirteen years—the most powerful healing had begun. Ann had stepped out of the perimeter and into the center and we had finally become a family.

In a downtown Oakland restaurant, with their mother in a Zen monastery and their Chicago Bulls hats pulled over their eyebrows, their $120 Air Jordan shoes and wannabe–Afro-American haircuts, my sons had poured out the love that had been poured into them, and then some.

I stare at Ann, captivated and self-conscious. I don't want to sound like some born-again Buddhist, but all I can think is, It's a gift. After four days of silence I don't remember how words work between people. "It's a gift," I say finally. "I feel like you've given me a gift."

Ann looks quizzical. Could four days of meditating, or four days of separation, have transformed her perennially discontented Jewish lover into this taciturn, appreciative Buddhist? Or could it be that I have been so affected by her pain and her distancing in our family that its ending can bring such tongue-tying relief? I see the wheels turning, and watch as she decides to rest her ever-analytical mind. We hug strongly and Ann leaves to go back to work.

WHAT IT'S LIKE
TO STAY ALIVE NOW

Biopsy

Ann parks the car in front of the surgeon's office. Without looking at each other or speaking, we get out and lock our doors. She loads the two-hour meter with change. I watch her feeding one quarter and then another into the slot. I think, In seventy-five cents' worth of time, either way, I'll be getting back into this car. In seventy-five cents' worth of time, I'll know if I have cancer.

Three months ago, on December 17, my best friend Wendy's left breast was amputated. On January ninth during a routine checkup my doctor, Maureen, found a walnut-sized lump in my right breast. Yesterday I asked Wendy, "How did you get into a car and willingly let yourself be driven to the hospital where they were going to cut off your breast?" "Some weird combination of numbing out and wanting to live," she answered.

And now here I am, delivering myself to the knife. Numb, yes. Wanting to live, yes. But, of course, this is only the biopsy. In a few minutes a piece of flesh—composed of mercifully benign or life-threateningly diseased cells, the pathologist and I will want to know—will be cut out of my body. Out of my breast.

Ann holds the door to the doctor's office open for me, offers to speak to the receptionist for me, and I let her. Not yet sliced nor diagnosed, already I feel myself to be the weak one, the invalid, the one for whom my lover and others will need to speak and cook and care. Ann sits down beside me on the pink velveteen couch. Facing us in a matching pink velveteen chair sits a Japanese man in a gray three-piece suit, flipping with determined concentration through a rumpled copy of *People* magazine.

I have promised to congratulate myself for every step of this process that I manage to accomplish, and I tell myself now: "You walked through the door. No one dragged you. You let Ann give them your name. You are sitting and waiting on the couch." Ann puts her hand on my thigh. I can feel its clamminess through my jeans.

A door into the waiting room opens. A sandy-haired nurse in a white polyester pantsuit and brightly flowered apron smiles at Ann, then at me. "Which one of you is Meredith?" she asks. There have been some interesting moments during my seven years of lesbianhood. This is definitely one of them. I glance at Ann, wondering if she loves me enough to go into the operating room and have her breast cut open in my place.

"I am," I say. As though I am already anesthetized, my lips are dry and my voice seems to echo.

"Then you must be Ann," the nurse says, smiling. "I'm Nancy. I know you're both really scared right now, but I want you to know that this will be easier than you think. I'm not just saying that. Only one out of twelve biopsies turns up a malignancy. We've done thousands of these and we can pretty much keep you from feeling any pain during the procedure."

Nancy sees she will get no reward for her efforts, and asks if either of us has a question. No, we've asked them all of the surgeon we call Barry, who accepts—indeed, seems to rejoice in the knowledge, or in his exemplary acceptance of the knowledge—that Ann and I are lovers. He hugs each of us in turn whenever we enter or leave his office, and asked Ann without embarrassment (on his part, anyway) if she'd felt the lump during lovemaking, if she's noticed any difference in its size or shape since it was discovered.

Barry has also encouraged Ann to be present in the operating room during my surgery. In exchange for agreeing to be locally, instead of generally, anesthetized, I get to hold Ann's hand as Barry cuts a hole into the breast that Ann's hand, that same hand, has caressed in tenderness and in passion maybe a thousand times.

I walk on my own legs to the surgery room and lie down on the table where, three months ago, Barry first confirmed Maureen's diagnosis: a large lump in my right breast. After which he ushered Ann and me into his office, turned on a tape recorder, and said, "I'm going to record everything I tell you because you're afraid right now and you won't remember much of it on your own." And then he told us that he was "ninety-five percent sure" the lump was benign—"ectopic breast tissue," he called it—and when I asked if it was possible that I was growing extra breast tissue to replace the missing breast of my best friend, Barry proved that he was worthy of referral by my nontraditional lesbian feminist doctor, and answered without hesitation, "Absolutely."

Because he was so sure it wasn't cancer, Barry wanted to give the lump a chance, through the next two or three menstrual cycles, to go away on its own. He said the odds were fifty-fifty that it would.

This talk of odds was sickeningly familiar. I'd heard a lot of it from Wendy's doctors in the past few months. Before her biopsy: a 75 percent chance the lump wasn't malignant. After her biopsy, the only unequivocal statistic: 100 percent chance she had cancer. Eighty percent chance of recovery if she had a mastectomy; 60 percent chance of survival if she had a lumpectomy instead. The likelihood of recurrence was 20 percent greater if she refused chemotherapy and had surgery only.

And the odds that she'd ever be able to conceive a child, they told Wendy, who, at age thirty-five, was finally in a relationship that promised her what she'd been yearning for all of her adult life—the chance to have a baby—were the same as my odds of avoiding surgery: fifty-fifty.

The process by which these authoritative-sounding numbers were derived seemed only slightly less mysterious to me than the process by which intelligent, instinct-driven people like Wendy and me were convinced to bet our lives on them.

"I'll take it out next week if you want me to," Barry said, "but if it was my wife, I'd recommend that she wait. It's minor surgery, but surgery is best avoided if you can stand to give it some time."

Could I stand to give it some time? No. From the moment Maureen put my hand on my right breast and covered it with her own and asked me calmly if I felt the lump that was there, I couldn't stand it. My chest ached from containing the pounding heart that woke me from fitful sleep night after night, frantically groping in the dark to see if the miracle had happened and all this waiting—measured in instants since the moment I left Maureen's office—might blissfully, peacefully, come to an end.

Yet I did wait. Although I called Barry's office every few days, and changed and was talked out of changing my mind, I waited—not one month, in the end, but two and a half months. Like the brave soldier I'd been praised for being as a sickly little girl, because I never cried or said how scared or hurt I was, I told myself that if Barry's wife was brave enough to wait (according to Barry, anyway), then so would I be.

Why did I wait? Because although terror kept me up all night and clenched all day, squeezing and measuring that lump while lying down and then sitting up in my bed, in my car, in the bathroom at work, when my kids weren't watching at the dinner table, in between holding Wendy's head while she vomited and retched and sobbed after chemotherapy every other Friday night, before I got my period, during my period, after my period, before making love, and furtively while in the midst of making love—something, ultimately, was stronger than the terror.

That lump was talking to me, and something in me was listening. Something in me knew that whatever it took to get through breast cancer or AIDS or an earthquake wasn't working in me yet, and that living with this lump, listening to what this lump had to say might teach me the skills I needed to face what life had to offer—which I was beginning to acknowledge, at age thirty-nine, was not guaranteed to be pleasant.

Somehow, while questioning my willingness to be tortured by this interminable waiting, I managed to breathe and mow the lawn and cook grilled cheese sandwiches for my children and edit catalogs and make

"My mother," Stephen says.

"Your mother?" I squeal, thrusting myself away from him. I glare at Stephen indignantly. Then I notice the tenderness in his eyes.

"It's like you're sending me off to my first day of school," he says. "Building up my confidence, making me feel good about myself. Like my mom used to do."

And then I remember that Stephen adored his mother, who was indeed a heroine—to her husband, to her four sons, and to the young activists who sought her nurturing and her counsel. I remember how much Stephen lost when she died of cancer four years ago, shortly after he and I met.

I reach out to Stephen, touch his sticky cheek.

"I'm flattered," I say. "Now go on—knock 'em dead."

love—while my best friend's hair fell out and her periods stopped, while another friend, herself a doctor and mother of two babies, was diagnosed and operated on and dosed with radiation, and a friend of a friend discovered not one but two lumps, one of them under the incision that marked the recent removal of her first cancerous breast.

Every day, I found something new that helped—sometimes by finding what didn't. I learned to carefully choose whom *not* to tell: the people whose faces I couldn't bear to watch as they registered the news and formulated the equation—lump=cancer=death—and reflected back to me the thought that coursed through me like my blood: I might die soon.

I didn't tell my children, who had seen and touched the jagged scar across the chest of their grandmother, my mother, from whom I might well have inherited this lump.

Night after night I sat watching *Fresh Prince of Bel Air* and *The Simpsons* with my sons, trying to laugh in all the right places while my fingers felt for that place in me whose disappearance I begged, bargained, and prayed for—for their sakes if not for my own. Staring at them sometimes when their soft faces were turned away from me, smooth with concentration and then crumpled in laughter, I imagined them as teenagers with no mother, as young men forgetting the absolute devotion of my touch, as fathers whose children would never taste my triple-chocolate-chip cookies hot from their grandmother's oven, carrying their grief with them through long expensive years of therapy my life insurance wouldn't cover and, finally, to their own graves.

I learned to carefully choose whom to tell, whom to ask for help— this after thirty-nine years of never asking for help, of never trusting or accepting offers of help, of scorning in envious contempt the people who could and did.

And so I got some.

I got some from Barbara, the acupuncturist and spiritual teacher Maureen sent me to, who brought me to meet myself by laying me down with needles protruding from my every extremity like a butterfly on a specimen board, and leaving me alone in a darkened, warm room with meditation tapes playing for longer than I could stand to be trapped that way, until my screams roiled around in my gut and swirled into my mouth but didn't come out. I made it through that first hour and in this way, each Wednesday at seven P.M., I began to learn to touch bottom and be still with myself.

I got some from Wendy, who offered to listen to my terrors and refused my refusals of her gift, who promised to tell me if it got too hard for her to hear—this fear of mine that what was chewing at her organs and her life was also chewing at mine. It made her feel less alone, she said, that her best friend was dealing with the same thing she was, although, she always added, she sure did wish I wasn't.

I got some from women who were dealing with that same thing too, women I'd never met, who'd heard about me through mutual friends—lesbians who called me to commiserate, to reassure, to offer referrals and homeopathic remedies and even child care, and through these conversations with strangers I was introduced to a subculture of my subculture, the network of lesbians surviving their own or their lovers' lives with—and deaths from—breast cancer.

I got some from my good friend Peter Babcock, who was, by the time of my lump's appearance, rapidly losing his once-unparalleled mental acuity to AIDS dementia, who nonetheless held me in his once-overdeveloped and now spindly arms and encouraged me to envision the lump as "my third breast"—like a third eye, he said, as wise and purposeful as a third eye. And as Peter dropped off to a restless sleep, his thirty-five-year-old, wizened head lolling in my lap, I remembered arguing with this very man, my closest man friend, several years back, the argument every lesbian was having with her best gay man friend: "If lesbians were dying of AIDS, would gay men be staffing the hospices and cooking the food and fighting for funding the way we're doing for you guys? And what are you guys doing for lesbians with breast cancer, anyway?"

I got some from the fourteen women I worked with in the Smith & Hawken Art Department, with whom I spent the day before the biopsy on a department retreat, to whom I confessed tearfully at day's end that I was having a breast lump removed the next afternoon. Who formed a healing circle around me, there on our boss's living room floor with

Mount Tamalpais our silent witness, and held each other's hands and closed their eyes and visualized that lump as benign until my own squeezed-shut eyes oozed tears at the wonder of letting love and help in, letting love and help in. After which one and then another of the women, the first one twenty-six, the second one thirty-two, spoke quietly to me of their own biopsies, both benign, of the pain and relief and the fear that never goes away.

I got some from my lover, who walked the fine line between reassurance and denial on a daily—and middle-of-the-nightly—basis, who reminded me that Barry had no motivation for putting me at risk by delaying surgery, who confessed to her own fear while ricocheting wildly off mine, who cried at the thought of loving me one-breasted but swore that she would, who drove me to Barry's office each of the many times I went there and resisted—sometimes gracefully, sometimes furiously— my persistent efforts to make this all her fault.

So in all of these ways, with all of this help and with the greatest aloneness ever known to me, I did wait, until two periods had come and gone and the lump had, I was almost certain, gotten correspondingly bigger and smaller but was, undeniably, still there. And the date for the biopsy rushed up and grabbed me and pulled me into Barry's office, where I never wanted to be.

I take off my shirt and my bra and lie on my back on the surgery table. Nancy covers me with a paper sheet, leaving my right breast oddly exposed. Barry comes in, takes my icy hand, and kisses Ann on the cheek. "Is it okay if I listen to a tape?" I ask him. "Of course," he answers. Without another word—he knows what I want, I want this to be over quickly and I want to have no cancer in my breast—Barry takes out a black pen and draws a one-inch line just below my right armpit. As Ann bends to adjust the Walkman headset over my ears, Barry adds, "If you feel anything even close to pain, just say 'ouch' and we'll give you some extra anesthetic. No point in being a martyr today, okay, Meredith?"

I nod and push the "play" button to start the precued Jack Korn-field meditation tape I'd been practicing with on my way to work these past long weeks. I'd chosen to be conscious for this surgery, but I hadn't promised to be present. As Barry injects the first dose of lidocaine into my breast, Jack's familiar voice guides me to "find what needs love in your body, and give it some now."

I feel the tugging I know is the scalpel slicing me open; at the same moment I feel Ann's hand clench in mine. Nancy has positioned her so that if she faints she'll fall away from the surgery table. The agreement Ann and I made was that, although I couldn't imagine how I could do what she was doing—watching some guy in green scrubs cut a hole in her lover—I would trust that she wanted to be here, trust her to leave if she needed to, so I could keep my attention focused on getting only myself, not both of us, through this.

Jack encourages me to "breathe, and notice the smells in the air, the feeling of the air in your lungs." I smell the Auschwitz stench of my own flesh burning as Barry cauterizes a vein. I know it might be as long as thirty minutes before Barry holds my lump in his hand and makes his preliminary diagnosis—"It'll only be a guess, but I'm right about these things ninety-five percent of the time," he said during our presurgical visit. I'd rather be with Jack than with Barry, Ann, and Nancy for these next thirty minutes.

Eyes closed, I retreat deep into my breathing and the hypnotic drone of a stranger's voice in my ears, until the feelings in my body and in my lover and all my predictions and projections recede from me as I fade away from them.

"You are whole, at one with your breath," Jack is saying. I become aware that someone in the room is trying to get my attention. I open my eyes. The first face I see is Ann's, pale but grinning. I turn my head toward Barry, who is smiling too. Nancy reaches over and gently removes the headphones from my ears.

"I don't see anything here that surprises me," Barry says, rather smugly. "You mean . . . ," I stammer. Nancy puts her face an inch in front of mine and says firmly, "It's not cancer, Meredith."

I look back at Ann, who now holds both of my hands in hers. Her blue eyes brim with tears. My own eyes are burning. "I love you," she says. "I love you," I answer. We hold each other with our eyes and our hands for a silent moment, Nancy and Barry beaming around us. "I feel like we're getting married," I say to my lover. "I feel like we're getting married right now."

"I'm going to close," says Barry, and bends to complete his work. I can't take my eyes from Ann's. I've never known how much she loves me, how rare and precious her love is, until this instant. How could we ever have fought? "I did it," I tell her, tears dripping down both sides of my immobilized face. "I'm proud of you, Babe," Ann says.

I think I've never been this happy. Even before the pathology report, even though I've promised myself not to count on this preliminary diagnosis, I believe Nancy that I don't have cancer. I believe that I can carry myself through something as difficult as this has been—not just the waiting but the surgery, not just the surgery but the waiting. I feel the way all those psychedelics all those years were supposed to make me feel, but didn't. Life is good and I'm good enough for it. There is love for me, and a chance to live. I am so euphoric I wonder if I'm high on the lidocaine.

"Great work you're doing, Barry. Are you gonna sew your initials in there?" I tease, watching him carefully stitching closed the flaps of flesh that will hold my breast together again. "I just might," Barry answers without looking up. "You're going to love me when you see how well this heals."

"I love you now," I answer immediately and honestly. Even though you're kind of arrogant and you get off on having all these needy terrified women depending on you, I think, but don't say.

Barry pats my shoulder and turns away from me. "Where's the lump?" I ask him. "Can I see my lump?" He hands a small jar to Nancy. "Are you sure?" he asks me. I nod.

Nancy holds the jar in front of me. It's nearly full of a mass that looks like a brain or a fetus—like the baby that was sucked from my womb twenty years ago, the child I never saw. I speak to that flesh from my body now.

"I'm sorry," I say to my first, unborn child. "I'm sorry it was so much easier to conceive you than it would have been to care for you. I'm sorry that my nineteen-year-old life couldn't have sustained yours. And that I snuffed our chance to know each other . . ."

"I'm sorry," I say to the little girl who grew up believing she didn't have what it takes, who needed to prove to herself, all these years later, that she was stronger than the fear.

"Thank you," I say to the lump that did just what it was supposed to do, to the people who loved me through this, to the god or goddess above or within or my own healthy body or whatever it was that gave me the miraculous good fortune of not having breast cancer right now.

Up the Hill

SEPTEMBER 1992

"I'm really excited about renting your cabin this weekend, Meredith," says Carla. We're standing back to back in the copy room at work. She's faxing; I'm Xeroxing.

"Who are you going with?" I ask, scanning Carla's bare ring finger, then my memory for data on her personal life. Is she single? Straight and living with someone? Gay?

I've never heard, and it's hard to tell by looking. Like most of her coworkers in Customer Service, Carla's style is funky-androgynous: short spiky hair dyed bright orange one week, platinum bangs plastered to her forehead the next. Black Doc Marten boots laced around heavy black leggings. A riotous parade of sparkling studs and dangling silver crosses marching up and around her earlobes. Siren-red lipstick, thickly drawn black eyeliner, and ghostly pancake makeup yesterday; no makeup at all today.

"My mom and my . . . other parents," she answers. "Other parents?" Is Carla's *mother* gay? I retrieve my collated copies from the machine and turn to her for an explanation.

"I grew up in a commune in Berkeley," she says. "My dad took the yuppie route—he lives in Palo Alto now with his new wife and his

BMW. But I'm still really close to my mom and the other people who raised me."

She feeds the last of her Service Confirmation Notices into the fax machine. It sucks them up greedily.

"My mom's really cool," Carla adds. "She could never stand a regular job, so she teaches English as a Second Language through environmentalism—takes people out on nature walks and teaches them the English words for flowers and trees. She's broke all the time, but that's nothing new."

Carla laughs affectionately. "My mom's really creative. Come to think of it, Meredith, she reminds me a lot of you."

Gulp. Reflexively I touch my chin to see if I've actually sprouted a long white beard, or if it just feels that way. "Um, Carla," I say, "how old are you?"

Carla looks puzzled. "Twenty-three. Why?"

Frantically I do the math in my head. Forty-one minus twenty-three. *Am I really old enough to be this woman's* mother? "And . . . how old's your mom?"

"Oh, she's about your age," Carla says. "Forty-eight."

Big gulp. Carla peers at me. "Oops," she says. "Isn't that about how old you are?"

"About," I say. "Give or take seven years."

"Sorry," she says, blushing.

I shake my head. "It's not the age thing, really," I say. "It's an . . . *identity* thing." Carla raises her plucked-to-nearly-nothing eyebrows at me.

"When I look at you, I think . . . I think you look like me, like someone my age," I say, realizing this only as I say it. "I guess the truth is, you look like I *remember* myself looking. I just don't think of myself as being in anyone's *parents'* generation. I think of myself as being . . . young."

Carla regards me blankly. If I'm waiting for her to agree with me, it appears I'll have time to make a few copies of *War and Peace* while I wait. She doesn't seem to share, or even understand the source of, my delusion.

But Carla's a polite person, and besides: I'm a vice president and the owner of the cabin in question; she's a customer service rep who's going to split the fifty-dollar rent with three or four of her still-principled but poverty-stricken "parents." I can certainly see why she wouldn't feel motivated to perform an act (however appropriate) of bubble-bursting under these circumstances.

"Uh *huh,*" Carla says, nodding at me as she backs rapidly out of the room, her papers clutched against her chest. "Well, see you later, Meredith. And thanks again for letting us use your cabin."

NOVEMBER 1992

Jesse and I are rummaging through the old family albums, looking for a baby picture he needs for a class project. We come across a photo of me in the bathtub in our house in Hayward in 1979, three-month-old Peter nursing at my breast and my ecstatic face beaming into Richard's camera.

"Mom, you were such a pretty girl!" Jesse exclaims. And then, with heartbreaking innocence: *"What happened?"*

DECEMBER 1992

Getting into a women's writing group in Berkeley in the nineties is the politically correct, postfeminist equivalent of getting into a country club.

Before a new member is accepted, group and applicant must first scrutinize each other for economic, philosophic, dietary, sexual, and artistic compatibility. Each must locate the other, with pinpoint precision, on all of the relevant continuums: between downward mobility and affluence; between Act Up activism and NOW liberalism; between macrobiotics and junk food; between 0 and 6 on the Kinsey scale; between raw but unrecognized talent and crass commercial success.

Should these initial criteria be satisfied, the applicant must then go on to audition her talents as both reader and listener. The successful candidate will demonstrate before the group the optimum balance, as reader, of self-revelation and containment; and, as listener, of kindness and adherence to rigorous—not male-identified, but certainly not "girlish"—literary standards.

So it was with great trepidation that I put out the word I was looking for a writing group to join. And it was with equal gratitude that I received my invitation to attend (once, on a trial basis, and then forevermore should I emerge triumphant from my confirmation hearing) a group that sounded right for me. The women in it had been published, but not intimidatingly; they were straight, lesbian, and points in between; they met a reasonable twice a month; and rumor had it that cookies were served.

But from the moment I entered the Berkeley bungalow in which the group met tonight, I felt out of sorts, unhappy. Waiting now for the call that will tell me whether I've been accepted or rejected, I still don't know why I felt that way.

The subjects of the well-crafted stories the women read were certainly of interest to me: raising children with different fathers; joining an encampment in the desert to protest nuclear testing; long-distance lesbian love; the waxing, waning, and rewaxing of a twenty-five-year marriage. And the women's feedback on the piece I read was constructive and encouraging—exactly what I was looking for when I decided to subject myself to shopping for a writing group in the first place.

Maybe, I think, it was the cookies. They had that good-for-you, sawdust-stuck-to-the-roof-of-the-mouth texture that makes my lips ache for the sloppy kiss of a dark, damp brownie. And, adding gastronomic insult to injury, there were only twelve on the plate: a paltry two of the offensive tidbits for each of us.

Maybe, I reflect, it was the ambiance of the house in which the group met: interesting, attractive, but—it occurs to me now—disconcertingly reminiscent of my mother's.

When my mother moved to Berkeley in 1978 she quickly adopted, and has transported to each of her apartments since, the style of home decor favored by many of her fellow feminist-grandmother friends: an imaginative if eclectic, yard-sale-based, seemingly timeless motif. Voluptuous sofas possessing in character what they lack in stuffing. Found and homemade objects of steel and pottery and cement poised menacingly on earthquake-stressed mantels. Threadbare rugs and kilims whose value has long since shifted from commercial to solely sentimental.

True, I'm troubled by my mother's decorating style. (*Who's the grown-up? Shouldn't a* grandmother *have matching dishes?*) But I don't think I would now be considering—and I realize that I am now considering—not joining a writing group just because the house where it meets reminds me of my mother's. I picture now the faces of the women who sat with me in the circle of charmingly mismatched chairs a few hours ago. Perfectly nice, intelligent women. Perfectly nice, intel-ligent . . . older women.

Pay dirt! And I do mean dirt. I'm ashamed of myself when I realize the true nature of my problem with the group.

It wasn't the landscape of the living room that bothered me. It was the landscape of the faces. It was, very simply, that the women in the group are older than I am: in their fifties, and thereby situated on the scary side of the midway marker between my age and my mother's.

I realize that I'm afraid to sit before the mirror of these fifty-something women. I'm afraid to see my not-so-distant future self as I saw them: squinting over and under the glasses they seemed to be still getting used to, as if they were already wearing bifocals, shoving them up against the bridges of their noses as they read their poems and stories. I don't want to have to peer through the masks, reamed with wrinkles, of their faces as they are today to find the smooth young skin of the beautiful young women they used to be . . . we used to be . . .

Years ago, a friend with severe acne told me that when she was a teenager no one would sit next to her in class. "They thought they'd get bad-skin-by-association," she said. Well, aging is no more contagious than acne, but now I seem to be afraid of becoming fifty-by-association.

The women in the writing group are the kind of older Berkeley women that younger Berkeley women look up to: energetic, iconoclas-tic, questioning; living out in their middle years the values they helped introduce to the culture at large in their youth.

"Berkeley's the best place for a woman to get old," my mother told me when she moved here from London at age fifty. "It's great to have all these role models of strong gray-haired women."

But I'm not ready to be one of those role models. I'm not ready to get old—in Berkeley, Oakland, or anywhere else. Not yet. I want ten— okay, okay, nine—good long years before I am fifty, please. I may be up the hill, but I'm not over it. Not yet. And until I get there, I don't want to be reminded of the inevitability of my destination.

As if I could escape *that,* writing group or not.

Already it happens daily: I glance into a mirror and see furrows across my forehead that weren't there yesterday. Already when Jesse turns his merciless caricaturist's pencil on me, people mistake his portraits of me for portraits of my mother. Already I have had that conversation with my haircutter—me! Who never even learned to properly apply mascara!—about options available when the gray hairs begin to overpower the black and vanity overpowers denial.

Already I understand the disgusting phenomenon of middle-aged men and their twentysomething trysts: the yearning to lie beside, if not within—to touch, if not to possess—such a sweet, sumptuous feast of fine, firm flesh . . .

Yes, yes, I know: aging is traumatic for everyone in a culture that glorifies youth and impossible standards of beauty. Yes, I know that Mick Jagger is older than the president, that Bob Dylan has grown a few chins and Wavy Gravy has been prehumously memorialized as an ice cream flavor. That aging is as inevitable as death and taxes.

But please understand: there are major expectations at work here. I am a member of the generation that denied the inevitability of anything. The generation that hoped to die before it got old! The generation that refused to pay taxes! The generation that claimed credit for no less than taking on death and winning: for ending a war that couldn't be ended. And for changing the meanings of sex and gender and education and work—reputedly immutable institutions, altered, every one, by my generation's sheer refusal to accept their immutability.

So surely I cannot be expected to lie down and die before this most mundane of opponents.

And while I'm figuring out how to exempt myself from the human condition, I'll be damned if I'll spend every other Thursday night staring into the wrinkled face of the enemy.

JANUARY 1993

Maureen was the perfect doctor for me. Lesbian-feminist, and out as hell about it. (When she married her lover last year, the wedding was featured in a PBS documentary.) A great proponent and teacher of holistic treatments as substitutes or support for drugs and surgery. A big-boned, buxom, maternal body; a creased, comforting face; kind eyes that had obviously seen more than a few breast lumps in their time; and enough salt in her long, peppery hair to reassure me that she might well know a lot of things I didn't know.

But Maureen and her lover had always dreamed of moving to the country before they got too old to enjoy living there. So when Maureen finally found a rural hospital that would let her practice her brand of maverick medicine, they sold their house in Oakland and headed for the hills. Sitting in the examining room now, awaiting my first meeting with Maureen's replacement, I swear I can hear the echoing keening of all her devoted patients, abandoned by our irreplaceable Mo.

The door opens; my heart sinks. "I'm Janet. Janet Arnesty," my new doctor says, extending her hand and shaking mine firmly. She makes the properly direct eye contact. She uses the properly egalitarian first name. She wears no improper makeup. Her feet are shod in properly unprofessional running shoes.

But already I feel my head shaking *no,* my mouth forming the words: "I'm sorry. I need to see a different doctor. *You're younger than I am.*"

VALENTINE'S DAY 1993

This is how lucky I am: I have a lover who believes in me so deeply that for our ninth Valentine's Day together, she gives me two gift certificates: one for classes at Studio 6000, where they offer street funk dance lessons, and another for the Capezio Dance Store, where they sell street funk outfits.

She gives me these gifts because every Sunday night when our family gathers 'round the glowing cathode ray tube to watch *In Living Color,* I eagerly await the two or three moments in each show when the comedians clear the stage, the house music revs up, and the street-funk-dancing Fly Girls explode onto the screen. Then I hush my family into reverent silence and assume a prayerful position so I can properly worship at the Doc Marten–shod feet of my idols—or is it idolettes?

Just when the Girls are really getting into it, just when I'm sure I've committed to memory the complex configurations of their clothes and their moves, just when I've been transported by the breathtaking pleasure of watching them, moving with them, *being them*—my reverie is interrupted by some inane commercial.

Abruptly, cruelly, the music stops. Abruptly, cruelly, I'm dropped back into my real life, my real self, my real living room. I'm the mother of teenagers again, wearing my stained sweatpants and faded *Utne Reader* T-shirt. I hoist myself up on creaking knees and slink back to my reclining position on the couch, muttering, "I could do that. I *know* I could do that."

Many Sunday nights ago my children recognized the futility of arguing the probability of my assertion. But Ann, my greatest fan, never argued it at all. No, my dream girl got herself instead to the aerobics studios and boutiques of College Avenue, where she procured for me the procurable tools of Fly Girlhood, the trade of my dreams. And I am moved to tears by her offering.

When the kids get home from school I can't wait to tell them my news. "Look what Ann got me!" I shriek, waving the gift certificates in their impassive faces. "I told you! I told you! Now I'm really gonna be a Fly Girl someday!"

Jesse decides that he can participate not one moment longer in the perpetuation of this particular one of his mother's myriad fantasies.

"Mom," he begins, in that long-suffering, eye-rolling tone of his. "Even if you could dance—which you can't . . ."

Out of the corner of my eye, I see Peter nodding gravely. I've embarrassed him more than once in his own living room, dancing at parties.

"Even if you could dance," Jesse repeats with calm conviction, "you're too old to be a Fly Girl."

I am stunned into momentary silence. How can this be? A child of mine accepting conventional limitations? A child of mine refusing to believe that anything is possible?

"Jesse," I declare, with all the authority vested in me by my age, my accumulated wisdom (however questionable), and the cesarean scar that bisects my belly. "The whole point of *In Living Color* is to expose discrimination. If they tell me I'm too old I'll . . . I'll sue them for age discrimination."

My twelve-year-old son doesn't miss a beat. "Mom," he says pityingly, "that's like a blind person suing because they won't let him be a bus driver."

May 1993

This is Peter's big day: the moment he's looked forward to through all the years he was forced to suffer the indignities of elementary and then junior high school. At last, his age has caught up to his aspirations: he stands now in the hallowed halls of Berkeley High, where he awaits registration and orientation with the barely suppressed pride and eagerness of a young warrior preparing for knighting.

Accompanying Peter to his appointment with destiny (in the form of his guidance-counselor-to-be) are his biological parents, severed matrimonially but reunited amicably by such family milestones as this one. Clutched in our hands, once adorned by matching gold bands, is the requisite documentation of Peter's birth, immunizations, academic record, emergency phone numbers, and the all-important proof of his father's Berkeley address, which qualifies him to switch from the Oakland to the Berkeley school district.

The Guidance Department secretary shows the three of us to a round table and hands us a tall stack of forms to be completed in triplicate. She gives Peter a pen, too. (*He's not a little boy anymore.*) As I bend to the task of building the paper trail that will follow my son forevermore, I am reminded of the era, many years before his conception, when I vowed to have my babies at home, school them at home, do whatever it took to render them invisible to the government bureaucracy that would otherwise reduce them to numbers—or, in the event of war, corpses.

"Who should I put for them to call if there's a big earthquake?" Peter asks without looking up. "They want it to be someone out of state."

Jesus, I moan to myself. My brain treats me to a full-color instant preplay of the scenario that would make such a phone call necessary.

"Jackie and Marty," Richard says. He dictates the phone number of his sister and brother-in-law in Colorado. Then he glances knowingly in my direction. "Hurricanes in Florida, Meredith," he says flatly. "Tornadoes in the Midwest. Standard operating procedure in schools from coast to coast, I'm sure."

"Are you folks finished with your paperwork?" the secretary asks. "Mr. Rosenbaum can see you now."

Richard, Peter, and I surrender our papers and pens and follow her into a small office. I note that there is a metal grate covering the window, and graffiti sprayed onto the glass. I wonder where we would have put Ann if she hadn't had to miss this meeting for an unmissable one at work—the three of us are kneecap to kneecap as it is. I wonder how many times Peter—and then Jesse, when he follows his older brother to Berkeley High next year—will sit in this office awaiting punishment for the kinds of misbehaviors that have caused both of my sons to spend so much time in the offices of each of the schools they have attended. We're still shifting ourselves around to establish the desirable ex-spouse-to-ex-spouse, parent-to-child distances when Mr. Rosenbaum enters the room.

"Oh wow!" he hoots. "Rich! Meredith! It's you!"

Richard and I jump to our feet. " '*Mister Rosenbaum?*' " I chortle. "Ron! I didn't even know you were a teacher!" He bear-hugs and kisses me, then hugs Richard.

"I'm not a teacher, Meredith," Ron says, mock-sternly. "I'm the head of the Guidance Department. I've been here for three years now. I was in the Oakland system before that."

I see that Peter is staring at us curiously.

"Dad and I have known Ron—um, Mr. Rosenbaum—for a really long time," I explain.

"How long *has* it been?" I ask. I don't know whether it's my lack of math skills or denial, but I can't seem to remember.

"Well, let's see," Ron answers, unbuttoning his tweed jacket as he settles in behind his institutional-issue desk. "The band—that was in seventy or seventy-one," he says. "And then there was the Workers' Defense Committee . . ."

Richard, Ron, and I burst into laughter. "I knew Ron when he was in a radical rock group called the Red Star Singers," I tell Peter. "And then a few years later Dad, Ron, and I were in an organization together— when we were trying to organize factory workers." *Doesn't it all sound silly, pretentious,* outdated, *now?*

Ron looks at Richard and then at me. "Hey—didn't you guys split up?"

"Almost ten years ago," Richard says. "You too, huh?"

Ron nods. "Diane and I haven't lived together since seventy-five. Remember you guys used to do child care for Carey? She's twenty now."

Peter shoots me an impatient look. *Cool, Mom—you're friends with the head counselor. But enough with the sixties stuff. We're here about my future, remember?*

"We'll have to catch up another time," I say, smiling at Ron. "Right now, let's get this boy off to a good start in high school, okay?"

"Definitely," Ron agrees, and starts punching Peter's program into the computer beside him. That done, Ron swivels his chair around and looks intently at Peter.

"I'm going to make you part of my family, Peter," he says. "I'll look out for you as long as you're at Berkeley High, Peter. But you're gonna have to keep your wits about you. Don't use the locker room in G building in the morning; you'll flush the homeless people out of their nests. Don't buy your pot on campus, and don't buy anything from anyone in Provo Park across the street.

"If you have any kind of problem at all, you come directly to me. Here's my beeper number in case you can't reach me in my office. Any questions?"

Peter asks Ron what to do if he changes his mind over the summer about the elective classes he's chosen. "No problem—I'll handle everything for you," Ron answers. "Your parents are good people. Just call me, whatever you need. Okay?"

Peter nods. Ron ushers us out of his office. More hugs and kisses are exchanged; Ron and Peter shake hands solemnly.

Richard, Peter, and I walk down the fluorescent-lit corridor together. I can't tell whether the people we're passing are students or teachers. I'm wondering how long Peter will be able to tolerate the risk he's taking: any minute now, one of his Berkeley High friends might see him here with his parents.

"Uh, Mom," Peter says to his custodial parent of the day, "I'm gonna meet Carlos and Sara for lunch. See you later, okay?"

I nod. Richard gives Peter's shoulder a loving little pat. Then Richard and I watch our older son stride away from us across the campus. It's one of those moments. There have been an awful lot of them lately. But for a change, Richard and I are sharing it.

"I guess that's about it," Richard says, his eyes following Peter. I know he doesn't mean the appointment with "Mr. Rosenbaum."

"I guess so," I sigh. "We're in the home stretch now, huh?"

Richard walks me to my car. There's a parking ticket stuck under the windshield wiper. I flip the ticket over to determine the nature and the price of my offense.

"Back end in red—$26," it says, and for some reason this strikes me as very funny. "My ass is in the red," I say. "Thanks to this damn ticket."

Suddenly I'm laughing uncontrollably. Richard just watches. Then I realize what's really funny.

"I guess we're regular pillars of our community now, Richard," I say between giggles. "Friends in high places and all that." I crack up again.

Richard smiles wryly. "Hey—whatever works. Public school is a tough system to crack. I want our kids to get as much out of it as they can. If an old friend can help, great. It's our version of the good old boys' network."

"The good old boys' network?" I say. "That's *us*, now?"

AUGUST 20, 1993

My friend Stephen and I have just finished our bimonthly game of what I refer to as "Twelve-Step Racquetball."

The name refers not to the number of paces required for me to run from one end of the court to the other, as I pointlessly do every time Stephen hits the ball. Rather, it describes the codependent manner in which Stephen and I deal with the discrepancy between our skill levels.

Losing to Stephen doesn't faze me. I am an equal opportunity loser, bowing to all opponents regardless of gender, age, or sexual orientation: the young lesbian to whom I willingly submit for humiliation every Tuesday; my lover, who picks up a racquet maybe once every six months; my kids—everyone.

But Stephen, bless his postfeminist heart, is troubled by the socio-dynamic implications of our competitive imbalance. And so he has developed a wide-ranging strategy for coping with his discomfort, a repertoire that includes attributing to my score points unearned; serving so loopily that even I can return the serve; and, occasionally, taking brief stand-up catnaps while the ball is in play.

When his ruse becomes embarrassingly transparent (conveniently, this usually transpires after I've accumulated a few ego-salving points), I haughtily accuse him of patronizing, unsportspersonlike behavior. At that point Stephen makes sincere self-criticism and goes on to win the game—but never by a more patriarchal margin than ten or twelve points.

Today, Stephen has beaten me by an unprecedentedly close score of 21 to 18. I attribute my relative success to Stephen's nervousness. Today is his first day as a UC Berkeley grad student. Stephen hopes that four years from now he will have evolved from a brilliant activist to a brilliant activist with a master's degree in environmental sciences.

"Thank God at least I'm not the oldest person in the program," Stephen tells me now, as we sit slurping our usual postgame lunch of frozen fruit bars salted with the sweat that still drips from our beet-red brows.

"Hard to believe," I tease him. Stephen and I are "about" the same age. Now. But when we were children I was six years older than he was. And this business of his going back to school has made our usually insignificant age difference suddenly seem quite poignant to me. (*Who's the grown-up?*) Especially today, the day before my forty-second birthday.

". . . but I probably am the least accomplished," Stephen continues, ignoring my jab. "The program's full of whiz kids from Harvard and Yale." He looks at me glumly.

"Oh, honey, you'll be great," I tell him, feeling protective. "Whatever you do—you're always great. Think of all the perspective you've got, the experience. How many of those kids have founded a grass-roots nonprofit organization? How many of them have been the director of social inventions for an international socially responsible business?"

Stephen considers my protestations for a moment, and seems to brighten slightly. Then he glances at his watch and jumps to his feet. "I've got to be at orientation in half an hour," he says. "I'd better go shower."

I grab Stephen's clammy body to me and hug him tightly. "You'll do fine," I repeat. "Call me later. Let me know how it went."

Stephen hugs me back. Our sweaty chests make squooshing noises against each other. "You know who you remind me of?" he asks, his nose against my ear.

Long ago Stephen and I, both vividly married individuals, put to rest the pulse of attraction that initially throbbed between us. Still, I am easily transported back to the early days of our friendship, full of flattering innuendos and comparisons to mutually revered heroes and heroines.

"Um . . . Jennifer Beals? Cher?" I prompt him, naming the celebrities to whom I was, at one time in my life (long before I met Stephen, or, for that matter, my children), occasionally compared.

Line of Fire

I'd never been so isolated, so much in need of a friend, as I was the year after Rich and I moved to San Jose. So when Rich came home with Jesse from a union organizing meeting one day and told me he'd met a woman who'd spent most of the meeting on her hands and knees cooing at Jesse—a woman he thought would make a great friend for me—I wasted no time calling her to make a date.

The first time Wendy showed up at our front door—the suburban tract house door behind which I was imprisoned with my two wild babies and my disintegrating marriage and my escape fantasies—she had a blue bandanna tied around her neck, a pair of well-aged Birkenstocks on her feet, no bra beneath her "Earth Camp" T-shirt, and a handful of freesias from her garden in her hand.

I could hardly believe my good fortune. Right in the middle of polyester-pantsuit-and-pumps-land, I'd finally found my soulmate! Like me, Wendy had never quite left the sixties behind. Like me, she was bisexual; unlike me, she'd actually had the nerve to act on her sexual versatility. She was politically active, artistic, adventurous, domestic, funny, psychologically savvy, and kind.

Best of all, Wendy loved kids in general, and—instantly, it seemed—two-year-old Peter and six-month-old Jesse in particular.

Bored out of my gourd, buried alive in Pampers and his-and-his playpens, I was rescued from mute motherhood by this miracle worker, Wendy. Saturday mornings, Thursday afternoons, Monday nights she'd appear, ready to throw the kids and me and all we entailed—diaper bags and strollers and blankies and car seats—into her funky but functional '72 Ford Maverick, its cracked dashboard littered with feathers and seashells and stones. Then she'd whisk us off to the Santa Cruz Board-walk, or out for ice cream, or over to her house for home-baked shortbread and hot chocolate and art projects in front of the fire.

No—best of all, Wendy loved me. As no one had ever loved me before. Her X-ray vision bored through the lead-lined labyrinth of my defenses, through every "bad" thing I'd ever felt or said or done, to the good—if hurt—person she unwaveringly believed me to be.

I attributed this beneficent perspective of Wendy's to her training in "co-counseling," some scary-sounding self-help therapy group she belonged to and kept urging me, unsuccessfully, to join. Wendy said that after completing a four-month fundamentals class, I'd be ready to ex-change no-cost sessions with other co-counselors with whom I'd take turns being counselor and client. But I couldn't bring myself to attend a class. I couldn't imagine making myself as vulnerable with strangers as I regularly made myself with Wendy: in seven years of marriage I hadn't cried in Rich's arms as often as I'd already wept in Wendy's. In thirty years of living I hadn't trusted anyone the way I was quickly coming to trust her.

There was just one problem with this romance-at-first-sight: some-thing was wrong in Wendy's body. And throughout the first year of our friendship, it kept getting worse.

At first it was the sore throat that wouldn't go away. Then it was her skin: she itched all over, all the time, and even the touch of her clothing against her skin made her wince. She started running low-grade fevers during the day, waking each night drenched with sweat. She quit her job at a graphic arts studio, too exhausted and in too much pain to do much besides search for a diagnosis. At Jesse's first birthday party, she barely had the strength to hold him as he blew out the two candles on his Oscar the Grouch cake.

Wendy's family doctor prescribed antibiotics for flu. A new age holistic clinic sold her a hundred dollars' worth of vitamins for hypoglycemia. A year and fifteen doctors after her symptoms began, Wendy was on Medi-Cal: unemployed, broke, scared, and depressed. One rainy day just before Christmas, 1981, I drove her to the county health clinic, where a technician suggested a chest X ray to rule out TB.

That night I was in bed, nearly asleep, when the phone rang. I heard Rich answer it in the kitchen; I heard his voice catch and then fall silent. I heard him put the receiver down on the kitchen counter and I heard his footsteps approaching and then I knew what he was about to tell me. And I knew what would happen to me when I heard it.

"Meredith," he said into the darkness of the bedroom. "It's Wendy. The clinic just called her." He sobbed, once. "They found a tumor the size of a grapefruit in her chest."

Everything in me froze: my blood, my brain, my heart, the tiny growing soft part of me that Wendy had discovered, that Wendy had believed in and cherished and tended. Without Wendy, it would wither and die. And now some doctor had found something growing in her. Something that could take her away. Without Wendy I would . . .

"Tell her I'm sleeping," I told Rich through clenched teeth. My whole body was quaking.

"Meredith—she wants to talk to you," Rich said. *"She just found out she has cancer."*

My teeth were chattering. I felt an icy wind whipping through me. *Without Wendy* . . .

I said it to him again. "Tell her I'm sleeping." I pulled the covers over my head until finally I heard his footsteps retreating down the hall.

The next morning Wendy still had a tumor in her chest. The next afternoon I took her back to the county clinic, where a doctor told her the truth and a lie about what she had. "It's Hodgkin's lymphoma," he said. "But don't worry—it's not really cancer."

It was really cancer. And for the next year Wendy spent every other Sunday night at our house, preparing to deliver herself to Stanford

Hospital every other Monday morning for the chemotherapy and radiation that she described as "getting hit by a car and then walking back into the same intersection every other Monday and getting hit by a car again."

Somehow Wendy survived both the disease and the treatment, and somehow my heart survived the fear of loving her and losing her, and I took a big chance and stayed by her and she took a big chance and stayed by me.

1985–1987: Fairview Street, Oakland

We weren't supposed to be friends, Peter Babcock and I. The rules of the co-counseling class in which we met were clear: relationships formed, as ours was, for therapeutic purposes were to remain so—unsullied by the inevitable disappointments of real-life friendship.

It's an overstatement to say that in the course of offering each other solace and insights, performing psychic high colonics on each other every Thursday night for six months or so, Peter and I fell in love—but it was something like that that happened between us.

We simply had too much to talk about, too much we could imagine doing together that had nothing to do with our pasts or our individual healing—and everything to do with our futures and the world's—to limit our relationship to its initial intention. We were a study in opposite and overlap: graphic designer and writer; New England WASP and New York Jew; gay man and bisexual woman; both in our thirties, both lifelong activists, both self-appointed officers of the fashion police, impatient and opinionated and driven.

I had no shortage of people to do co-counseling sessions with, and a dearth of gay male friends. Peter, the perennial social alchemist, was eager to mix us up in his lab to see what kind of fission might result. So we agreed to end our counseling relationship and open ourselves to whatever might emerge from the secrets we'd already shared.

Our new agreement made it possible for Peter and his lover, David, to move into the house across the street from mine when it came up for rent in 1985. Now Peter and I saw each other every day. No longer bound to provide each other with unconditional, therapeutic understanding, our inner children's honeymoon came to an abrupt end and our relationship ripened like a sharp cheese. It turned out that our adult selves had well-matched appetites for acrimony; the exchange of conflicting opinion became our daily bread.

Should the United States retaliate against the PLO? Should San Francisco close the gay bathhouses? Should he and David keep the exercise equipment in the living room or the study? Everything was fodder for argument between Peter and me; we butted our pig heads together regularly and enthusiastically, declaring truces in between for hugs, kisses, and the occasional Sunday brunch with Ann, David, Peter, and Jesse.

When David was away on business Peter would invite himself to dinner, mock-self-pityingly imploring me to rescue him from "widowhood." My own "little" Peter, and Jesse, got attached to "big Peter," too—with them my irascible co-contestant was nothing but loving and gentle. Over and over they would ask him; over and over he would repeat the story of how he'd lost his left eye, playing with knives when he and his brother were Peter's and Jesse's ages.

One night in '86 Peter knocked on my door waving a piece of paper. "I want to start a magazine," he announced, charging past me into the kitchen. "Look at this list of ideas and tell me which you think is the best one."

Fortunately Peter disregarded my advice, as usual, and launched *Out/Look,* the first national gay *and* lesbian magazine. He got the money and the people together; designed the logo; found writers and artists who met his exacting standards and persuaded them to donate their work; and fought it out with the multitude of naysayers (including me) who didn't believe lesbians and gay men could work on a magazine staff together, would read the same magazine, appreciate the same jokes or aesthetic, support the same advertisers.

Just before the '87 gay march on Washington, Peter sat in my kitchen with that gleam in his right eye again. First he convinced Ann and me to go to the march, and to participate in the mass wedding to be held there. That accomplished, he extracted from me a commitment to write a personal account of the ceremony for *Out/Look*'s premiere issue—the first time in my journalism career that I was called upon to write straight (so to speak) from my heart, and fully in my own voice.

The first issue was well received; the magazine needed a bigger staff. In the spring of '88 Peter pounded on my door again—this time to recruit me to the all-volunteer *Out/Look* editorial board. We had the magazine to do together now: his baby, my adopted child. So it was less of a blow when Peter and David bought a house and moved to Berkeley, a couple of miles away.

JANUARY 1987: FAIRVIEW STREET, OAKLAND

Four A.M. I am in my bed, sleepless, in hell in my head. In the bathroom today I noticed a spot on my back. Turned on the light and examined it in the mirror. It was purple, like a bruise, but it didn't hurt to the touch. Breath left my body.

I made it through the workday somehow, through dinner with the kids, through the phone call to Ann. She said the purple spot was probably not a KS lesion. I made it through homework and TV and snuggling and through the six hours since I first laid my head on this pillow tonight knowing I was not to be granted an instant of sleep.

I think of calling my therapist. I think of calling an exorcist. I close my eyes and see myself anesthetized, inert, on the operating table in the moments after my first son's birth. *1978, before the virus had a name.* I feel the jab of the needle as the doctor starts the IV in my arm, feel the warmth in my vein as the transfusion flows in, replacing the blood that flowed out when they cut me open, yanked my failing baby from my womb.

I see the blood gushing into me. I see the virus in the blood. *The virus that will start to kill me now.*

I call my doctor, Maureen, as soon as her office opens in the morning. The receptionist hears the flat-out panic in my voice, connects me immediately.

Maureen asks me detailed questions: about the bruise, about

Peter's birth, about my sexual and drug histories, about my health. She says the bruise is probably just a bruise; that children seroconvert more quickly than adults and that if I had the virus, Jesse would likely have AIDS by now. She tells me to come in for a test if I'm still worried, if the bruise hasn't faded by tomorrow.

The bruise has faded by tomorrow.

NOVEMBER 1987: BERKELEY

Tonight's bimonthly *Out/Look* editorial meeting is a potluck dinner at Mikey's group house in Berkeley. Gathered around the huge, food-strewn dining room table are Kim, Chas, E.G., Jackie, Tomás, Dorothy, Jeffrey, Peter, and me. Our most junior member, Noah—Kim and Chas's infant son—is asleep in his car seat in the middle of the table, next to the steaming bowl of vegetables with peanut sauce that Mikey made.

There's a big argument in progress—nothing unusual there. That's what the editorial board is supposed to do: debate among ourselves all the difficult, confusing, touchy issues that keep our community divided and therefore prevented from exerting its potential power—then, present the debate to our readers.

Tonight the question on the table is incest. We all agree that the magazine needs to address the subject; on the question of how, as is often the case, we are split along gender lines.

The men say *Out/Look* should expose the link between the increased reporting of child sexual abuse and the rising tide of sexual repression. That many gay boys come out of the closet by having sex with older men; and teenagers can make empowered decisions about sex. That the gay community—especially the gay press—must fight for sexual freedom: if we don't, who will?

Most of the women are outraged. Two are in tears. All of us know women—several of us are lovers with women—who are suffering the aftershocks of childhood sexual abuse. How can the men, our gay brothers, be so insensitive, so unaware of our pain, of the repercussions of their position?

"I'd rather have been sexually abused by my father," declares Mikey, "than have been forced to play Little League. They're both parental power abuses. Why should we treat one differently than the other?"

I stare from one person to the other, hoping someone will express the despair I feel. How will this wound between men and women ever be healed? I look to Peter, sitting next to me, but he turns his head away.

And then I see it: bulging beneath the skin now stretched tightly across his neck, the hugely swollen gland. I don't care about incest anymore, or *Out/Look,* or *anything.* All thoughts but one fall from my brain:

He's got it. Peter's going to die.

MAY 1988: OAKLAND

I'm furious at Wendy. Over happy hour chicken wings at Yoshi's tonight she let it slip that she hasn't been going to Stanford for her post-Hodgkin's checkups. I asked if she'd rescheduled, offered to take her to her next appointment, but she recoiled from the anger in my voice, changed the subject.

I hate our relationship—the way we hide out instead of fighting it out when we're mad at each other. I hate Wendy's doctors for not going after her when she misses her appointments. I hate the medical establishment for not curing AIDS and cancer, already.

I hate worrying that I'm going to lose Wendy.

JULY 1988: SAN FRANCISCO

I'm looking forward to meeting Ann after work in the city tonight. Her old friend Sharyn is in town; we're going to visit her in her fancy, expense-account hotel room and then go out for a funky, non-expense-account dinner.

But when I see Ann standing at the agreed-upon corner on Market

Street I know that something is terribly wrong. She opens the car door, sits down heavily, looks over at me, and bursts into tears.

"It's Doug," she says. Doug is her closest man friend, one of the three or four people she's stayed deeply connected with since she left Boston four years ago. Doug and his lover vacation in the Bay area every year or two; Ann sees him whenever she goes to Boston.

Please don't let this be what I think . . .

"He's got it, Mer," she cries. *"Doug's got AIDS."*

APRIL 1990: MAL WARWICK & ASSOCIATES, BERKELEY

The phone on my desk rings, the short urgent buzzes that tell me the call is from someone else in the company.

"Got a minute, Mer? I need to talk to you," says Peter from his desk a few yards away. Instantly I'm worried: since Peter helped me get this job six months ago I can't think of a single time he's felt the need to call before coming to see me.

"Sure," I answer, my heart pounding.

"I'll be right there," Peter says.

This is it, I think. Since I first saw that lump on Peter's neck I've been holding my breath, dreading the inevitable. I tried fighting the dread with foolish optimism—just because he's a gay man that doesn't mean he can't get plain old swollen glands; he comes to work every day; he hasn't lost any weight. But I've known for years that Peter is HIV-positive. I've known for years that this moment would come, as surely as I've known that neither protracted denial nor preemptive grieving would make it one bit easier to face when it did.

"I have something exciting to tell you," Peter says, closing the door behind him. He's never closed my office door before; he always shrugs off my efforts to engage him in office gossip and intrigue. But . . . *exciting?*

"I've been diagnosed with KS," Peter says, looking into my two eyes with his one good one. "And I'm going to be the first person ever to survive it."

Take it back, I demand silently. *This isn't funny, Peter.*

"I'm working with a great doctor," he goes on. "We've come up with a really innovative treatment plan. I'm not going to take AZT or any of that shit. This could be a major AIDS breakthrough." He looks at me as if expecting me to share his "excitement." "I need you to do some things to help," he says.

"Anything," I croak. I stand up to grab him, pull him to me, but his stiff body refuses my touch before it is offered. I slump back against my desk.

"First," he says calmly, "don't tell anyone besides Ann and the kids. I don't want anyone at work to know until I'm ready to tell them. I don't want to deal with other people's reactions. Okay?"

I nod and he continues, as though he's reading me a list of groceries he'd like me to pick up on my way home.

"Here's the most important thing: *I need you to believe me that I'm going to get better.*

"If you can't believe me, I want you to act like you do. I don't want to ever see fear on your face. I don't want to hear pity in your voice. I don't want you to bring up my physical condition unless I bring it up first. If I want anything from you, I'll ask. Don't offer me anything from now on that you wouldn't have offered me yesterday."

His face softens almost imperceptibly. "I know you'll have feelings about this," he says. "But I need you to deal with them somewhere else—not with me. I need to stay"—he snickers ironically—"positive."

I am dumbstruck. *He's demanding the impossible of me. The son of a bitch. He's gonna do this on his own terms, too. No AZT—he'll be dead in a year. Don't I get a vote?*

"Okay?" Peter asks insistently.

How can I be close to him when he's forbidding me to show him what's in my heart? Do I lose him just like this—right here, right now?

But this isn't a news event or an issue of a magazine. This is his life, and his death. Unlike every other damn thing we've disagreed about, this is nonnegotiable.

"Peter," I say, "I love you. I'll support you doing this the way you need to do it.

"Anyway," I say, actually managing to contort my face into something resembling a smile. *See, Peter: I'm doing it your way.* "This isn't exactly the first time you've asked me to take a roller-coaster ride with you, is it?"

He grins at me, that twisted little lopsided grin. Now I am permitted a hug. *From now on I'll be taking what I can get, and grateful for it.*

"If anyone can beat this disease," I say, meaning it, "I'm sure you're the one."

Peter extricates himself from my arms, glances at his watch. "I've got a meeting. I'll talk to you later," he says, and leaves the room.

JUNE 1990: MT. VERNON STREET, OAKLAND

Midnight. Ann and I are falling asleep. Suddenly she sits upright in bed.

"Doug just died," she says. "I felt it in my body. Doug just died." She starts to cry.

The next morning we find out that Doug died at three A.M., Boston time.

AUGUST 1990: MAL WARWICK & ASSOCIATES, BERKELEY

Peter brings a futon to work, sets it up near his desk in the big open room where the designers work. He takes naps on it once or twice each day.

At first it's hard not to stare at him, lying flat on his back, slack-jawed and wheezing softly. I remember the night we slept beside each other at an *Out/Look* retreat, how I kept kicking him to interrupt his snoring. How we joked in the morning about the sleep-deprived marriage we would have had, if we'd been straight, if we'd been husband and wife.

I want to kick him now: wake him up so he can tell me this is all a bad dream. Kick him out of his denial, scream at him: "No one has *ever* recovered from AIDS!" Force AZT down his throat so he'll live just a few months longer. I want to buy him the world's finest eiderdown quilt and tuck it around him tenderly. I want him to be as easy to love awake as asleep. I want to lie down next to him. I want this whole fucking epidemic to be over before it takes Peter away from me.

After a while we all realize that we don't need to whisper, don't need to alter our normal routines. Peter sleeps through everything. We maintain the pretense, avoid his eyes and each other's. We learn to work around him.

SEPTEMBER 1990: OAKLAND

Wednesday night has been my Wendy night every week for ten years now. In the old days we'd hit the happy-hour hot spots of Silicon Valley, paying a dollar plus tip for a glass of club soda, scarfing up our body weights in free chicken wings and cubed jack cheese and peanuts while exchanging the intimate details of our psyches, hearts, and lives and ignoring the lecherous looks of engineers wearing blue jeans and wedding rings.

Now that we both live in Oakland we often eat in real restaurants where we actually pay for our meals. Since I took up co-counseling five years ago, our dates usually end at my house or hers for sessions: first Wendy counseling me, then me counseling Wendy. (Fortunately our relationship is exempt from the no-friendship rule, since it began before we were counselors to each other.)

Tonight when Wendy arrives at my house she doesn't have her happy-hour face on. She barely greets Joe. She looks grim. She wants to do sessions before we go out to eat. And she wants her session first.

In her session she tells me that she's found a lump in each of her breasts.

NOVEMBER 1990: SMITH & HAWKEN, MILL VALLEY

Wendy's biopsies kept getting put off because she had the flu, then a bladder infection, then a kidney infection. Her holistic doctor told her not to worry because he doesn't see cancer in her aura. Her Stanford doctors reassured her that the lumps don't feel malignant.

I have hated every moment of this waiting. But I hate this moment even more. The results of Wendy's biopsies are due today, and I can't imagine anything but bad news, or worse.

I go to a meeting, come back, hold my breath, punch in my voice mail code. The mechanical voice tells me I have one new message.

"Mer, it's me," says Wendy. Her words are blurred with tears. "Call me as soon as you can, okay?"

Outside my office window the birch trees are bare, battered by winter wind and rain. This time there is no blanket to hide me, no shelter of night. I don't want to call Wendy. I don't want to hear another one of her doctors' statistical analyses or lies. I don't want to watch her walk into that intersection again.

I don't call Wendy. I leave work in a crowd of women who are going out to drink margaritas. I think I am on my way to Wendy's house but when the women ask me to join them I agree. I am numb now, bobbing along in the clear uncomplicated waters of my coworkers' worries about office politics and layoffs. I am grateful for every moment that I am able to resist the undertow that is pulling at me. I am grateful for every moment I can live without knowing that Wendy has cancer again.

In the bar I suddenly feel sick. I imagine Wendy lying in her bed thirty miles from here, both breasts sliced and bandaged, her new boyfriend, Michael, by her side. I want to be by her side. I want every moment with her. I can't get to her fast enough. I cradle her face in my hands.

"I have breast cancer, Mer," she says, tears streaming down her cheeks.

"I know," I say. "Both breasts?" The lumpy bandages that swaddle her chest reveal only the damage that was done.

"Just the left one," Michael says. "The other lump was benign."

I know I can't fix what's wrong with Wendy. I can't undo what the doctors did, the doctors who planted a tumor in her breast when they overdosed her with the radiation that helped save her life eight years ago. So I do the best I can. I stroke her arms and fluff her pillows. I bring her organic raspberry juice and decorate her room with angels. I fight the urge to run and succumb to the urge to stay by her.

January 1991: East Bay Family Practice, Berkeley

I'm in for my annual checkup and breast exam. Maureen, my doctor, starts the familiar, frightening probing and squeezing, her face furrowed with concentration.

Her fingers circle and linger, move away, then return to a spot just beneath my right armpit. She reaches for my hand, places it beneath hers.

"Do you feel that, Meredith?" she asks me.

I do, of course. I do feel the lump in my breast.

November 1990–June 1991: Oakland

All I can do is be with her. I help Wendy to her bed when she comes home from the mastectomy. I hold her head every other Friday night when she vomits the poisons from her body. I put my arms around her in sessions when she cries and pounds out her rage and her terror. I help her eat the absurd overabundance of soy loaf and banana bread and lentil soup with which her panicked mother continually stuffs her refrigerator. I buy her bright teal cotton socks and slip them onto her icy, twitching feet while she shakes with chemo sickness.

Wendy decides to skip her last two treatments. She tells me her oncologist says it's okay for her to do that. Michael says it's okay with him. It's not okay with me.

I want to drag her to the doctor's office and stick the IV in her arm myself. I want to have a big screaming fight with her about my rights as her best friend, and I want to win the fight. I want to learn to love her on her terms, the way she deserves to be loved. I want her to never have cancer again. *I want her to outlive me.*

We don't have the fight. We have never known how to fight. I've never known how to disagree with her, get angry at her, without causing a fight. I distrust my anger, anyway: is it about our relationship, really— or her illness? Or both? She stops her treatments. I see that I have no control over this at all.

Six months after her treatments are finished Wendy moves with Michael to Santa Cruz, seventy miles away. Now that she is going to live, after all, she is going to live without me. Abandoned doesn't begin to say how I feel. And still she expects me to love her, as much as I did all the years between cancers, maybe more. *Impossible.*

The way we are together is different now. I feel the strain of silence beneath the chatter, the anger and disappointment and fear, the distance that comes from the seventy miles, the not saying, the not fighting. Still we don't let go of each other. In time I hope we'll find our way back. I hope for time for that and more.

JUNE 1991: MT. VERNON STREET, OAKLAND

Since I changed jobs last summer I hardly ever see Peter. Neither of us goes to *Out/Look* meetings anymore, and I don't feel as free to stop by his house as I used to. When I call on Peter's line, David answers. He tells me that Peter never goes to the office anymore, that night sweats and blinding headaches and bone pain keep him awake most nights, so he sleeps when he can during the day. I don't want to interrupt his rest, or his time alone with David, or the co-counseling sessions he has in his bed several times each week.

A few times I call first, then bring them dinner. Peter complains that the bland fresh pasta I've cooked to David's specifications is too spicy. He leaves his plate full and burrows under a pile of blankets on the couch. I follow him there, stroke his burning forehead. He sleeps, shakes, awakens, tells me excitedly about a new environmental magazine he's going to start next year. I look over at David; David shrugs, his eyes clouded with pain. Peter offers me a job as managing editor, then falls back to sleep. I don't know how to be with this, with him.

My kids haven't seen Peter in over a year, since before he was diagnosed.

So I'm thrilled when Peter calls one Saturday afternoon and asks if he can come over, finally see the house that Ann and I bought together. He sounds lucid, coherent—not like the last few times we spoke on the phone, when he kept forgetting who he was talking to and what we were talking about. After I hang up I remember that David doesn't like Peter to drive anymore. I consider calling David to check in—lately it seems my relationship is with David-about-Peter, not Peter—then decide to let this happen just the way Peter wants it to.

I watch through the window in my front door as Peter unfolds himself from his car, walks slowly toward the house. His body is bent and emaciated, his skin and what's left of his hair matte gray. I know better than to offer to help him up the four porch steps. So I watch his painful progress, wait for him to ring the bell.

The kids greet Peter with feigned nonchalance, as though he just bopped over from across the street the way he used to; as though his appearance doesn't make it clear that this will probably be the last time they see him alive.

Ann hugs him gently, offers him tea. He says he likes the house, the garden. He tries to make it up the ladder to see Ann's attic, but his legs are shaking too badly. He offers no decorating advice, no barbed jokes about how long it took Ann and me to decide to live together. He doesn't ask to see Jesse's latest artwork. He simply is not Peter anymore. He is suddenly in a big hurry to leave. As the door closes behind him, the teakettle starts to howl.

OCTOBER 1, 1991: SMITH & HAWKEN, MILL VALLEY

Peter is in the hospital. I don't go see him there. Every hour I think about Peter being in the hospital. Every hour I decide again not to go see him there. I don't want to see him dying. I don't feel I can do him any good. I don't want to face my guilt about how I've let go of him already, not like the kinder, more loving friends who sit day and night at his bedside. I can hardly remember how it felt when Peter was Peter and he and I loved each other.

The phone rings on my desk, the long tones that indicate a call from outside the building.

"Meredith?" I recognize the voice. Ruth is a co-counselor of Peter's, and the coordinator of the phone tree that keeps the twenty-odd people in Peter's support system connected to him, and to each other.

I know why she's calling, although that doesn't make her words any easier to hear.

"Meredith, Peter died early this morning."

OCTOBER 20, 1991: MT. VERNON STREET, OAKLAND

I wake up to the thought: today I say good-bye to Peter.

His memorial service is scheduled for one o'clock this afternoon. At eleven-fifteen the air outside the kitchen window suddenly turns orange. The sun becomes a burning red ball in the sky. Soot falls like black snow from billowing gray clouds of smoke. By noon our backyard is littered with tiny singed fragments of other people's cookbooks and photographs.

Ann and I stand at her attic window watching through binoculars as flames leap to hallucinatory heights above the mountaintops and fire eats every tree and house in the hills. A chorus of sirens screams; prop planes drop thimblefuls of water onto the roaring blaze.

"But it won't come to our house, right?" says Jesse, flipping the TV from station to station as one football game after another is replaced by coverage of what is now being called a "firestorm."

"We hope not," I say.

We don't need the binoculars anymore. The hill behind the Claremont Hotel, a mile or so from our house, is being devoured. Maybe two hundred houses, including a few belonging to friends of ours, reduced to smoking ash in fifteen minutes flat.

"Maybe we should pack some things, just in case," Ann says quietly. "What should we do about Peter's funeral?"

The church where the service is to be held, the church I helped David find, is midway between our house and the Claremont. I call Peter's number, the number on which David has been leaving updates since the last time Peter went into the hospital.

"This is David," the message says. "Peter died, surrounded by his friends, at two o'clock in the morning on October first. There will be a memorial service on October twentieth at St. John's Episcopal Church in Berkeley."

No fire update. "Do you think they'll still hold the service?" I ask.

Ann shakes her head. "I don't know," she says.

From across the room I hear the newscasters announcing the number of houses believed to have been destroyed so far. In the last hour the count has gone from twenty to five hundred.

"The Santa Ana winds have whipped the fire completely out of control," some official is saying. "The only thing that could help contain it now is rain. And no rain is forecast for the next several days."

There is only this one chance to say good-bye to Peter. To say I loved you, I'm sorry we fought so much, I'm sorry I didn't come to see you in the hospital, I'm sorry you won't be having all your crazy ideas on earth anymore, I'm sorry I didn't love you better.

Already people have died in this fire, cars and people melting on congested roads engulfed in flame.

"Let's pack," I say to Ann.

And so just when I should have been sitting in a church pew with several hundred other people who loved Peter Babcock, remembering him and losing him together, I was dodging burning embers instead— driving my car full of photo albums and insurance documents and the people I love most and still have in my life to safety, for the moment, out of the line of fire.

WHAT IT'S LIKE
TO PURSUE HAPPINESS
NOW

Not Waiting to Write

FRIDAY, JANUARY 30, 1993

I'm whirling around the kitchen getting ready for Sabrina's going-away-from-Smith-&-Hawken party: trying on one unsatisfactory tablecloth and then another (the only time I remember to buy a good one is at moments of need like this one); stuffing white plastic forks into the blue ceramic vase Melissa made (and presented to me, filled with Hershey's kisses, at *my* going-away-from-Smith-&-Hawken party a year ago); splaying pink paper napkins, petal-like, I hope, around stacks of flowered paper plates and cups.

Diana is sitting at my desk in the front room, struggling to create a cover for the homemade photo album she's putting together for Sabrina. Surrounding her is the assortment of art supplies I dredged up from all corners of the house: glue stick and colored pencils from Jesse's room, markers from Peter's backpack, stamps and several colors of stamp pads from my collection. I hear my Macintosh chime. Diana must have given up on the old-fashioned method and decided to seek a higher-tech solution.

In my bedroom on the second floor Sabrina is dressing for her party. Unknown to her, each of the thirty people who will come here tonight will be wearing only black and white—with the exception, it is hoped, of our guest of honor. This secret sartorial theme is intended to ensure that Sabrina stands out.

"Everyone's been acting so weird all week, M," Sabrina complained when she called yesterday to ask if she could come over early and hang out before the party. "I swear, at least ten people have told me what they think I should wear tomorrow night. Do you know what's going on?"

"Umm . . . don't worry about it, S," I'd demurred. I'd received about that many calls myself from my former coworkers, frustrated in their efforts to convince Sabrina to wear bright colors tonight without revealing why. Having decided two weeks ago to quit the job she's had for three years, leave the city and the friends she's lived in and with for ten years, and move to Manhattan for a high-powered job that starts Tuesday morning, Sabrina had been too preoccupied with movers and yard sales to chitchat much about her party outfit.

I'd sneaked a peek at the clothes slung over Sabrina's arm as she headed upstairs to change; through the cloudy wrap of the dry cleaner's bag, I saw only muted mauves and grays. Luckily, we have a backup surprise: our going-away present to Sabrina is a gift-wrapped vibrator with all optional attachments included.

Tossing the fourth and final tablecloth choice over the kitchen table, I'm feeling torn: anticipating the pure pleasure of being with the people who will soon fill my house—and wishing there were no reason for this party.

I'm rarely happier than when I'm encircled by this group I still hold to me as family: the people I worked with in the Smith & Hawken Art Department (no, that doesn't say it—because the spiffy catalogs we produced were merely backdrop to the real business of our being together: the hugs and hilarity, lunchtime beach hikes and tearful happy-hour confessionals, daily dream-telling and company-wide rainbow alerts—the loving, loving, loving that hummed between us as we edited copy, propped photographs, wrapped type) until I left our cozy nest just before its ultimate disintegration, of which Sabrina's departure is final proof.

The phone rings. I answer it, expecting a partygoer asking for directions.

"Meredith?" asks a vaguely familiar voice. "It's Felicia."

Felicia! Reminding me of what I've spent this last week struggling to forget: that Felicia, my . . . (I can't quite spit out the word) *agent* is in New York peddling my . . . (dare I call it a) . . . *book*.

(Since we first met for lunch three months ago, Felicia has un-flinchingly referred to the hundred pages I stumblingly call "my writing" as "your book." She knows why I don't share her optimism: the last two almost-books I almost-wrote, ten and then five years ago, were almost-sold by snooty agents who wouldn't return my phone calls but did eventually return my nonbooks to me, along with dozens of rejection letters from wouldn't-be publishers.

But Felicia has invested considerable effort in cajoling me through my third—third time's the charm? Three strikes and you're out?—attempt at book-proposal-writing. And since that investment will only pay off if what I am writing is a book, as far as Felicia's concerned I am, indeed, writing a book.)

My heart pounds. Felicia! Ten years of receiving good publishing news and bad has taught me that the bad kind rarely comes by phone . . . and almost never ahead of schedule. Before she left for New York a few days ago, Felicia said I wouldn't be hearing from her until she got back to California next week.

She's calling me from New York. This can't be bad news. "I've had some interesting conversations in the past couple of days . . . ," Felicia is saying. *Interesting conversations?* ". . . with editors I've showed your pro-posal to. There's a lot of interest here, Meredith. A lot of very serious interest in your book.

"As a matter of fact," Felicia continues, "I'll have an offer from Bantam on Monday morning. I'm sure there will be other offers. I thought it might make your weekend to know."

My breath rushes through and out of me. The sound grabs Ann's attention; she dashes to my side. I feel my face and my life changing. I can see Diana at my desk two rooms away . . . but everything looks a little tilted, unfamiliar.

"Felicia—this isn't a joke, is it? You're not kidding, are you?" Ann's eyes, six inches from mine, grow wide. I tip the receiver away from my ear so Ann can listen in.

"No, Meredith, I'm not kidding. You should think about coming to New York to meet some people. I'll call you when I know something definite. Have a good weekend."

I put the phone down, grab Ann close to me, and whisper in her ear, "It's happening. Did you hear that? It's really happening."

"Oh, Babe," she breathes, hugging me tight. "I'm so happy for you."

"It's you I want to tell," I say, pulling back to look at her full-on. "I want to tell you first."

Ann's eyes fill with tears. "Really, Mer?" I nod, take a few steps to see if I can still walk, take a deep breath, and let loose a scream from the bottom of my bubbling innards.

Diana spins around in my desk chair; Sabrina comes galloping down the stairs. "What happened?" Sabrina gasps, trailing chiffon scarves in various (pale) colors, her (gray) pants half-zipped.

"My book . . . ," I stammer, tasting the words, for the first time, as if they belong now in my mouth. "My agent . . . it looks like she's gonna sell my book. The publishers love it."

"Wow," Diana says quietly, her dark eyes fastened on mine.

"Ohmigod," says Sabrina. "Does this mean you're gonna come visit me in New York? That's so great, M!" She squeezes my shoulder, glances at the clock, yelps, and bolts back up the stairs. Diana walks toward me slowly, grabs me, and says again, "Wow, Mer."

I can't think anything but the feeling is clear. The feeling is, my dream is coming true.

"Don't tell anyone tonight, okay?" I say to Ann and Diana. I don't know where this impulse for secrecy comes from; telling everyone everything immediately is more my usual style. "This is Sabrina's night," I say, "and anyway nothing's definite." But the truth is I haven't made this new information mine yet. I don't want to give it away until I do.

The doorbell rings and then rings again, and again. Our tuxedo-jacketed and black-T-shirted and white-Converse-high-topped friends stream through the door and into the kitchen bearing their assigned bowls of grilled chicken, grated cheese, diced onions, and chopped cilantro, and grease-stained bags full of whole-wheat tortillas and cinnamon *churros,* and six-packs of Dos Equis beer and lime Calistogas, and platters of lemon bars and brownies—throwing off their coats, hugging and kissing, loading their plates with roll-your-own fajitas, settling in around the coffee table to eat and laugh and talk and eat some more. Sabrina gets the black-and-white joke, duly admires everyone's adherence to the dress code, promises to wear red to her coming-back party.

It's always dreamlike, being with these people—more so since a year ago when I stopped being able to see them without planning it. But tonight I am truly floating: in my living room passing the salsa and feeding logs into the wood stove; under the covers hours after my mother has put me to bed writing stories by the dim beam of my Ringling Brothers circus flashlight; thrashing around in my marriage bed praying the agent will call and rescue me from the job and the life that are strangling me; showing my first-grade teacher my Arbor Day poem published in *Highlights for Kids;* Melissa's head in my lap, Diana massaging my feet, Ann sneaking secret smiles at me from across the room.

My writing is becoming a book. My ideas are being believed. My dream is coming true.

Sabrina unwraps her vibrator, blushes, gasps, dives behind the couch to hide. The women start swapping ultimate orgasm stories; the men, showing signs of embarrassment and titillation, escape one by one to the kitchen. From behind the couch I hear Sabrina's giggles as she unwraps each attachment; from the kitchen I hear the clinking of bottles as the men empty half-drunk beers into the sink and toss them into the recycling bin.

My house is full of happy noise but the usual clanging in my head ("IwantIwantIwantIwant") is blissfully silenced. I hold my secret tenderly to me like a sweet fragile newborn, cord yet uncut.

MONDAY, FEBRUARY 2, 1993

I'm sitting at the round table in my office discussing a direct-mail campaign with Terese and Tod when the phone rings at three-fifteen. It's bad office etiquette to take calls during a meeting, but office etiquette has been suspended for the duration: I'm waiting for life-altering news from New York.

"Meredith?" I recognize Felicia's voice by the adrenaline rush it prompts. "I can't talk long—I'm in a phone booth and it's freezing here. I just called to tell you I'm turning down a preemptive offer from Bantam for seventy-five thousand dollars. It would be good for you to come to New York as soon as possible."

"Oh my God," I gasp. I remember I am not alone. "Felicia: hold on a sec, okay?"

I turn to my coworkers, who know nothing of the parallel universe I've been inhabiting since Friday night—the universe for which, it now appears, I am likely to abandon them in the near future. "Sorry, guys— this is important, and . . . personal. Can I come find you in a few minutes?"

Tod and Terese look at me, intrigued, then silently gather up their recycled manila folders and pens and close my office door behind them.

"Felicia! What's a preemptive offer?"

"Preemptive means Bantam wants to be the only house bidding. If we accept their offer we don't get to show it to anyone else, or take any other offers," Felicia explains.

"But . . . seventy-five thousand dollars! Why'd you turn it down?" I'm trying hard not to shriek.

"Frankly, Meredith," Felicia says carefully, "because I took you at your word. When we first talked about this you told me you wanted to meet the editor you'd be working with before we made a deal. So I'm telling everyone here we can't accept an offer until you come to New York. You did say that, didn't you? Do you want to change your mind?"

Well, yes, I did say that . . . but I didn't expect you to listen, or remember, or believe me . . . I didn't really expect there to be an editor, or an offer, or a book . . .

"No, I guess not," I answer slowly. *But for $75,000 I could hate the editor and still be happy, couldn't I?*

"Okay then. You'll come to New York next week, meet all the editors who want to bid on the book. When you get home I'll take their offers and you'll tell me who you like. Then we'll decide which one to go with. I'll talk to you in a couple of days," Felicia says, and hangs up.

I fall into my chair, stunned. I'll *tell* you *who I like?* I'll *decide which one to go with?* In one phone call I've been transformed from beggar to queen.

One phone call. Two years ago exactly I was stumbling through my workdays waiting for one phone call . . . waiting to hear whether the lump that had been surgically removed from my right breast was benign or malignant. Then, too, the news was good. Then, too, I felt a new life had been given to me. But this . . .

In the few fantasies I've allowed myself to entertain since Felicia and I began, I never even imagined the possibility of more than one interested publisher. I thought getting a book contract would be like trying to get pregnant: searching for that one editor who would connect with my words like the one valiant sperm that finally connected with my eager egg.

I'd hoped—wildly, I thought—that that one editor would offer enough money so I could cut my work week back to four days, maybe three. Enough money to buy distance, if not disappearance, from the job at Working Assets—the job that's never felt as right to me as the one that got away a year ago. Enough money to be a writer. Not an editorial director, not a creative director, but a *writer*.

I'd hoped that some publisher would get invested enough in promoting my . . . book (if what I was writing should become one) that it would stand a chance of being read by more than the six people (five of them my mother) who bought copies of the youth culture treatise my first boyfriend and I published with Random House twenty years ago.

I'd hoped to learn the unknown pleasure of writing for long leisurely stretches—hour after hour for whole luxurious days. To write in time slots longer than the moments I'd been stealing from my over-stuffed life for the past year: the shrinking interval between the kids' bedtime and my own; the hour or two on cabin mornings, rousing myself and my PowerBook at dawn while Ann sleeps next to me and sunrise peeks through fingers of fog in the valley; slipping away from a still-warm computer at the end of a long workday in San Francisco, dashing to BART and home (on no-kids nights) to another unergonomic chair, another blinking cursor, a few paragraphs set down while my head throbs with exhaustion and a warm bed beckons.

What I am being presented with now is the granting of all these wishes, and more.

As difficult as it is for any part of my being to believe—my brain scans memory fruitlessly for previous experiences of such abundance, my Jewish DNA clangs a warning of holocausts to follow, my limbs grow rigid in defense against easing into the warm seductive soup of contentment—it seems undeniable that I will get not only some of what I want, but more. And more.

And despite my lifelong intimacy with scarcity and deprivation, some renegade cells in my body open to this feeling: of a vessel being filled to overflowing.

Later, walking home from the BART station at sunset, I hear the slap of Jesse's basketball against the driveway, punctuated by the snap of Ann's *gi* as she practices karate *katas* around Jesse's dribbling, shooting, and grunting: "Yes! Swish!"

"Hi guys," I call to my girl, and my baby boy. They run to greet me with the same question on their faces. Today, they know, was "the money day."

"Bantam offered seventy-five thousand dollars," I tell them. "Felicia turned it down. She's expecting other offers."

Jesse's big brown eyes get bigger. I see him turning inward, sorting out the zeroes, trying to understand the amount. This twelve-year-old boy—who asks periodically whether our house cost $2,000 or $200,000 and why I complain about paying $125 for his Air Jordans when I earn "like a million dollars a year"—is trying to sort out the meaning of this money.

"It's about time, Mom," Jesse says quietly. As is so often the case when my younger son speaks, I wonder if I have heard him correctly, or if he is channeling some being several lifetimes older than either of us. "What do you mean, Sweetie?" I ask.

"You're such a good writer," he answers, and because Jesse is so deeply disdainful of the concept and the mechanisms of flattery, his words send my spirit soaring. "Sometimes I read stuff like Stephen King, and it hooks me into it. Your writing hooks me into it that way."

I could die happy now, I think. I go into the house and find Peter in his usual tableau: watching ESPN with the remote control in one hand, the cordless phone at his ear in the other, a bag of salt-free tortilla chips, a bowl of medium-piquante salsa and his size ten, Reebok-shod feet on the coffee table in front of him.

"Babe . . . ," I say. He looks up at me, mutters a few words into the phone, and hangs it up. "It looks like I'll get at least seventy-five thousand dollars," I say.

Peter's face goes back in time . . . loses its fourteen-year-old jaded mask, crumples into ten-year-old excitement. "Oh boy," he hoots. "Here comes Hawaii!"

"Well, maybe," I say, reflecting on the role reversal I've just witnessed: Jesse, the age-appropriately self-centered one, instantly placing my news in the big picture of literary justice; Peter, the adult-pleaser, focusing immediately on the impact of this development on his chronic yearning for surf.

I realize suddenly there's something wrong with this picture: Sara, Peter's new (and first real) girlfriend, was supposed to be with us for dinner tonight.

"Where's Sara?" I ask, hoping, as I have every day for the past month, that they haven't broken up yet. The light leaves Peter's eyes; his mouth tightens.

"She's with Leda . . ." Peter looks at me intently; I see his little-boy longing to be protected, and his grown-up urge to protect me, both. Fourteen is such a strange age.

"Mom . . ." Peter's hazel eyes are burning. ". . . Leda's mom died today."

Like a punch to my gut, Peter's words double me over. I fall heavily onto the couch.

Breast cancer three years ago. Six months ago a recurrence. Two weeks ago, before she became comatose, Leda's forty-four-year-old mother said her good-byes to her husband of twenty years, her fourteen- and six-year-old daughters.

Today, Peter's friend Leda came home from school to hear that her mother is dead. Today, Peter came home from school to hear that his mother's wildest dreams have been given birth.

How can both of these things be true?

February 16, 1993

Ann and I are sitting on the burgundy velour couch facing the brown leather chair on the edge of which Arlene, our couples counselor, is perched, watching us intently. Ann and I are arguing, which isn't unusual—embarrassing as it always is, we've learned the hard (and expensive) way that there isn't much point in paying Arlene to witness our relationship unless we expose it to her: arguments, warts, and all.

What is unusual is how our bodies are arranged, and what we're arguing about.

Usually Ann and I take preemptively adversarial positions at opposite ends of the couch: Ann closest to the door, I closest to the box of Kleenex; both of us addressing our remarks to Arlene (or, in the worst of times, to the oriental rug on her hardwood floor as well as—white-noise machine notwithstanding—the neighborhood).

But tonight Ann and I sit laced together: legs intertwined, fingers in each other's hair, eyes fixed lovingly on each other's faces. And what we're arguing about is whose "fault" it is that we've been doing so well together for the past couple of months.

"It's you," my lover of nearly—incredibly—nine years informs me with great conviction. "You feel so present and *open.*"

I smile into her, remembering a particularly hot encounter at sunset in our cabin bed this past weekend. Ann reads my smile accurately, returns it, then shakes her head.

"I don't just mean sexually"—I steal a glance at Arlene and see that she is beaming proudly—"although that's been great too. I mean your softness. Your sweetness . . ."

"I think it's you," I argue. "You've been so patient, so supportive. I can't believe you're encouraging me to write this book when it's blowing your privacy to bits."

"I worry that you're just being so nice to me because you're high about the book," Ann frets, shrugging off my appreciation as effortlessly as she has, in the bad moments—when our old and recent wounds have flared and we have railed against each other, not hearing, not loving—shrugged off my accusations.

"No," I tell her. "I've had so many ups and downs with this thing; normally that would make us fight. Something else is different."

Ann is frowning with concentration. Just as she turns maps inside out while I drive around stopping strangers for directions, she is struggling to figure this out by herself, while I turn impatiently to Arlene for her opinion. Arlene turns the question back to me.

"Do you *feel* any different, Meredith?"

Safely held in the caring cradle of these two women who want the best of and for me, I take a deep breath to summon courage, reach inside, and say, without censoring, what I find there.

"I feel like I can meet you now," I say to Ann. "I can stand where I am. This whole process with the book makes me feel like I'm solid, grounded. Being believed by the world makes me believe my own truth more. I'm not as afraid as I used to be that you can take it away from me when we're fighting. So I guess I have less to fight you about."

"Ahhh . . . wonderful," Arlene breathes, leaning back in her chair.

For a long moment the three of us sit silently together, aglow. Then my mind starts clacking.

"But it disgusts me," I say, "that it took this kind of external affirmation to make me strong enough to stand in a room and be with my lover. Why should a book contract make so much difference?"

Arlene leans forward again, shaking her head vehemently. "It's not just the book, Meredith," she says. "It's what you went through two years ago with your biopsy. It's what you went through a year ago wrenching yourself away from that job at Smith & Hawken and those people you loved so much. It's everything you went through in your childhood, everything you're working on in your own therapy, everything you and

Ann have worked on so hard for all these years. This is just the culmina-
tion."

I feel teary but good. I believe her. It feels true and right that I'm
happier, wholer than I've ever been—and that the happiness, strangely,
is made possible by all the unhappiness I've known and struggled
through and survived.

It was unhappiness that brought me—as it did when I was six and
ten and fifteen years old—to writing. And the writing gave back to me—
as it did when I was six and ten and fifteen years old—a mirror to reflect
and integrate a lifetime of refracted reality, disbelieved truth.

I made a promise to myself the day I sat down to begin this writing,
a year ago: that I would honor the process above any outcome—that no
hopes or enticements of wealth or fame would derail me from this
bumpy road to meet myself.

Even in making this promise I doubted myself, my intention to
keep it. Suspecting my own motivation, repeatedly I self-administered
this quiz: If there was to be no agent, no publisher, no money, no chance
to change my worklife, no magazines clamoring for excerpts, no drama
fix—would I still keep waking up at dawn to write and staying up late to
write and crying and shaking and laughing my way through these stories
of my life?

And this is how I began to believe myself, this past year, about my
writing and my reality and my truth: each time I asked myself these
questions, the answer came back clearly, and it was always: yes, yes, yes.

"Learning to hang on to my truth," I say to Arlene and Ann now, "is
what all of this is about. And that is . . . ecstasy."

Jewish to Buddhist and Back

"We have yarmulkes here for anyone who wants one," says my friend Sam, his own black velvet skullcap strategically placed to cover the spreading circle of hairlessness atop his pate. Sam gets up from his place at the head of the Seder table and walks around it, proffering a yarmulke to each of the men and women. He stops beside Peter, nods at Jesse. "Boys?"

Jesse looks at me questioningly—"Do I have to?" his eyes ask. I shrug, releasing him from obligation; he turns his glance to Peter across the table. "Do I want to?" Peter peers appraisingly at the varicolored collection of yarmulkes in Sam's outstretched hand. "We've got one to match every outfit," Sam says encouragingly.

A frown flashes briefly across Peter's face. Insulted by the suggestion that his spiritual choices might be swayed by such superficial motives, he shakes his head. "No thanks."

True to his second-child developmental task, Jesse immediately chirps up, "I'll take one."

Jesse chooses a maroon satin yarmulke the precise color of his massively oversized Girbaud denim jeans, and perches it precariously atop his sawed-off haircut. An instant later, he reaches up and flattens the yarmulke against his forehead so it covers his eyebrows like a backwards baseball cap. Surreptitiously, he checks himself out in the breakfront mirror across the room, then buries his eyes in the copy of the Haggadah that's been placed before him. Each of the seven adults around the table is struggling to squelch a smile.

I wince, imagining Jesse's reaction if he should notice theirs. Both of my children—but Jesse especially—are allergic to condescension real or imagined. I give Jesse's back a compensatory reassuring rub. The slight pressure of his body against—not away from—my hand tells me that he accepts my sympathy.

"Before we begin," says Sam, "I should tell you—this Haggadah is from the forties and it's full of sexist language. So as we read, let's just substitute 'she' for 'he,' 'humans' for 'mankind,' and so on. Frankie, do you want to start?"

I pick up my Haggadah, place it in my lap, flip quickly to the back (oh yes, I remember now: the back is in the front) and check the page count: One hundred and seventy-three pages. Jesus.

I steal a peek at my watch. Six-thirty already. I wanted to celebrate Passover, but—I didn't want to celebrate it all *night,* for God's sake. And if I'm going to make it to morning meditation tomorrow, I've got to be at Zen Center at five forty-five A.M.

In front of me, and my hungry children, and my lover who worked through lunch today so she could get to the Seder on time, are square stacks of matzos, bowls of hard-boiled eggs, the special Seder plate upon which Frankie has placed a few sprigs of parsley, a mound of *haroset,* and a large bare bone.

How long will it be until we get to put any of this food into our mouths? Scanning my memories of Seders past, I recall getting to eat a piece or two of matzo, maybe an egg and a bit of *haroset,* during the ceremony itself; then more reading, then the meal, then more reading . . .

I didn't remind the kids about this ceremony when I cajoled them into coming here tonight. In my argument I focused on my favorite part of the Seder: the dispensing of lots of good Jewish food. (A double redundancy, that: Jewish food only comes in one flavor: scrumptious;

and one quantity: five times more than could possibly be consumed by the people present.)

"Do I have to go?" Peter asked last week when I told him that for the second year in a row, we'd be celebrating Passover with our only religious Jewish friends, Sam and Frankie, and their daughters, Sarah and Leah.

"Yes," I answered, surprising both of us. I've almost never dragged my kids anywhere they didn't want to go, especially since last year when Peter requested, and was granted, exemption from all preplanned family activities.

But it was also last year, after our first Seder at Sam's, that Peter (in recovery from a long stint as a self-described "black wannabe") became interested in his Jewishness. He made some Jewish friends, attended some bar and bat mitzvahs, and was sufficiently intrigued by the possibility of an ethnic identity (as well as the cash prizes awarded thereupon) to ask Sam how he might get bar mitzvahed.

I was thrilled—until Peter asked me if I'd attend bar mitzvah classes with him, maybe even get bat mitzvahed myself. Then I hit the brick wall of my lifelong ambivalence about all things Jewish. I had to tell my son, truthfully but sadly, that I was lacking the energy or the conviction to do what I'd wanted to do as a child, and now wanted him to have the chance to do: learn to be, and learn to love being, what he is—a Jew.

"I've always wished I knew enough about Judaism to teach it to you and Jesse," I told Peter, "but I don't—because of how *I* was raised. I want to give you guys enough experience so you can choose to be religious or not, and raise your kids religiously or not. Luckily we have Sam and Frankie to educate all of us.

"Anyway," I added, resorting to the argument I'd used, ultimately, to convince myself, "you know the food'll be great."

And indeed, it seems that it will be—whenever we get to eat it. From the kitchen, smells swarm into my quivering nostrils—smells that snap my blurry Passover memories into sharp focus. The long-untasted flavors of my childhood: tender chicken, soft, sweet carrots, and fluffy matzo balls simmering in rich golden broth; crusty beef ribs roasting astride whole heads of garlic; chunked yams bubbling beneath a browning blanket of melting marshmallows.

My DNA sings for joy, easily overpowering the dissenting whispers of my ambivalence, and my recently taken vegetarian vows. The last time I had a homemade matzo ball was at my Grandma Sophie's Seder table nearly thirty years ago.

The "dining nook" in my grandparents' gloomy three-room apartment on West Eighty-sixth Street was far too small to accommodate their three sons, two daughters-in-law, and four grandchildren. So each Passover we'd arrive to find their sunken living room filled from end to end with card tables pushed together and covered in starched linens upon which, my cousins and brother and I were warned repeatedly, we were not to spill a single drop of the syrupy purple Manischewitz wine that we were served in shot glasses on Passover only.

The oldest (and most outspoken) grandchild, I sat each year at my grandfather's right shoulder and recited the four questions—a little proud, a little embarrassed, mostly eager to get on to the feast whose aromas suffused the small apartment as we hurried our way, skipping all of the songs and most of the words, through the Haggadah.

"*Why, on this night, do we eat bitter herbs?*" I would read, following my grandfather's creased, liver-spotted finger across the page. "*Because our forefathers were slaves in Egypt . . .*"

At my grandparents' Seders there were no politically correct revisions (or discussion) of the sexist text; no yarmulke fashion statements; no jokes, no tears, no laughter. There was only this incomprehensible ritual, parts of it conducted in an incomprehensible foreign language, which seemed to mean something (but what?) to my grandparents and nothing much to anyone else.

I never understood what the Seder was actually about, let alone the bigger questions it raised. For instance: what it meant to be a Jew, and why my parents—both of them Jewish-educated, bar mitzvahed, and confirmed—seemed so determined to be and associate with anything *but* Jews. But the rituals that signaled the end of the Seder, at least, became predictable over the years.

When the last flourless crumb of honey cake had been eaten, my uncle Mitch (the thinnest of the Maran boys) would stand up, burp contentedly, pat his flat stomach while peering down at his shoes, and ask loudly (with a sidelong glance at my grandmother, at whom his compliment was directed), "Are my shoelaces tied?"

Then my uncles would light their fat brown cigars and my grandfather would send me to search for the piece of matzo he'd hidden, invariably, under the pile of monogrammed handkerchiefs on his dresser. Upon surrendering the matzo to him, I would receive (along with the approving nods of my aunt and uncles and the envious glares of my brother and cousins) a crisp new dollar bill, purchased from the bank especially for the occasion.

This transaction completed, the men would begin dismantling the makeshift Seder table and moving the plastic-covered couches back into place. And my grandmother would scurry to the kitchen, where she went to work dividing the mountains of intentional leftovers into scrubbed-out mayonnaise jars she would fill, wipe clean, then pack into A&P grocery bags she'd press upon each set of guests as we left.

Equally predictable were my parents' complaints—for days before and after Passover and the three or four other family gatherings they reluctantly attended each year—about having to show up "just to make Sophie and Jake happy." Even as they emptied the contents of the mayonnaise jars into their wedding-present Revere Ware, sighing contentedly as the fragrant steam rose from my grandmother's homemade sweetbreads and chicken fricassee, they would bemoan the wasted evening spent with people they disdained, honoring a religion they'd long since rejected.

It confused me then and it confuses me now: the pure pleasure of my grandmother's buttery chicken melting on my tongue; the bored, boring voices of my uncles as they read from the Haggadah; the buried treasure I searched for in the gobbledygook of Hebrew and English— the sense of something there that belonged to me, yet wasn't mine; something that would welcome me, make for me a place in the world and the family from which I felt so alienated.

My parents' eager escape, while the special Passover plates still dripped in the drainer, from my grandparents' joyless apartment; my grandmother's devotion to feeding us, in her home and then for days after we'd returned to our white-carpeted, three-bedroom apartment (to which she was rarely invited) on the more posh East Side of town.

Why didn't my family go to synagogue, as all my friends and cousins did?

Why wouldn't my parents let me go to temple with my best friend Michelle Blumenstein on Saturdays—or at least on my favorite Jewish holidays? (The ones that involved special foods and boisterous behavior.) I could only imagine the mysterious Jewish ceremonies, the sense of belonging she had enjoyed without me when Michelle returned at last: her taffeta "temple dress" crumpled, her patent leather shoes scuffed, slick-faced from excitement, with noisemakers in her hands and bits of candy apple still clinging to her cheeks.

Why did my mother drill me after school until every trace of my classmates' New York Jewish accent was purged from my tongue and I was disconnected not only from the religion and the rituals that bound my friends to their families and their history and each other, but finally, from the dialect they shared?

Why was I the only kid in my class who got presents on one morning in December while school was out for "Christmas" break and there was no one except Michelle to brag to—instead of every night for eight nights while school was in session and my classmates huddled together each morning of that interminable Hanukkah week, ardently exchanging descriptions of last night's bounty?

(Shunning Hanukkah, excluded from Christmas, my mother invented a secular rite involving neither menorah nor tree. On Christmas morning my brother and I would wake to find our presents hidden throughout the apartment, each gift attached by a strand of yarn to our bedroom doors. It was creative, but it wasn't Hanukkah.)

Why did my friends' fathers speak with thick throaty accents, work as tailors and graveyard-shift butchers, have blurry blue numbers tattooed on their forearms—while my father left for his downtown office each morning dressed in crisp tailored shirts my mother delivered to, and then fetched from the Chinese laundry, fastened at the wrist with shiny gold cufflinks?

Why were my friends' parents never invited from upstairs or across the hall to the rib roast dinners my mother prepared from the best meat in Manhattan, procured for us at wholesale prices by Herman Blumenstein, Michelle's butcher father? These dinners my mother cooked only for my father's bosses and coworkers and their wives—starched, hairsprayed, suited, and nyloned, with clean, manicured fingernails; no numbers tattooed on their arms, and flawless diction.

And why, when I left my parents' house, did I live fully fifteen years without once considering my Jewishness? It wasn't until Christmas Eve 1981, when I came upon my three-year-old firstborn son—he of upturned freckled nose, blond ringlets, and Episcopalian father—sitting enraptured in his yellow Dr. Dentons before the blinking lights of the Christmas tree we had decorated happily together in our suburban San Jose tract house the night before, that some sleeping Jew in me was startled awake. And she shrieked above the Christmas carols playing merrily in the background, "How did my life turn into this Norman Rockwell painting?"

I realized then that despite my childhood yearning to belong to the society of Jews, I had absorbed through the leaky membrane between my parents and me their apparent conviction that to keep themselves and their children safe from anti-Semitism, they must distance themselves from that group and every member of it.

Jew-hating in the world seemed to have engendered Jew-hating in my parents. Self-hatred had engendered anger—and anger's helpless twin: fear. My parents feared, and ran from, the equation they saw between being Jewish and being victimized—condemned to hoisting bloody sides of beef onto meat hooks at three in the morning; living their final years in an airless three-room apartment; being herded into cattle cars bound for death camps. And that equation had taken root in me.

I thought that in the fifteen years since I had separated myself from my parents—physically, politically, emotionally—I had examined every mark they'd left on me. I was well into the expensive, disturbing process of coming to know (and in rare sparkling moments, to accept) the many parts of me unknown to, and unaccepted by, my parents.

But now I saw before me a vast terrain of unexplored territory: my parents' rejection of their Jewish selves, and my own mindless rejection of the Jewish part of me.

Here was the legacy of that unexamined heritage: I was living my life and raising my children without knowledge or celebration of their Jewishness—and without a single Jew in my life not related to me by blood. My husband, my brother's wife (and, according to Jewish matrilineal law, their children), my friends, my coworkers in the factories where I'd been building trucks, tin cans, and socialist consciousness for the past eight years—not one was a Jew.

It took me two years of clearing psychic underbrush to begin inching and stumbling my way toward the part of me called "Jew." I began down this path not knowing what I was looking for. Self-acceptance? Religion? Culture? Ethnicity?

I went to the library and read children's books on Judaism. (The adult texts were boring and cerebral, but the kids' books were full of goose-bump-raising action stories, villains, heroes, and heroines.) I crept into the back row of a progressive Berkeley synagogue on Yom Kippur. I bought a Jewish cookbook, and a thick manual called *The First Jewish Catalog: A do-it-yourself kit.*

Finally I was ready to go public, starting with my closest and toughest audience. On Christmas Eve 1983, I introduced my family to Hanukkah.

To ease us all into our first Jewish holiday I created a ritual I called "Hanuchris." With the presents stacked under Drew and Berta's popcorn-and-cranberry-draped Christmas tree (I'd added a few wrapped in blue-and-silver Hanukkah paper to the green-and-red-wrapped pile), and with my mother in (unusually reticent) attendance, we ate the first latkes I'd ever cooked and spun the first dreidel any of our kids had ever touched.

(The spiritual context may have been unclear, but the concept of *gimmel*—or "gimme," as the kids called it—was eagerly grasped, along with several dozen gold-wrapped coins of chocolate *gelt*.)

When the honey cake was finished, I read the condensed and simplified version of the Hanukkah story I'd compiled from the books I'd been studying. After every sentence or two I'd stop reading to encourage questions—not just "the four questions," but as many as the kids had.

"Why didn't they just buy more oil at the store?" asked three-year-old Jesse.

"Did they have bombs for their war?" asked Peter. And then, his eyes darting to the redwood menorah his father had carved for the occasion, "Can I light all the candles?"

"How come they had women soldiers?" asked five-year-old Josie, adding gravely, "Candles are dangerous."

"You did that, huh, Rita?" three-year-old Nicholas asked his grandmother. "You fought for the Jewish people with Grandpa Sid, huh?"

"When do we get to open our presents?" asked Peter.

And so we all moved from the gelt-strewn dining room table to sit beneath the boughs of the Christmas tree and Roberta put the Christmas music on and my husband played Santa and we ate candy canes and squealed over our presents.

Hanuchris was a hit. I had visions of stitching this new ritual firmly to the fabric of our extended family—the kids' questions growing more sophisticated, their connection to their heritage more solid each year it was repeated; repairing in Peter, Jesse, Josie, and Nicholas's generation the damage of inherited, internalized anti-Semitism that had nearly rent me from my heritage.

But by the next December the rupture in our family had rendered Hanuchris irrelevant. Peter and Jesse spent Christmas at their father's house in San Jose, where they decorated a tree with our family ornaments and woke at dawn to ravage the stockings hung from the mantel.

And they spent Hanukkah at their mother's house in Oakland, where they ate latkes and took turns lighting the menorah and opened two presents each (one from me, one from Ann) on each of the eight nights.

Newly divorced, raising my children as a single mother with a freelance journalist's income and a $950 mortgage to pay, I became more focused on survival than spirituality. Anyway, my sense of urgency had been alleviated. I'd established a baseline of Jewishness in our lives: however confusing they might have found this information, Peter and Jesse now knew that their maternal grandparents were Jewish (although they didn't identify themselves as such) and their mother was Jewish (although she was learning and teaching them Judaism from a catalog), and they were Jewish (although their father wasn't, and they didn't go to synagogue or observe most Jewish holidays).

Living with me near the Berkeley border, Peter and Jesse were no longer the only Jewish kids on their block or in their classes. They came home from school each December with construction-paper menorahs along with tinfoil angels; they sang "Dreidel dreidel dreidel, I made it out of clay," along with "Silent Night."

Even if I hadn't quite achieved the religious experience I'd hoped for, my exploration had yielded some measure of self-awareness, a few new holidays to celebrate each year, and a move to a more Jewish-populated neighborhood. As my children and I slipped comfortably into our new, assimilationist environment, our nascent Jewish education slipped by the wayside.

I never missed it.

Until the day, years later, when my doctor found a lump in my breast and in my uncontainable panic I searched every interior corner of myself for a spiritual perspective to help me understand, breathe, live through this—and found nothing there to sustain me.

Where was the G-d whose name Michelle was forbidden to write but who surely would see her through a crisis like this one, in return for the hours she had spent in synagogue worshiping and shaking noise-makers at Him?

Where was the family of Jews who died in defense of each other's Jewishness in the blood-spattered streets of Warsaw?

Where was the faith that my forebears packed up in suitcases of string and cardboard and fled with to America, forsaking their homeland and all that was familiar in order to go on practicing Judaism?

It wasn't in me.

I'd learned some Jewish history, and made contact with my ethnically and culturally Jewish self. But my inherited ambivalence was still stronger than my fledgling Jewish identity. The spiritual benefits of Judaism were as inaccessible to me as ever.

And so in my desperation to keep my mind intact, whatever the fate of my body, I was willingly led by my lesbian feminist doctor to a lesbian feminist spiritual teacher who, in the three months between discovery and biopsy, slowed my racing heart with acupuncture needles, odoriferous Chinese herbs, a sugar-free diet, and Buddhist meditation tapes.

As I lay in Barbara's darkened treatment room with the heat lamp warming my feet and an ink drawing of Gaia above my head, the voice of a Jew named Jack Kornfield urged me to "take the one seat in the center of the room" from which, he said, a student of Buddhism—now, suddenly, me!—might sit and calmly regard all the comings and goings, the breast lumps and loving caresses, the terrors and the passions, as benign blips on the big screen of the universe.

I could scarcely believe my ears: here was a Jew who *aspired* to relinquish control, and urged others to do the same—as if trust was not toxic, but a reasonable default mode. A Jew who believed in attentive breathing and surrender, not hyperventilation and hypervigilant struggle, as a way to heal not only one's self, but the world.

Unexpectedly—my Marxist-Leninist training notwithstanding—I was comforted by this notion of myself as a speck in the universe, whose life and death had no greater significance than that of Adolf Hitler, Harriet Tubman, or the mosquitoes I slapped to death on my arms each summer.

I, who at age forty still believed, secretly and deeply, that I was as powerful in my world as a six-year-old, responsible somehow for everything wrong and for righting it all as well—was profoundly grateful to have stumbled upon a belief system that relieved me of this unbearable burden.

In my weekly sessions with Barbara she offered neither diagnoses nor prognoses, modeling a method of nurturing previously unknown to me: no answers, no solutions—just presence. With her blunt fingers pressed soothingly against the racing pulses at my wrist, Barbara interrupted, with her gentle Buddhist parables and her tiny needles and the meditation tapes she played for me, the tape loop of despair that was blaring in my aching brain.

For the first time in my life I could imagine freedom from the self-punishing disaster scenarios I'd inflicted on myself daily since childhood. "What's the worst thing that could happen?" I would ask myself— ostensibly to self-soothe but in reality to make contact with the throb of familiar, immobilizing fear—when I couldn't find my mother at the skating rink, when I'd swallowed more LSD than I should have, when Jesse was late coming home from school in the dark, when I'd found a lump in my breast.

But according to the Buddhists, my deepest fear—and the deepest fear, instilled through generations of pogroms and holocausts, of the Jewish people—was not worth fearing, for it had already come true. I *was* out of control: of my breast tissue, my body, my fate, the world.

Once I'd consulted the best doctors, eaten the purest food, written the most generous will, there were no answers or solutions to exhaust myself by chasing. I could rest, rescued from the inherited belief that if I just made the right choice, took the right turn, I could outsmart, outrun, or prevent disaster.

What, then, was truly "the worst thing that could happen"? I could condemn myself to living the rest of my life, whether fifty weeks or fifty years, locked in struggle against that immutable truth. There was no question that I would die; the only question was: what was to be the quality of the time between now and then? I couldn't control the earthquakes or heartbreaks or breast lumps, but I could control (or try, anyway) my responses to these events.

In the months after the biopsy, as the scar on my right breast faded from angry scarlet to subdued pink, I set about keeping the promise I'd made to myself in the surgeon's waiting room: to move these new ideas from my head into my body, to create for myself a spiritual practice—

whether I had cancer or not, whether I "needed it" or not. (I needed it. And I knew it.)

I briefly considered turning to Judaism, picking up where I'd left off; this time putting enough into it to get back what I needed. But it felt too overwhelming—despite everything I'd worked through, too *scary*— to undertake a struggle against my fearfulness while embracing the religion that was still so deeply associated, in some dark corner of my psyche, with the cause of it.

Buddhism was readily available to me. It was unassociated with anyone or anything that had ever frightened me. And it had already given me a dose of exactly what I wanted from religion: it had seen me through a major crisis, in better shape afterwards than I'd been in before.

So I took a week off between the end of the job at Smith & Hawken and the beginning of the job at Working Assets and—resisting the urge to stay home and reorganize closets, or retreat to the familiar solitude of our cabin in the woods—gave myself a spiritual kick in the butt and checked myself into Sonoma Mountain Zen Center.

What did I know from Zen Centers, a nice Jewish girl like me? Only that this one had agreed to have me, for twenty-five dollars a day including meals—even after I admitted that I'd never set foot in a Zen Center before, didn't have a *roshi* or even a *zafu* to call my own, had never in my life sat still, let alone sat *zazen*—on the condition that I'd follow the rules and routines of the resident monks. And how was I to learn these rules and routines? Upon my arrival I was instructed, simply, to watch carefully and mimic everything the residents did.

Imagine my surprise: being awakened at four forty-five every morning by the insistent percussion of a wooden clapper outside my cabin; being led along a dark, frost-crusted path by black-robed, glowingly bald monks of indeterminate gender; bowing solemnly be-fore, during, and after entering the dimly lantern-lit *zendo*; sitting with my legs crossed, motionless, facing the rough-hewn pine wall, for six hours each day.

And—most incredibly—I was expected to perform all my func-tions at Zen Center: sitting *zazen*; shuffling slowly around the *zendo* in walking meditation; pulling weeds from the *roshi's* yard and blackberry

brambles from the orchard; eating lentil curry and praiseworthy blackberry muffins; washing and meticulously drying bowls, teacups, and
chopsticks—not only with my eyes averted at all times, but in complete
silence.

Silence! Me! Never had I felt so Jewish as when I was deprived of
what my Grandma Sophie had diplomatically referred to as my "gift of
gab."

The biggest surprise was that it worked. Although I spent most of
the first day (silently) plotting my escape—They can't keep me here!
They can't make me weed some guy's yard when my own yard needs
weeding! This is so patriarchal! What will I *do* while I'm meditating all
that time?—I began to notice that the silence, at first torturous, was
moving inside me, where it became less deafening and unexpectedly
comforting.

I noticed how much there was to notice when words (my protec-
tors! My armor!) didn't get in the way, and how I was coming to know
the people I was sitting and eating and working with, although we'd
never spoken to each other.

Having joked for years about being "the only living lesbian in
California who's never read a book or been to a meeting about addic-
tion," I noticed the core of codependence that kept me from myself: how
I'd step into the *zendo* or the dining room and immediately focus on the
man who coughed, the woman whose teacup was empty, the *roshi* whose
special attention I wanted—everyone other than the person I'd checked
into Zen Center to focus on.

In meditation and in enforced silence, the game of looking for a
mirror in every reflective surface lost its appeal. Slowly I closed my eyes
and sank into myself, lonely and relieved.

I left Zen Center feeling I'd gotten what I went there for. I found a
calmer place within myself to go—a place that goes with me now, when
I'm jammed into a BART train feeling bummed out by all the shut-down,
suited-and-tied commuters around me; when I'm starting to cue the
terror tape before my annual mammogram; when I'm slipping away
from myself in a fight with Ann; when I push myself to sit *zazen* two or
three times a month at the *zendo* five blocks from my house.

"I don't know why you're shopping for a religion," said Sam, shaking his head when I told him I'd been at Zen Center for a week. "You've got a perfectly good one of your own."

Maybe if I'd been raised to know and love, instead of fearing, Judaism, I would be looking now for what I need closer to home. Maybe someday I'll find it there—or maybe Judaism is, and always will be, *too* close to home.

For now, I'm grateful to have meditation tapes that calm me when I start to whir around, a menorah to light on Hanukkah and sons and a lover who expect to light it with me, a place for my sneakers on the wooden rack outside the *zendo,* a good friend and spiritual teacher named Barbara, and good friends and spiritual teachers named Sam and Frankie who cook foods that smell and taste like forever and invite me and my *meshuggeh* family, along with other Jewish "orphans," to learn and laugh and celebrate with them on *Shabbas,* and Yom Kippur, and Pesach.

"Why, on this night, do we eat bitter herbs?" Jesse reads, his deepening voice clear and sure. *"Because our forefathers and, um, foremothers were slaves in Egypt . . ."*

I close my eyes for a moment, reaching inside as I learned to do in the *zendo,* welcoming the tears that well up from the depths. Pride is not an emotion I have often allowed myself to feel in relation to my children—because I am so aware that they are themselves, not adjuncts of me. But proud is what I feel right now.

A thousand years ago in a tent inflamed by blazing desert sun, or fifty years ago huddled in an unheated hidden attic—on this first night of Pesach my son would be reading these very words. My eyes would be filling with these very tears of sorrow and pride.

"Why do we dip the herbs twice tonight?" Jesse continues. *"As a sign of hope; the hope of freedom."*

I touch my hand to Jesse's back, feel the ancient words resounding through his strong young body. From what source or sources will Jesse draw his hope of freedom?

Maybe next year he'll want to be bar mitzvahed, or maybe next year I'll have to talk him into coming to Sam and Frankie's Seder with me.

Maybe next year we'll have a Seder at our house, and Sam and his family will come and celebrate with us.

Maybe someday I'll be invited to a Seder at Jesse's house, or Peter's.

As for me: on this night, and on all other nights, I wish for my sons—and for myself—freedom from self-hatred and fear, wherever and however each of us may find that freedom.

Therapy Dreams

Therapy Dream, May 24, 1993

"We have to stop now," Miranda says, as she does at the end of every session. What do you mean "we"? I think sarcastically, as I always do. I don't have plans. Let's stay another hour or two.

Instead of waiting for me to leave, saying good-bye to me from her chair as she always does, Miranda gets up and walks into the next room. I'm still sitting on the couch, check in hand, waiting for a normal ending. I hear water running. I know that Miranda is in the kitchen washing dishes. I also know that to go in there, to watch her doing a normal life thing, will demote her instantly from the superhuman status upon which our precious, precarious dynamic depends.

But I find it irresistible to test this limit, and so I move to the kitchen doorway, where I stand silently watching her lather and rinse, lather and rinse mug after matching white porcelain mug. Sunshine streams through the window above the sink, framing her face with light like a golden lion's mane. I think what I have secretly thought during most of my sessions with Miranda: She's so pretty.

I wonder if she serves tea to her other clients in those mugs. She has never offered me tea, although she sometimes sips water from a ceramic cup during my sessions. I wonder if she gives tea to them, not to me, because she cares more for them. Doesn't she realize what she's showing me by washing all those mugs in front of me? How can she be so insensitive? Or maybe she's forcing me to confront this evidence that she sees other people, endless streams of strangers who pay her and depend on her as I do—but to whom she serves tea in clean white mugs.

Miranda finishes and dries her hands on a blue checked dish towel. I follow her out of the office, out of the building. Once we're on the sidewalk I realize that I'm in New York City, the place in the world I least want to be. Although I grew up here, I no longer know my way around.

I focus on projecting how helpless I feel, and it works: Miranda takes my hand protectively. I am at once soothed and horrified. Finally, I'm getting what I've always wanted from her: she is reaching to me across the boundary that defines and restricts our relationship. At the same time, I dread the repercussions, the inevitable loss that will result from violating that limit.

I say to Miranda: "I've had recurring nightmares about being forced to move back to New York." I point across the street to a hulking gray gargoyle-laden edifice. "That's the building I always dream I'm forced to live in."

Miranda says to me: "I used to work in that building."

We approach the steps to a subway station. I'm so terrified to be in this awful city, so grateful to have Miranda taking care of me that I've given up worrying about the long-term effects on our relationship.

As we go down the steps (Miranda still holding my hand) I notice that she is limping. On closer examination I see that one of her legs is encased in metal braces; she is badly crippled. How could I have failed to notice this in all the years I've been seeing her? Come to think of it, have I ever seen her standing up before today? Has she been deliberately hiding her disability from me? Or did this just happen to her now, as we were walking down the street together?

I slow my pace, falling slightly behind her, to preserve the good feeling that she is leading me.

Inside the subway station Miranda sees a woman she knows—an obvious lesbian. "Hi, Frannie," Miranda says. "This is . . . um . . . Meredith." My despair resurfaces. Now I know what I've always wondered and never wanted to know: Miranda's a lesbian.

"You see what happens when you break the rules?" I want to scream at her. Sure, I liked having her hold my hand—but she's the one who's supposed to be in charge, the one who's supposed to withhold anything that, if given, might threaten our relationship. "Now I'll find out *everything* about you!"

Miranda drops my hand, limps over to Frannie. The two of them stand a few feet away from me, whispering together. I feel humiliated, certain that Miranda is explaining to her who I am (a particularly needy, desperate client). But wait a minute: shouldn't Miranda be at least as embarrassed as I am? Isn't our being together in a subway, our holding hands, her transgression as much as it's mine?

A train explodes into the station. I want to tell Miranda about another recurring nightmare of my childhood, the one in which the subway platform I'm walking on suddenly shrinks to the width of a wire and I teeter, about to fall to my death beneath the wheels of an oncoming train. But Miranda is way ahead of me now, pushing through the crowd to be first on line.

The train squeals to a stop. Miranda is waving to get the conductor's attention, pointing to her shriveled leg. Before my eyes she suddenly becomes an old, fat, homeless woman, wearing a tattered rag of a house dress and thick beige stockings rolled around her swollen, scabby ankles.

The conductor understands her gestures and rolls out a special boarding platform for the disabled. All the aggressive (nondisabled) New Yorkers in the station rush to take advantage of this—including me.

Once I'm on board I look around. I can't find Miranda. The train doors slam shut. My throat, my whole body is clenched with fear. I look through the filthy, cloudy window and see Miranda still standing on the platform. I scream frantically to the conductor to stop the train, but it's too late. I don't know where this train is going, where Miranda was taking me, where I'm going now without her. All I know is, I'm on my own.

THERAPY SESSION, MAY 26, 1993

"I had a big dream about you the other night," I tell Miranda. I am lying on my back with my eyes closed, grateful for this acceptable way to keep from looking at her. Out-of-season rain drums fiercely against the skylight above my head. Lying this way, I can almost believe she can't see me either.

For a long time the rain is the only sound in the room. I like this about Miranda, about the understanding between us: there is, in this room, respect for silence. As in the *zendo,* there is time to breathe, to slip into a trance of *feeling, not thinking.* Yet somehow Miranda senses, reels me back, when I start to spin out instead of in.

"Do you want to tell me your dream?" Miranda asks finally. My throat constricts; I inhale noisily.

"It's scary . . . embarrassing," I say. I hear her earrings—she's wearing three: a lapis stud and a dangling silver one in the right ear; a dangling silver one in the left—making tiny ringing sounds as she nods her head.

"The intimacy of it?" she asks.

"The intimacy, yes," I answer.

Eyes still closed, I start to remember the dream. And then into my mind springs a picture of the orthopedic cushion set into the crook of Miranda's chair. I noticed it for the first time two sessions ago. The cushion was there again today. I wonder if she's having back problems. I wonder if she's in pain right now. I wonder how she can possibly concentrate on me when she's . . .

"Meredith? Where'd you go?" Miranda asks.

I sigh deeply. And then I tell her my dream.

Once I'm into it it's not so bad. It's like telling a story. Except for telling the feelings. I leave out the part about thinking—in the dream, and in real life—that she's pretty. I am quick to reassure her that there was nothing sexual in our hand-holding. I laugh self-consciously when I tell the most embarrassing parts: the jealousy about her other clients; the happiness when she took my hand; the wondering—in the dream, and in real life—whether or not she's a lesbian.

"Let's go back to that building," Miranda says. "The one you felt trapped in. What does it mean to you that I said I used to live there?"

"*Work* there!" I snap. As astonished and delighted as I am when Miranda remembers, often more accurately than I do, the details I've mentioned to her over the years—I am doubly infuriated when she misquotes me. Anyway, I thought the thing about the building was the least interesting part of the whole dream. Why is she wasting my time?

"Sorry," she says evenly. "What does it mean to you that you dreamed I used to *work* in a building where you were forced to live?"

"You tell me," I mutter, still sulking. "Isn't that what I pay you for?"

After two years with me, Miranda knows when to zero in on my anger at her and when to simply short-circuit it. "I think it means you want to know that I've been through what you've been through—that I've been in your worst, most trapped places. So you can be sure that I understand and empathize with you."

"Hmm," I murmur, impressed and mollified.

"What about those leg braces?" she presses on. "That made me wonder if you feel you're a burden to me."

"Not a burden . . . ," I say, reaching around inside for a more resonant truth. "That part reminds me of my mother—the way she always seems to fall apart as soon as she starts to take care of me."

I feel Miranda leaning forward, her head closer to mine. "A child blames herself for everything bad that happens, every weakness in her parents. It wasn't your fault that your mother didn't take care of you, Meredith."

And just like that: zoom, I'm gone. I am dizzied by the sensation of Miranda and my connection to her receding from me at the speed of light.

Therapy 101, I sneer silently. That old mother thing again. And to think I'm *paying* for these so-called insights.

Sometimes—in the moments and in the years when it's working—I feel about therapy the way I do about loving my children, or patting homemade compost between the tender baby leaves of lettuce in my garden: that it's a sacrament, a holy thing I do in a life and a world nearly devoid of reverence. At those times the therapy room is my temple, Miranda my spiritual guide, the process we engage in together my salvation.

And then there are the moments and the years when it's not working—as well as moments like this one, when it's working too well—and the raging bull of my cynicism puts its head down and charges. When my bullshit detector gets stuck in the "On" position, and everything Miranda says to me sounds canned, rote, banal. When I imagine legions of therapists nationwide sitting in their gray wool-carpeted offices with R. C. Gorman prints on the walls, "designer" tissue boxes on oak end tables within arm's reach of their Haitian cotton couches, and white-noise machines whirring in their hallways—each therapist intoning to each middle-class neurotic like a mindless mantra the very incantation Miranda repeats endlessly to me: "It's not your fault, it's all your parents' fault, you're a good person, we have to stop now."

As I do in each session with Miranda, I have wobbled on the thin line between faith and cynicism through nearly every one of the approximately seven hundred therapy sessions I have undergone in the past twelve years.

Arguing in favor of faith: incontrovertible evidence, at any point along the way, that I'm in better shape after than before. That I am closer to reaching the goals I set in my first session with my first therapist, a nun at the United Way agency in San Jose who charged me five dollars a week to help me recover from my beloved mother-in-law's sudden death, and then to help me prepare to separate from my husband.

"I want to be a nice person," I told Mary the first time I sat facing her, both of us perched on folding metal chairs in her musty church room full of dusty institutional furniture. The muffled shouts in Spanish of the immigrant workers playing basketball in the gym downstairs echoed through the peeling green walls as I told her what I hoped therapy would do for me.

"I want to be able to lie in the sun and relax, to stop thinking I have to be doing something all the time to justify being alive. I want to feel happy at least some of the time."

Twelve years and seven therapists later, some of those dreams are in the process of coming true. I now believe I am an essentially okay person. (Believing this to be true has either made it *be* true, or made it *seem* true; in either case, I am less inclined than I once was to consistently think the worst of myself.)

I am able, once in a while, to lie in the sun—or even in my waterbed on the fault line—and relax. (When I am unable to do this, I am usually dimly aware, at least, that I am entitled to the pleasure of doing it nonetheless.)

I do feel happy some of the time. I know more what makes me happy. It mostly boils down to love: good contact with my kids, my lover, my friends; and some satisfying work thrown in to keep the brain cells oiled and clicking. I know better how to let happiness come to me, instead of battering at the doors I used to feel were locked to keep it from me. I'm better at slowing down and noticing when there's happy-making stuff around me: "Kodak moments," as Peter calls them.

Arguing in favor of skepticism: Maybe I'd be just as mentally healthy—and quite a bit more financially healthy—if I hadn't spent the $35,000 or so that I've shelled out for: individual therapy (1981–present); marriage counseling with Richard (1981–1982); sex therapy with Rich (1983); divorce counseling with Rich (1984); relationship counseling with Ann (1985–1986; 1987–1989, and 1991–present); brief family therapy with Richard and Ann (1990); and even briefer family therapy with Richard, Ann, Peter, and Jesse (1990).

And there's this, too: why should I—and nearly all of my friends, and all of those faceless people whose mugs Miranda was washing— have to *pay* to get the support and nurturing that every single generation of humans preceding ours was able to obtain at no cost and as a matter of course from tribe, deities, family, friends?

Finally (and more to the point): how can I believe that Miranda cares about me when her caring is timed by the clock strategically placed on the wall above my head, whose ticking dictates the moment at which I am to be evicted from my temple, the same moment at which I am to hand her a check, my tithe for the privilege of having entered there?

"Meredith?" Miranda interrupts my silent diatribe. "Do you want to tell me what's going on?"

Here, in this moment—and in all the moments in all the sessions to come, in this relationship and every other one—is the choice that I know I am paying all this money to learn to make, and to make well. Do I open up, push through privacy to trust, tell Miranda the truth—or do I hold back, protect myself, reinforce the crumbling retaining wall around my heart?

It's like a 45 rpm record being played first on 78, then suddenly on 33⅓, this damn therapeutic relationship. All the choices and all the fights, all the distancing and all the embracing are slowed to a standstill, examined microscopically from every angle—yet somehow this is accomplished within the accelerated space of fifty minutes, once a week. Everything that happens between Miranda and me happens between Ann and me, Wendy and me, every boss and me, and every friend and me, and oh, yes, between my mother and me. Only slower—and faster.

"What you said about my mother . . . ," I begin. I'm still not sure which path to take, how far to go, where I might end up with this. "It just sounded so . . . I don't know . . . so trite . . ."

I sneak a peek at Miranda. Her face is tranquil, her body relaxed. Her lips aren't twitching with anger; her knee isn't jiggling nervously. I see no evidence of the reaction a normal person, a friend or a lover, would have to my accusation.

It strikes me that I have criticized Miranda often—sometimes in honesty, more often like throwing trash cans in her path, fleeing to escape her as she chases me ruthlessly through the dark alleys of my psyche—and that she has never retreated, never retaliated, never failed to catch up with me, always listened and responded calmly to my complaints.

Is *this* what I am paying her for? To teach me how I want other people to be with me? To teach me how I want to be with other people? And to what end am I learning these lessons—to be set up for endless disappointment? Because who else—who in my *real* life could be even half as forgiving, as maternal, as perfect as Miranda?

"Did what I said about your mother feel false to you?" Miranda asks me, sounding sincerely concerned.

How much time could we waste chasing that one around, I wonder. Could I get through the rest of the session without having to say any more about the damn dream? I picture myself a half hour from now, pedaling my bike furiously south on Grant Street, berating myself all the way home (*again!*) for letting my defenses run my therapy off the tracks.

I take a deep breath and plunge straight ahead.

"No," I sigh. "I just got mad at you. The truth is: the dream, telling you about the dream . . . I get mad at you because I hate realizing how important . . ."

I swallow, summon courage. Why is this so hard? What if this woman gets hit by a truck tomorrow? Or decides to move to Montana?

". . . how important you are to me." A shudder quakes through my body.

Miranda says, "I know that scares you, Meredith—feeling it, and acknowledging it to me." We breathe together through a long silence. When Miranda speaks again I hear the hint of a smile in her voice.

"At the risk of seeming . . . *trite*," she adds, "I do want to say that, given your childhood, it's not surprising that you keep dreaming about me violating your boundaries."

"*Keep* dreaming?" I ask, confused.

"This is the third dream like this that you've told me about," Miranda says. "There was the one about a year ago, when you dreamed that my husband walked in on our session. And the one when I asked you to come to my house for a session, and when you got there I didn't have time for you because I was feeding my daughter.

"Now," she continues, not giving me time to respond or disappear, "back to this dream. I turned into a lesbian right before I turned into a homeless person. If I was a lesbian, would that be a bad thing?"

Checking for internalized homophobia, I think, pleased. Not bad for a straight therapist . . . or whatever she is.

"That's not it," I answer. "It's just so strange: I know nothing about you. I feel so . . . close to you, you know all these intimate things about me, and I don't even know if you're straight or gay."

"You've said clearly and repeatedly," Miranda reminds me, "that you don't want to know anything about me."

"Because of Stephanie," I say, knowing she'll understand this shorthand reference to one of the thousands of my life stories that now occupy space in Miranda's memory.

"Because you felt so betrayed by Stephanie's disclosures," Miranda amplifies.

Oh yes. Betrayed. The rage fills me in an instant. Stephanie, my first therapeutic body worker, with whom I desperately sought relief, six months after the earthquake had shaken my sanity to rubble. When I first lay down on Stephanie's table it had been half a year since I'd dared to exhale, for fear it was the tension in my body that was holding the world together.

Stephanie, whose firm touch and quiet, insightful murmurs offered me such rare comfort that I would count the days and then the hours between Thursdays at six P.M. when I could climb once again the blue wooden steps to her gabled garret and slip between the pale yellow flannel sheets, craving the warmth of her hand on my back like an infant shrieking to be swaddled.

One year later, my final session with Stephanie: lying facedown on her table, crying and shaking in the grip of terror, Stephanie's steadying touch my only firm ground. Crashing through the dense, dark thicket of my childhood in search of clues that might shed light on—or, better yet, end—my crippling reaction to the natural disaster from which everyone else, it seemed, had long since recovered. And then coming up for air, needing contact with the present, a reality check.

"I'm not crazy to keep living here, am I?" I asked Stephanie. "An irresponsible mother? Raising my kids in California when there could be a big earthquake at any time?"

Stephanie was uncharacteristically silent. Her only response was a slight stiffening of her hands on my shoulders.

"Sometimes I walk up and down College Avenue for hours," I told her, a secret I'd never told anyone. "I look into people's faces, trying to see if they're anywhere near as scared as I am. Trying to figure out how they stand to go on living here. I see pregnant women, men pushing strollers. People are still having babies here! As if they think this is a reasonable place to live! It makes me feel a little better to think that people—parents—aren't leaving California because of earthquakes."

Stephanie's hands were still for several moments. When she spoke at last, she was no longer touching me.

"Actually, Meredith," Stephanie said, in a tremulous voice I'd never heard her use before, "some people *are* leaving the Bay area. Because of earthquakes."

Through the blurry haze of raw, unfinished emotion, I felt a sharp stab of dread. I wanted Stephanie to stop, to undo what she'd begun, but

I knew she wouldn't. So I waited, my body suddenly cold and rigid between the soft sheets.

"I've been meaning to tell you . . . *I'm* leaving the Bay area. My lover is terrified of earthquakes. She doesn't feel she can tolerate living here any longer. We're moving to the Midwest in three months."

I don't remember, now, how I got myself untangled from the flannel and dressed and down the blue steps and into my car and home. I remember building a fire in the wood stove, although it was April, and sitting on the couch staring at it dumbly for hours.

I remember that for days a liturgy drummed through my mind, the litany of unwanted information Stephanie had given me, the reasons I could never see her again: I now knew that she was a lesbian (and I could no longer reassure myself that her touch was the guaranteed nonsexual contact I required). I now knew that there *were* people wiser, more prudent than I, who were uprooting themselves to be safe from earthquakes. I now knew that Stephanie was at least as imperfect as I, and—I knew that she had disappeared, in an instant, from my life forever.

"I'm not Stephanie," Miranda says now, as she has said to me and proved to me many times and in many ways during the past two years. "I'm not going anywhere. And I won't tell you anything about myself that you don't want to hear."

"I know . . . ," I say, although I don't. I'm always waiting for her to screw up, leave, make me sorry that I ever began to trust her.

"Even though you don't want to know if I'm a lesbian, in your dream you were wondering . . . ," Miranda prompts me.

"Just because I don't want to know doesn't mean I don't wonder," I interrupt her. "I wonder about *everything*. I wonder if you're a lesbian—you seem to have quite a few lesbian clients—or if you're married to that guy who shares your office, John whatever his name is."

"John *Hoover*?" Miranda gasps.

"Now don't give me any hints," I admonish her. And then I go on. "Every time I come here I wonder if you live in the house next door with him, although the fact that you park your car in a different place each week would indicate that you don't."

It's exhilarating, opening the floodgates and releasing two years' worth of unacknowledged questions. Trusting Miranda not to answer them, I decide to spill the whole lot.

"Then there's that car seat I saw in your car a few months ago. Do you have a kid? Probably not—I've never seen the car seat again. Or did she outgrow the car seat? But if you do: is it your lesbian lover's kid? Or yours and John's? Did a baby come out of your body?

"I wonder who does all that gardening in the front yard. If it's you, you're a tidy gardener like I am. Did you plant those begonias in the pots? Are pink ones your favorites, too? Is that calico cat in the garden yours, or John's, or both of yours? If you don't live here, where do you live . . . ?"

I open my eyes now, sit up, see Miranda smiling at me.

"Don't say anything . . . ," I warn her.

"I won't," Miranda assures me. She pauses, then looks at me intently.

"Meredith: Most of what I know about you I know from how you are with me. And I think you know a lot about me—all the important things about me—from how I am with you."

I consider this for a moment, then shake my head.

"How you are with me," I say. "I think that's just . . . technique. I don't trust it."

Miranda gazes at me steadily. If I didn't know better, I would think the look in her eye was one of . . . love. Then she glances at the clock above my head.

"We have to stop now," she says.

"See what I mean?" I retort.

Miranda and I look at each other openly, fully. The space between us feels clearer now, as though a slightly out-of-focus lens has been adjusted into sharp focus.

"Just kidding," I say, with a nervous little laugh. "You know I'm kidding, right?" I bend to find my wallet, busy myself with writing the check.

"I know you're *sort of* kidding," Miranda says, grinning and leaning back against the orthopedic cushion in her chair.

I nod, rip out the check, stare at it briefly. At the end of one of our first sessions, I walked over to hand the check to Miranda while she was sitting in her chair. I didn't like the feeling of towering over her, and I've never done it that way again.

I lean toward Miranda, check outstretched. She reaches out to take it; our fingertips touch. I stand to leave, gather up keys, raincoat, wallet.

"You remember, don't you, Meredith: I told you I'll be on vacation next week. So I'll see you on June ninth."

"Yeah, I remember. Have a good vacation," I say. I open the door, hear the dim roar of the white-noise machine. I turn back to look at Miranda. Two weeks until I see her again.

Through the window behind her chair I see the rain has stopped; the heavy gray clouds are outlined in light. She's so pretty, I think. I let that thought come into my eyes when I smile at her.

"Have a good vacation . . . *with John*," I say.

I close the door behind me, and stand outside her office, listening. I smile with satisfaction when I hear Miranda burst out laughing. Stepping out into Miranda's garden, and then pedaling my bike down Grant Street, I'm laughing too.

Wanting Not to Want

Ann and I are having a city weekend for a change: going to the movies with friends, rolling around in the sheets till noon, solving the world's problems and our own over lattes and cranberry-whole-wheat scones in our favorite cafe, and shopping.

Friday night's movie, *The Wedding Banquet*—the latest cinematic testimonial to the demise of heterosexism—I loved. The rolling around in the sheets, I simply cannot live without. The lattes are a treat; we haven't yet equipped the cabin with a solar-powered espresso machine. The scones remind me how lucky I am—despite stratospheric real estate prices, the ever-looming specter of the Big One, claustrophobically congested streets and freeways, and all the nameless terrors of the night—to live near Berkeley, exotic baked goods capital of the Western world.

But the shopping . . .

When Ann and I need new wicks for the kerosene lamps in the cabin or a wrench to fix the basketball hoop in the driveway, we shop at Ace Hardware on University Avenue, where the ancient floorboards creak with satisfying authenticity, the prices bear a credible relationship to the value of the goods, and the salespeople are as tried and true as the dusty ceiling fans that whir soothingly overhead.

When we "need" new clothes we go to the 100 percent cotton and discount designer boutiques of College Avenue, or to the recycled swap-shops like Buffalo Exchange and Wasteland. For a good bread knife or a briefcase we go to Whole Earth Access—once a tiny, overstuffed storefront that sold potbelly stoves and work boots to fleeing radicals on their way to the country communes of Mendocino; now a mini-chain of maxi-emporiums that sell Cuisinarts and computers to the affluent and domesticated graying boomers who have nicknamed the store, with unself-conscious irony, "Whole Earth Excess."

Recently Ann and I identified a need for some drinking glasses—the eight we bought a couple of months ago having been reduced to three by our teenage dishwashers-in-training. So our destination this afternoon is the yupscale antimall of Berkeley's Fourth Street, home of (among many, many other things) the Crate & Barrel outlet store.

I park my long-unwashed Honda wagon on Fourth Street behind a gleaming burgundy Jeep Cherokee and survey the scene before me. This is not the Berkeley I know and sort of love. Expensively dressed people with actual hairstyles are strolling along the sidewalks sipping foam-capped coffee drinks from environmentally correct cardboard cups; lolling on teak benches eating foccacia sandwiches and elegant little cookies; crisscrossing the street to duck into one shop and then another, emerging with recycled-paper shopping bags topped with tufts of colored tissue swinging from their arms. It all looks so very attractive.

Ann and I decide we have time to browse. As we bypass Crate & Barrel en route to the trendier, pricier shops, my heartbeat quickens and the heady seduction of retail therapy begins to work its spell on me. Who knows what treasures are waiting to be perused, admired, perhaps even purchased? Who knows how my life might soon be enhanced by some thing I don't yet know I need?

We begin at Hear Music. In this burnished maple and Plexiglas palace you can plug yourself into the Listening Bar and hear any CD in the store on state-of-the-art headphones, or stand inside an acoustic bubble and be drenched in the mellifluous melodies of Duke Ellington. If pressed for time, you may also select a CD sight-unheard and proceed to the Paying Bar, where you'll spend a paltry extra dollar or two for the privilege of buying music-to-go in such a sublime milieu as this.

"Sixteen bucks for a CD?" I squawk. But when I find a rare Crosby, Stills, Nash & Young retrospective (with cover illustration, as Ann points out, by Joni Mitchell), I swallow my never-pay-retail pride and fork over the big bucks.

If I'd never seen that CD I never would have thought to want it, I reflect uneasily as Ann and I push through the store's heavy glass doors and are hailed by the street sounds outside. *Do I need it, really?*

What's need got to do with it?

Now that we're here, we might as well jog across the street to inhale the lavender-scented air at The Gardener, where dollar-apiece narcissus bulbs are artfully arranged in antique bushel baskets, tiny handmade shovel earrings are priced at twice the cost of the life-sized genuine article, and the Brahms concerto issuing softly from hidden speakers leadens the eyelids and loosens the purse strings.

"Mmm," I murmur, stroking a spun mohair lap blanket that's draped across the rungs of a knotty pine ersatz kiva ladder.

"*This* is the kind of throw I wish *we* could have on *our* couch," I whine. The flimsy plaid acrylic one we've got was on sale last year at Bed Bath & Beyond for $16.99. It is neither warm nor lovely; its sole redeeming quality is its machine-wash-and-dryability.

"When we have our next house," Ann begins, the opening words of the mantra the two of us chant together with increasing frequency as the departure of our sons from their childhoods and, therefore, our home, grows increasingly imminent, "we'll give the kids all the furniture we have now and buy ourselves some really good stuff."

"Like this hook," I say, pointing out a patina-mottled copper salamander from which a starched French cotton dishcloth dangles perkily. "We won't buy *anything* tacky. We'll wait till we can afford really nice things like this. Every detail will be *perfect.*"

I know I can count on Ann not to mention the seven years or more that will elapse before we embark on the search for our cozy country cottage. Nor will she spoil the mood by raising the sticky question of where the money might come from to pay for it—not to mention its oft-discussed perfect furnishings. What is the basis (if any) of our shared assumption that we'll have more money, somehow, someday? What price might we pay, someday, when reality demotes that assumption to the fantasy it is?

But now is not the time for such unpleasant explorations. Nor is it the time to discuss the ambivalence each of us experiences when we face the reality of putting a hundred miles or more between ourselves and such gentrified, decadent city debaucheries as those in which we are, at this moment, so enthusiastically immersed.

It's all about the future, this wanting and wanting. And you know what happens when you dwell in the future . . .

In Devony's Linens, Ann fingers the sleeve of a sumptuous white flannel robe, moaning softly with pleasure. "I'll have to get rid of my old terry-cloth robe one of these days," she says, fumbling for the price tag. I read it over her shoulder. $150.00. Ann sighs and straightens the robe on its padded satin hanger. "Not today, I guess," she says.

I wish I could buy it for her, I think, gazing longingly at the robe as Ann wanders off to sniff the scented soaps. *I could buy it for her. But does she want this more than she wants anything else?* I feel disappointment—the familiar flip side of desire—welling in my chest. *I can't buy her everything she wants.*

The futon shop has meditation bells and kimonos and bolts and bolts of Japanese ikat fabric. "I like the simpler patterns best," Ann says, watching for my reaction. For the next seven or eight years, I know, we'll be trying each other's tastes on for size in furniture stores, nurseries, real estate offices. At this rate, by the time we're ready to furnish our fantasy house, we're likely to have every decision made, every yard of fabric ordered, and every dishtowel hook chosen.

"Me too," I say. We smile at each other. Maybe we *are* compatible, after all. Maybe both of us can have what we want. In the next house. In seven or eight years.

We ooh over the $750 cashmere cardigans and too-cute-to-be-true saleswoman at Carolyn Clement. We ahh at the rice-paper lamps and deco halogen sconces at The Lighting Studio. We roll our eyes at the five-dollar organic whole-grain dog biscuits at EarthSave, and share a giggling sexual fantasy on a four-poster bed at Z Gallerie. It's easy to imagine replacing the functional black mailbox we bought at Ace Hardware with the gleaming copper model on display at Restoration Designs, and dumping our plastic recycling bin in favor of the $85 wicker one at Slater Marinoff.

By the time we've gone through Crate & Barrel and picked out our eight new $1.50 glasses and our one new $1.25 candleholder, my head is pounding. The faint queasiness in my stomach has ripened into full-blown nausea. I feel as if I've eaten too much, drunk too much, wanted too much. I feel as if I'm crashing off a bad drug high, overdosed on excess. I feel like putting the glasses and the candleholder back, returning the CD, slapping myself out of this consuming trance.

"We just wasted three hours of our lives," I mutter at Ann as we emerge from Crate & Barrel, single half-empty shopping bag in hand. She nods. I notice that she looks like I feel: dazed, hung over.

"It's fun, shopping," she says. "But I know what you mean. Kind of empty, huh?"

We were planning to go out tonight, maybe dancing, but now we agree we're too tired. "Dinner and bed," Ann proposes. I accept and drive toward home. I have a sudden urge to empty my closets and shelves and drawers, to reduce what I have—to play the movie of my wanting in reverse so I'm getting rid of instead of acquiring more things, and with them, more wants.

What is wanting about?

I pull into our driveway and sit looking up at our house, the house that has survived two big earthquakes and thousands of little ones, and ninety years of toddlers pounding and teenagers gallumping and husbands and wives and lovers fighting and lovemaking, and carpenters hammering, and rainstorms thrashing. I squint at it critically as I always do, see it through narrowed eyes as the house-until, the house to be tolerated between now and the acquisition of the mythical house-to-be.

I try for just a moment to gaze at it lovingly instead, to see it as the house where I live contentedly, here and now.

Wanting has always been my motor. Without it I would stall out—motionless, useless.

Not just my motor but the culture's.

Not just the culture's, but most especially, my generation's.

The international youth tribe I joined when I fled my family was *defined* by what we wanted—by the difference between our wants and "theirs," by the dreams and demands we invented and shared. It was what we wanted and how and why we fought for it that made us uniquely qualified to change the world; and provoked the same incessant entreaty from our detractors and sympathizers alike: *"What do you people want?"*

While scorning the uptightness that prompted the question, we reveled in each opportunity to expound upon the purity, the high-mindedness of the answer. Not Buicks and promotions but community and enlightenment; not the clenched jaws of war but the innocent open mouth of pleasure. We want the world and we want it now.

Lofty wants, but wanting, still.

Like all wants, ours sprang not from acceptance, but from opposition. Like all wants, ours grew and multiplied in the ambient incubator of self-righteousness. And even more than most wants, ours were compelling and convincing: the urgency of the times made our unchecked desire to change *everything* even more alluring than a cashmere sweater, even more persuasive than a marked-down price tag.

Wanting makes the future look better than the present.

For all of these reasons and others, I'm afraid to give up wanting, to succumb to satisfaction, to call what there is now "enough."

Contentment would immobilize me. What there is now has never been enough.

Long before I took the vows of the youth revolution, and since, I've been driven by the next thing to do, to make happen, to be. There was never a choice to sit with things-as-they-are, to un-know what I knew, un-want what I wanted—to let the war rage, the family swallow me alive, the boyfriend disappoint me one more time; to let the plum job go unpicked, the woman's lips go untasted, the baby unconceived, the evil empire unchallenged.

Never a choice to turn off the motor and drift.

I've always had a list going, my own personal Top Ten of Things-Not-To-Be-Happy-Until-I-Have.

Never a choice to rest.

It's laughable, really, to look at that list, to see how it's changed and stayed the same and fed and contradicted itself over the years. To realize that the wanting is as pervasive, as enduring, as the objects of the wanting are fleeting, ephemeral.

Still, the present is never quite good enough. And so the wanting goes on.

What I want (1993):
1. To write a great book.
2. Less time alone, more time with my kids.
3. A cure for AIDS and cancer.
4. More tears, more sex, more laughter with Ann.
5. A plain-paper fax machine.
6. More closeness with my friends and more friends to be close to.
7. A green Miata.
8. To lose five pounds.
9. For the Clinton administration to fix the economy and end racial and sexual oppression and homelessness and violence.
10. To feel less fear and more compassion: peace inside and out.

What I wanted (1988):
1. A stable job in a progressive company.
2. More time alone.
3. A cure for AIDS and cancer.
4. Fewer tears, more laughter, less fighting with Ann.
5. A country cabin.
6. More friends, more of a circle of friends.
7. Enough money to stop worrying about money.
8. To lose ten pounds.
9. Gay liberation.
10. To be a really good, famous writer someday.

What I wanted (1983):
1. A divorce.
2. Custody of my kids.
3. A way to earn a living.
4. A house in North Oakland.
5. More time alone.
6. A community of friends in which to raise my kids.
7. To lose twenty pounds.
8. The elimination of every nuclear weapon on the face of the earth.
9. An affair with a woman.
10. To be a really good, famous writer someday.

What I wanted (1977):
1. To get pregnant.
2. A stable job in a really oppressive factory.
3. To get pregnant.
4. A more passionate, less predictable relationship with Rich.
5. To recruit workers to the October League and make socialist revolution.
6. To get pregnant.
7. Less mandatory overtime.
8. To get pregnant.
9. A Ford Mustang.
10. To get pregnant.

What I wanted (1972):
1. For Danny to love me as much—okay, half as much— as I love him.
2. Women's liberation.
3. A more predictable, less volatile relationship with Danny.
4. To be accepted by the lesbians in the Berkeley Women's Health Collective, even though I'm in love with a man.
5. For our group house to become a conscious, committed commune.

6. To get through nursing school without losing any more weight.
7. A new sunroof for my '65 VW bug so it won't rain on me anymore.
8. To have sex with Judy Goldstein.
9. To have Danny's baby.
10. To be a really good, famous writer someday.

What I wanted (1967):
1. To end the war.
2. To be with Paul forever.
3. Youth revolution.
4. Straight hair.
5. The nerve to be more militant and to take more drugs.
6. To have sex with Pasha.
7. To have sex with lots of other people.
8. A commune in New Mexico.
9. To be a revolutionary rock-and-roll star.
10. To be a revolutionary writer.

There was always this gnawing wanting, this sense of something missing, something better to be found or made to happen that might make the emptiness go away. Early on I stuck the carrot of that unnamed something-better in front of my own nose; I've been chasing it around the track ever since.

A year ago I sat in a meditation instruction class, waiting my turn to ask the question I ask myself every time I cross my legs to sit in any *zendo,* the question I never had to ask all the years before, when revolution was my religion and the groups with whom I practiced it dismissed spiritual pursuits as the opiate of the masses, the search for pleasure in the present as bourgeois individualism.

The leader of the class was the abbot of a New York Zen community that puts homeless men and women to work building their own housing, baking the brownies that go into Ben & Jerry's ice cream, and feeding other homeless people. This man wouldn't be the first Buddhist teacher to whom I had posed my question. I hoped he would be the first to answer it.

"Buddhism teaches us to accept things as they are, to be in the present, to extinguish desire," I said. "But how do you reconcile all that with wanting to change the world?"

The abbot smiled knowingly. I'd seen that smile before. I just knew what he was thinking: Another one with that stupid question again. *Shit,* I thought, *he's gonna give me some damn Zen riddle for an answer, like these guys always do.*

"Let's say you plan a picnic," he began. "You invite your friends, prepare the food. On the day of the picnic you wake to see that it's raining.

"What are your choices? You can anguish over the disappointment—the day didn't turn out the way you wanted it to. Or you can plan an outdoor picnic for another day, have today's picnic in the living room, and enjoy it for what it is—not the picnic you'd imagined, but something equally pleasant."

Huh?

The abbot beamed at me expectantly—anticipating, no doubt, my epiphany. It was not forthcoming. I drew courage from my surreptitious observation that the other students in the room seemed as baffled as I was.

"Whenever I sit *zazen,*" I pressed on, hoping to zigzag around his parable and finally hit the straight-answer button, "I find myself wondering if the twenty people in the *zendo* would do more good if we got up and went outside and cleaned up a vacant lot or something. So many well-intentioned people just *sitting* there . . . I know I'm supposed to be watching my breath, staying in the moment, but . . ."

The abbot's smile widened.

"The trick," he said, "is to do both. To rejoice in the present while wanting something better for the future."

Huh?

I was reminded of the bumper sticker, ever popular in Berkeley: "You cannot simultaneously prevent and prepare for war." *How can you simultaneously rejoice in the present and fantasize about the future?*

The abbot glanced around the room. "Does anyone else have a question?"

Of course, even the Buddhists—the faith-healers I turned to in my search to cure the lifelong itch of my wanting—want things. There are always plenty of BMW's and Jeep Cherokees among the beat-up Toyotas and Hondas in the Zen Center parking lot, and Mephistos and Rockports mixed in among the rubber flip-flops and scuffed clogs in the *zendo* shoe rack.

Is the answer to want only what you need?

The Zen Centers themselves want things, too. They want to earthquake-proof the dining room and print a monthly newsletter in two colors of ink and buy the property next door when it comes up for sale. And so, like the prochoice groups and credit card companies and aluminum siding brokers whose unwanted appeals fill my mailbox every day, the Zen Centers send me elaborate (if uniquely tasteful) direct-mail solicitations, in hopes that I will want them to have what they want enough to give them some of my money.

Who's to say what the difference is between a want and a need? Or that Zen Center's need for a newsletter is any "better" than my need for a fax machine?

The best and the worst things have happened in the world, as in my life, because people wanted things: territory, freedom, technology, equality, escape, peace.

During the long tearful years when I wanted a baby more than I'd ever wanted anything—even proletarian revolution—I got the same bit of cruel advice from several of the dozen or so fertility doctors from whom I sought salvation.

"Try to relax," one and then another of them said, leaning back in their glossy leather chairs, the photographs of their smiling wives and children neatly positioned on their elegant desks. "The best way to get pregnant is to stop worrying about it so much."

And then would follow the inevitable reciting of the legend that "proves" the strength of this unfillable prescription: the stories of the long-infertile women who finally get pregnant the day they bring their adopted children home, or some other variation on the theme—promoted with equal enthusiasm by new age sages and AMA assholes: "Give it up and you'll get what you want."

"Well, gee," I never quite had the nerve to snarl at these overpriced charlatans, "now that you've convinced me I'll only get pregnant if I give up wanting it, I'll just stop wanting it. Why didn't I think of that myself? Here's your two hundred bucks."

But the truth is, I did get pregnant after I finally gave up.

Four years after I'd started trying to "relax" about getting pregnant—while simultaneously undergoing surgeries and toxic hormone treatments and womb-splittingly painful tests—Rich and I were on our way to a labor rights demonstration in Sacramento when the car ahead of us skidded out across all four lanes of the crowded freeway. In the elongated instant before our Camaro smashed into the center divider, only one thought flashed through my brain: *You've wasted years of your life mourning over something you can't have. Now you're going to die.*

But I didn't die, and as Rich and I stood on the side of the freeway in the rain, shaking but miraculously unhurt, watching the ambulances and the tow trucks hauling away the mangled bodies and cars, I told him, "That's it. I'm not wasting another day crying about having a baby. No more tests, no more drugs. If it happens, it happens. If it doesn't, I'm going to start enjoying life anyway."

The trick is to rejoice in the present while wanting something better for the future.

Two weeks later I was pregnant.

But still, I went on keeping my list. I did go to a publishing conference in Dallas in 1983 looking for a lesbian to fall in love with, and I did find Ann and fall in love with her. And I did visualize the attributes I wanted my next job to have, and I did get exactly that job at Banana Republic. And I wanted a country cabin and a house in North Oakland with bleached pine floors and for Ann and me to fight less and the chance to write a book—I wanted all those things, and never gave up wanting them, and I got them, despite or because of wanting them.

The trick is to rejoice in the present while wanting something better for the future.

For the first time in my life, now, I have what I want. I have, in fact, what other people want. I have an abundance of riches, and, thanks to—what? Extraordinarily good luck? Sitting *zazen*? Years of wanting? Years of therapy? Years, period?—I'm able to notice and appreciate my blessings.

And so I'm able to imagine a life beyond the tyranny and the sweet itch of wanting.

Ann is gathering up the detritus of our day from the car: the bulky brown shopping bag and the trim little CD bag, the chocolate-stained latte cups and wrinkled wax papers.

"I'm starved," she says as she gathers up the mail from our funky metal mailbox. "Let's go out to eat."

"Okay," I say. "But I'm dying to hear my new CD. Can we go in a few minutes?"

Ann rolls her eyes at me. "Can you ever *wait* for *anything*?" she asks, with equal parts affection and exasperation.

"Good thing I couldn't wait to find *you*," I answer, my usual response to her chronic impatience with my chronic impatience. I can see I've worn out this particular rebuttal; Ann's still standing in the doorway looking hungry and determined.

"Just the first two songs, I promise," I wheedle.

Ann shakes her head. "Five minutes," she says, and goes off to greet Joe. I slip the CD into the snazzy Sony CD player my brother gave me for my fortieth birthday, and reverently await the sounds I've been longing to hear.

I hear nothing. I smell smoke. I see smoke, rising from the Technics receiver Rich awarded me in our divorce settlement ten years ago. I turn everything off, wait a minute, turn it all on again. No sound. More bad smell. More smoke.

"Ann!" I bellow. "My stereo's fried!"

Damn, I think. Who knows how much this'll cost to fix? Who knows how long it'll take, how long I'll have to wait to hear my new CD.

I know! I think, cheering up immediately. *I've never really liked this receiver anyway. Tomorrow's Sunday; Whole Earth is open all day. I'll just bop over and buy a new one.*

WHAT IT'S LIKE
TO LIVE HERE NOW

The Murder

DECEMBER 30, 1992

Eleven o'clock at night. The night before New Year's Eve. Where is Ann? I've been pacing for half an hour, flopping down across my bed to read a few paragraphs of the scary book I can't stay away from, jumping up again to peer through the blinds at the dark street below.

My Breast, the book is called. The journey of one woman through breast cancer and out the other side. As if there *is* any out, or any other side for any woman, with or without a personal or family history of benign or malignant breast lumps, these days.

January ninth two years ago my doctor discovered the lump in my right breast. January ninth this year—ten days from now—I'll offer up my pregnancy- and biopsy-scarred breasts to be squeezed into submission between the clamps of the mastodon mammogram machine. This January, and every January for the rest of my life. Now that I'm forty, with the dread words "family history" (my mother's breast cancer) plus one lump of my own recorded in the chart that will follow me wherever I go, my only respite from the annual mammogram will be death.

Ann went to her support group tonight, even though Ellen, her best friend and ex-lover (a seemingly invariable combination in the lesbian world), is here, visiting from the suburb near Boston where they used to live together, and then apart. I first got worried about Ann's whereabouts an hour ago, when Ellen and I were chatting in front of the fire. Ann was later than usual for a Wednesday night. Later, and then later still. I couldn't keep my eyes from darting again and again around Ellen's knees to the blue digital numbers on the VCR clock: 9:43, 9:47, 10:01 . . .

"Oh, didn't Annie tell you?" Ellen asked. "She's stopping at Richard's on her way home—she said something about sorting through Jesse's clothes." I remembered then: as usual, Ann had volunteered to conduct the research necessary to deny or confirm Jesse's periodic claim that he had fewer than the allotted five "good" outfits at each house.

But now it's two hours later than Ann usually is, and it's dark and cold out, and the breast lump in the book (unlike my own) has turned out to be malignant. Nights like this always bring me back to the night four years ago when the phone next to my bed rang in the dark and a stranger asked, "Is this Meredith?", and that stranger told me she lived near the intersection where Ann's Volkswagen had just been broadsided at fifty miles an hour and flipped twice, the intersection from which an ambulance had just removed Ann to Merritt Hospital.

Where *is* she?

Eleven-ten. It's late to be making phone calls but I've got to start tracing her path. Peter answers the phone at his dad's house. He should be in bed, Christmas vacation or not, but this is no time . . .

"Hi, Babe. Is Ann still there?"

"She's not home yet?" Peter answers, and my heart thumps once, hard. She's not there. She's not there? I remember that this deep-voiced boy is my child. He loves Ann too, depends on her too.

"Not yet," I answer, struggling to keep my voice even. "When did she leave?"

"About ten, I think. Are you worried about her? Dad's in the basement—I'll go ask him." Peter puts the phone down and I imagine myself getting in my car, driving down Martin Luther King, Jr. Way, the street that Ann would have taken on her way home from Richard's, coming upon the flashing lights, the twisted metal wreckage . . .

My ex-husband's voice comes on the line. "She's just leaving," Richard says. "Sorry. We got started talking."

I'm drenched with relief. She's alive! I tell myself to put the book away, take a celebratory break from anxiety, but still the breast cancer story pulls at me. Several mammograms failed to turn up the author's tumor. The surgeon says it's probably been growing in her for five years. But he thinks it's the highly curable kind . . .

I hear gunshots. Pow, pow, pow, pow—fast and close, but muffled. Many times I've imagined noises in the night to be gunfire, never sure if I was dreaming or hearing a car backfiring, a branch snapping in the wind, firecrackers left over from some Fourth of July. But in this instant I am certain: there's nothing else this noise could be.

Someone is being shot.

Someone is being murdered.

With the noise still ringing in my head, I begin to see a movie there too.

I see Flint's, the barbecue place two blocks away on Shattuck. I see a young black man standing in front of Flint's, cradling a steaming grease-stained bag. I see another, slightly older black man walk up to him, jab the muzzle of a big thick black gun into his stomach. (Now I know what muffled the sound of the gunfire.)

I see ribs and potato salad and blood-red barbecue sauce splattering against Flint's plate-glass window as the bullets propel the young man backward and the gunman turns and runs away. I see the young man collapsed on the sidewalk, dead.

Before I can even begin to make any of this make sense, I see another picture: my dear dying friend Peter Babcock, shriveled to near-nothingness by HIV.

"Stop!" I want to yell before the blood has run out of the bullet holes. I want to run out into the street, find the fool who just used a human-made weapon to suck the life from a young, healthy body. "Don't you know there's a virus killing too many people already?"

Where is everyone I love? The kids are at Richard's across town. Ann? I reassure myself—she would have taken Martin Luther King, not

Shattuck, unless she stopped for half-and-half for our morning coffee. No, there's cream in the fridge . . .

I jump up, bolt to the window.

Directly below me an old Toyota is stopped in the middle of the street. One of the young white guys from the group house across the street is bent over talking to the driver. The people in the car and my neighbor are talking and laughing.

How could they be acting this way if they've just heard what I just heard?

As I'm staring down at them, wondering why they seem unaware that a life has just been snuffed out a hundred yards from where they are, I hear running footsteps approaching.

From the direction of Shattuck, from exactly where I have imagined (seen) the shooting taking place, a young black man runs toward the car below me. Numbly I note that the man is wearing a white sweatshirt, dark pants, white shoes—that his hands are empty, his arms are crooked at the elbows, and he is running without apparent panic, as though he's jogging leisurely on a college track on some sunny afternoon. But no—he is running from where a murder just happened, at eleven-eighteen on a dark winter night . . .

The running man approaches the Toyota without slowing. My neighbor looks up as the runner is nearly upon him. The two men make eye contact; the laughter from the car is suddenly silenced. I wonder if my neighbor and his friends are about to be shot before my eyes to keep them from recounting what they have just seen. Do they understand the significance of what they have just seen?

Do I?

I wonder if I'm making this whole thing up. I wonder if I should call 911 right now.

The black man jogs by, his eyes locked on my neighbor's until he jerks his head around in the direction he's running and disappears into the night. My neighbor peers into the darkness for only an instant, then turns back to his casual conversation.

Did that man in the white sweatshirt just kill someone? Is this my racism gone wild? Should I call 911—report the shots I heard, the man I saw?

I hear sirens approaching: one, two, five sirens screaming from all directions. They don't wail by as they usually do, but stop where I imagine (know) the murder took place. I feel certain that the running man was somehow involved, but did not pull the trigger.

The Toyota pulls away. My neighbor waves good-bye to his friends, then looks up (why?) and sees me peering through my miniblinds at him. He stares up at me oddly, coldly, without recognition or friendliness. My heart pounds; I am unable to look away. At last he turns his head, walks quickly down the street, climbs into an unfamiliar car, and drives away.

Suddenly my white, longhaired neighbor seems more sinister than the black stranger who ran past him. Yet I don't suspect my neighbor of anything worse than odd behavior.

Can I trust that what I saw is what I know—that what I know is true? Is my certainty a product of racism, or psychic power—or both? My mind spins out another scenario, one less racially charged: my neighbor and his friends conspirators in the murder, the jogger their accomplice; the deed done, they all rendezvous in another neighborhood to smoke a joint (a pipeful of crack?) and celebrate . . .

Ellen is upstairs in Ann's attic, presumably asleep (in the twin guest bed, or in Ann's double bed? I still fret, nine years later). I wonder if she has heard or seen any of this. I want to call out to her, to hear my voice aloud, to hear it answered by another human voice, to know that these events have not transpired in my mind alone.

I realize then that I am equally afraid that Ellen has, and has not witnessed what I have seen. If Ellen *has* heard the gunshots, the sirens, she has proof of all I wish I could deny: that in leaving Arlington Heights and her, Ann has chosen a neighborhood and a life devoid of the safety and security of Ellen's white-picket-fenced suburb. That Ann and I are choosing to raise our sons in the kind of violent, threatening environment that white-flight neighborhoods like Ellen's were designed to shield their inhabitants from.

Worse, in showing Ellen my fear I would reveal my shame. Ancient shame: that I have made a series of Wrong Decisions that now have landed my family in this unsafe place, where death lurks in wait around the corner. The kinds of Wrong Decisions that my ancestors believed (and passed on to me to believe) were in large part to blame for the pogroms, the humiliations, the incinerations.

The silencing shame that my rational mind knows is delusional (Genocide, like Shit, Happens; what Right Decision could any Jew in history have made to prevent it?) but my psyche clings to desperately—finding shame, it seems, more tolerable than the bottomless grief it masks.

If, on the other hand, Ellen has heard and seen nothing, I am shoved back into wondering if I have finally lost my mind to the paranoid holocaust demons installed before birth in my DNA and reactivated at moments like this.

The front gate latch jiggles. Ann's keys turn in the two deadbolts. She sets the burglar alarm, climbs the stairs, knocks on my closed door, comes into my room.

"I just heard a murder," I tell her. A flicker of skepticism crosses her face. "I heard shots. It sounded like they were coming from Flint's," I defend myself. "And then a whole bunch of sirens. I *know* what happened"—still she looks at me dubiously—"*I saw it in my head,*" I add, knowing she will understand what I mean, whether she believes me or not.

"There *was* a police car on the corner," Ann says.

"I know it was a murder," I repeat. "And I saw a guy running away. I feel like I should call 911, but . . . I don't want to be up all night waiting for the cops to come question me. And there must have been witnesses at Flint's. Plus there were some people in a car right in front of the house when it happened—they got a better look at the guy than I did."

And, I admit to myself, but not to Ann, I'm afraid of the people who sent the guy who pulled the trigger—whoever they are, whoever he was. I've heard the stories: brave grandmothers who stand up to drug dealers in their East Oakland neighborhoods, found shot full of Uzi holes in their beds.

"It wouldn't do any good to call the cops now, anyway," Ann says. "The guy's gone, right?"

I notice as if from a distance how calmly Ann and I are talking about this, that our faces are stiff and drawn. I can barely meet her eyes. I feel my shame spreading over her like slime. Both of us made this Wrong Decision; both of us are now numbed by the reality of its repercussions.

"What are you reading?" Ann asks, frowning at the book that lies open next to me. I shrug, embarrassed to be caught midwallow in one of my terrorfests. "Oh, Babe," she says, shaking her head. "Why don't you give yourself a break? Can I do anything to help you relax and go to sleep?" Without her, she means; tonight is Wednesday, one of the three nights of every week that we sleep apart.

I ask for a beer. She goes downstairs to fetch me one, hands it to me, kisses me good-night with cold, tight lips, goes upstairs to her attic and (I hope) her own solitary bed. I suck on the bottle hungrily, my eyes wide open and fixed on the windows. Where is that man in the white sweatshirt? What is he doing right now?

DECEMBER 31, 1992

Seven A.M., New Year's Eve. The movie of the murder plays in my head before my eyes open.

I roll over in bed, flip on the local news. Nothing about a murder in North Oakland. It strikes me as odd that I am disappointed—shouldn't I want to be proved wrong? Maybe what I heard was gunfire intended to frighten, not kill—shots fired into the air. Maybe the sirens rushed to the scene, caught the reckless but harmless jerk who couldn't wait till New Year's Eve to fire his gun for the fun of it.

I consider this possibility briefly; reject it unhesitatingly.

In the BART station on my way to work I buy a morning paper. Nothing. Did the murder happen after the paper was put to bed last night? Have murders in Oakland become so commonplace that the San Francisco paper doesn't even report on them anymore?

The mood at work is festive: there are New Year's Eve parties to look forward to tonight, a paid day off tomorrow. I feel as if I'm in a bubble, fogged in by shame. Lots of these people live in neighborhoods like mine, but I can't tell them, either. My Bad Decision follows me around all day like a diseased dog.

The plan for tonight was to share a quiet New Year's Eve nesting in front of the fire with a few close friends: Ellen, Diana, Diana's sister Vicky. An evening of silliness, optimism, cuddling, and laughter. Since the election two months ago, we've all felt this great yearning to relax into hope; this was to be the first New Year's Eve in my adult lifetime when the world was giving me reason for hope. When I planned this evening, I was so looking forward to having something to look forward to . . .

Now I wish tonight were an ordinary Thursday night.

I love Diana. I adore her sister Vicky. I have come to embrace Ellen, after eight years of jealousy, whining, and resistance, as a member of my chosen family. But these are women who walk alone in their neighborhoods at night. How can I tell Diana, who, with half my income, pays as much to rent a tiny Marin County cottage as I pay to own a three-story Victorian—who looks around nervously as she walks the few feet from her car to our front door—that my openness, my giggles, my hope have been sealed inside me by a murder I witnessed—or didn't witness—from my bed last night?

I can't, and I won't, and I know that my shame and my silence will seal me off from the very thing that might comfort and release me: the love of the people who will be in my house tonight.

But home is where there is to go, and so after work I go there. Ann is bustling around getting ready for the party; she takes one look at my granite face and gets busier. Ellen's got the corn syrup out, waiting to make my secret-recipe caramel corn with me. I discover we're out of brown sugar, so I have the excuse I need to do what I've been wanting to do—and dreading doing—since last night: drive to the scene, look for clues, for confirmation, for shattered glass and dried blood . . .

As I'm approaching Shattuck an Oakland police car turns in my direction. I roll down my window, flag him down. Most of the cops on this beat are burly black men; this guy is young, skinny, and white.

Twenty years after my last bust for pot or politics, it still goes against my every instinct to deliberately attract a cop's attention.

"I live on the next block," I begin, so he doesn't mistake me for a lost yuppie looking for the BART station. "I thought I heard gunfire last night around eleven."

The young cop looks me in the eye and says evenly, "There was a homicide."

Homicide? It takes me a moment to remember what the word means. Until now I've only heard it on TV. Murder. It *was* a murder I heard.

"Right over there," the cop continues, pointing at Flint's. His blue eyes never leave mine; his gaze is soft . . . sympathetic. I have the unexpected sensation of being cared for, as if he has come to my door to tell me gently that someone I love has been killed. For the first time in nearly twenty-four hours I am talking about the murder with someone who knows it really happened and understands its significance.

The cop looks at me questioningly before he says more. I nod and he says, "A guy in a ski mask walked up to a twenty-three-year-old kid in front of Flint's and shot him. It was drug-related."

I see the man in the white sweatshirt running down the street last night. The words rise to my mouth; I swallow them back down. Fear and guilt burn in my throat. Are the drug lords who arranged the assassination watching me talk to this cop right now?

"Did you catch the guy who did it?" I choke out the question.

The cop shakes his head, his eyes still locked on mine. I see the movie of the murder again, try to place the guy in the white sweatshirt at the murder scene. His hands were empty as he ran, but of course he would have tossed the ski mask before he took off running.

"The case is still under investigation," the cop says. His face crumples slightly. He looks apologetic, as if he is to blame for allowing this to happen in my neighborhood—as if by doing his job well last night, he could have prevented it. And if I had been a good citizen last night, I think, I would have called 911 the instant I saw the guy running away, and he could be in jail right now instead of . . .

"We're hoping to apprehend the perpetrator and solve the crime," the cop adds, shrugging as if to acknowledge the lameness of his remark. I wonder if this is a white-person-to-white-person-in-a-black-neighborhood thing—if he would be treating me this sensitively, apologetically if I were a black woman in a beat-up American car.

"Thanks," I tell him through clenched teeth, and he drives away.

I sit in my car a few feet from the murder scene. There's a puddle of auto glass on the sidewalk near the corner, but there are always puddles of auto glass on these streets. As usual there's a line of people spilling out Flint's front door and a plume of greasy hickory smoke billowing from its chimney. The windows of the bar next door are boarded up, but the plywood looks weathered and I seem to remember it's been that way awhile. The only evidence that a terrible thing happened here last night is the scattering of burned-out flares in the gutter.

What did I expect to see? The outline of the murder victim drawn with yellow chalk on the sidewalk? Black-ribboned wreaths placed at the spot where he was gunned down? Flint's closed for the day in acknowledgment of the murder that took place in its doorway?

I drive to the corner store three blocks away. Its owner, Bill, explained to me once that in the Palestinian village where he grew up, the market was where people went to hear the news, and that the business of his store is as much the exchange of neighborhood gossip as the exchange of cash for milk, midnight munchies, and newspapers. As if he were still in his village, Bill, in defiance of all that's true about our neighborhood, extends credit to his unemployed customers, keeping stacks of scribbled receipts next to the register and selling cigarettes to youngsters only after calling their parents.

As he rings up my brown sugar I ask Bill if he's heard about the shooting. He nods dejectedly. "That's the second one in a few months," he says. "Remember the one at the bar down Shattuck?"

Of course I do. One of the three people who died that night was the coach of the basketball team my kids often play against. The bar that was sprayed with bullets is across the street from the rec center where my kids' basketball games are often held.

"It's getting worse," Bill says. His conclusion—the conclusion of a man who bets his livelihood daily on believing the best about the people in our neighborhood—goes against everything I have hoped for and wanted to be true. But how can I argue with Bill's flat despair, the night after a murder five blocks from his store?

I drive home with the brown sugar and still more information I need to, and will not be able to, share. Sticking out of the mailbox on our porch is a flyer that wasn't there when I left. There's a picture of a lit candle and a handwritten headline, "STOP THE VIOLENCE TONIGHT." Next to the candle is written:

"Last night there was a shooting in *our* neighborhood! Join us in showing our care, concern, anger, unity in meeting. Let's meet in front of Flint's BBQ at 11 PM and walk around our neighborhood. Bring candles."

I stand with my key in the lock, the flyer in my hand, and my emotions in turmoil.

This is good: my neighborhood is organized; there are brave, caring people here. This is bad: who is naive enough to believe it's safe to go back to the scene of the crime? This is good: neighborhoods like this one have, in fact, been snatched back from the crack dealers by organized efforts like this one. This is bad: I want to go to the vigil to heal myself and my neighborhood, but how will I explain my absence to the friends who are expecting festivities at my house tonight?

I bring the flyer inside, catch Ann's eye behind Ellen's back, beckon to her to come upstairs with me. "I was right," I tell her. "There was a murder last night at Flint's. A twenty-three-year-old got shot—drugs."

Ann's face tenses. She hugs me. I can barely feel her touch. I show her the flyer. "I want to go," I say. "But I'm embarrassed to tell Ellen and Diana what happened."

"I already told Ellen what you thought you heard," Ann says. "She said she thought it was firecrackers."

The phone rings. It's Mark, the gay man next door, asking if I know who left the flyers in our mailboxes and if we're going to the vigil. I'm too ashamed of my shame to explain to him why it would be hard for me to go. "We're having people over, so I won't be able to get away," I tell him. "I heard the shooting, Mark. It was really scary."

For the first couple of years after he left the white-flight 'burbs and bought the tiny house next to ours, Mark was in a chronic state of panic, leaning on Ann and me for reassurance, for the names of alarm companies, fence builders, fellow gay neighbors, and city council members. But since we told him, a few months ago, that we were thinking of moving to a safer neighborhood, Mark's been playing the stoic. "We live in the inner city," he tells me flatly. "This kind of thing is a fact of life."

Mark agrees with me that the vigil is a great idea. But he's not going, he says, because rain is expected. He's going to a party instead. I'm not going, either.

And so our friends ring the doorbell, and I find I am able to move my clenched jaw through the motions of welcoming kisses, dinner, conversation. But the real conversation is raging in my head.

I want to be able to enjoy my New Year's Eve, my friends, my lover, the goodness that is here now. But even more than I want the pleasures of the present, I want to stay human. I don't want my ability to feel—to grieve when there is grief, and there is so much to grieve—to be stolen, along with my safety, by crime or AIDS or breast cancer or homelessness or any of the other terrible stuff I step through and around every day of my life.

I want to find a balance I haven't yet found—to be able to laugh at my son's jokes today although my chosen brother Peter died yesterday; to be able to enjoy dinner with Molly, knowing that Wendy is home puking up the chemotherapy that will either kill or save her; to be able to revel in the incredible amount of money I find myself earning these days, passing twenty homeless beggars in doorways on my way to work each morning; to relish the pure, mindless joy of lovemaking, knowing that somewhere a father is raping his three-year-old daughter.

I don't want to live in denial. But I do want relief. I want to find a way to choose what fills my heart and my head—on this New Year's Eve, in this new year, in my life.

Mark was right; at eleven o'clock rain pounds the roof, the windows, the sidewalk outside. In our living room the fire is blazing, the caramel corn is sweet, the touch of my lover's hands in my hair heartwarming, the movie we've rented—about a comedienne who uses her kids' lives as material—funny and touching.

While my friends laugh and chatter and tease me about being like the comedienne, I watch the clock and imagine what's happening at Flint's. I wonder if my neighbors have gathered there, if they're an all-white or a mixed group, if the dealers will retaliate, if anyone who loved the man who died will go there, if the man in the white sweatshirt will slip, unidentified, into the crowd; if my neighbors will be able to protect their candles from the rain that would snuff them out in the dark.

Staying Human

I *hate* being late for a movie, and Ann and I are almost late for *Husbands and Wives*. As I'm speeding down Shattuck Avenue, my compulsion to be seated in time for the opening credits overcomes my compulsion to park for free. So instead of running through my usual movie-night routine—expending half a tank of gas driving around greater downtown Berkeley in an effort to save two dollars on parking—I drive directly into the twenty-four-hour meter lot.

Eight quarters are required; between Ann, the schmutzy floor of the car, and me, we have only six. Noting that my eyes are now dilated and fixed on my watch, that my jaw is clenched and my breathing labored, Ann jumps out of the car waving a dollar bill.

"Do you have change for a dollar?" Ann asks one and then another of our fellow moviegoers. Several people walk by shaking their heads. Several others step around her disdainfully without acknowledging her presence. One woman stops long enough to say that she just put all the change she had in her own meter.

"Excuse me, sir," Ann says to a middle-aged man in a suit and tie, her usual reticence cranked up a bit by the urgency of the moment. "Do you have change for a dollar?"

Without breaking stride—neither making eye contact with Ann nor noticing the dollar bill she's proffering—the man digs in his pocket, tosses a few nickels and dimes in Ann's direction, and keeps on walking.

Ann turns to me, stunned. "He thought I was a homeless person," she says.

OCTOBER 1992: BERKELEY

I pull up in front of Richard's house at nine o'clock on Saturday morning to pick up the kids for the weekend.

There's a man in mismatched shoes and tattered clothing stationed in front of Richard's gate. His arms crossed, he glares at me belligerently, as though he's been hired to guard Richard's house and I'm about to challenge his authority.

I consider my choices. I could drive to a phone booth, call Richard, and ask him to go out and shoo the guy away. I could sit in my car for a few minutes and hope the guy wanders on down the block. I could walk past him, ignore him, and hope for the best.

I could close my heart and be annoyed by this unpleasant interlude, angry at this man who is inconveniencing me—or I could open my heart and let myself feel the grief.

I glance at my watch: 9:05. Jesse's due at a basketball game at 9:30. The man doesn't look dangerous—maybe just a bit deranged. I snap my fanny pack around my waist, lock my car door, and walk toward the house.

"Give me something," the man demands as I approach him. "A dollar, a quarter, something."

He needs so much more than a dollar, and I don't have it to give.

"Sorry," I mutter, my usual response to panhandlers.

Sorry? What a hypocritical thing to say!

If I were really sorry, I'd . . .

Give him a quarter? A dollar? The contents of my wallet? Buy him a meal? Take him home with me and cook him a meal?

This man is being so direct with me. What if I were to be equally direct with him? What if I were to tell him—tell myself—what I am really sorry about?

I'm sorry for you that I am unwilling to part with a sum of money I could lose on the floor of my car and never even miss.

I'm sorry for myself that I am faced, at every turn, in every city in this country, by the evidence that you and other homeless people present: of the abysmal failure of our economic and social system to do what it's supposed to do. And the abysmal failure of human beings like me *(I do care! It's just so overwhelming . . .)* to do a damn thing about it.

I'm sorry for both of us that the inability of this, the wealthiest nation on earth, to provide food and shelter (never mind the pursuit of happiness) for so many of its citizens has drained the very humanness, in this moment, from you, and from me.

I'm sorry for both of us that we stand facing each other now in opposition, frozen rigid, numbly acting out the roles assigned us: I, the Have; You, the Have-Not. I, hoarding what I have; you, wanting to wrest a bit of it from me.

I'm sorry that neither of us will ever know the person you, in a better world, might be—or the person I, in a better world, might be.

I'm sorry that I'm so afraid of the feelings you evoke that my heart closes like a lens until I barely see you at all.

This man doesn't do what most homeless people do when they see I'm not going to give them any money. He doesn't turn away; rather, his scowl deepens.

"You have this big house and everything," he says, gesturing toward Richard's front yard, enclosed now by the brand-new redwood picket fence that Jesse and Richard built together since I was here last week.

I don't bother to correct him. Maybe not this big house, but yes: another big house. And (the crowded pantry shelves; the bountiful garden, the Ben & Jerry's in the freezer), as he says, everything.

Guilt is nonproductive.

"You have everything," the man repeats. "I have nothing. Can't you even give me a quarter?"

NOVEMBER 1992: SAN FRANCISCO

It's not the job I hate so much as the getting to it.

Thundering beneath the bay on BART, I feel as if I'm trapped inside a sealed cattle car. The white- and pink-collar commuters sit stiff as corpses: the men in their starched oxford shirts and polished oxford shoes and locked leather briefcases, the women in their flesh-colored nylons and rapier-length fuchsia fingernails and ersatz Gucci purses.

Nearly every one of the people around me looks depressed, insensate. Nearly every one of them reads his or her copy of the morning *Chronicle*. Page One, Atrocities in Bosnia, turn the page. Page Two, Baseball superstar gets $43 million contract, turn the page. No one talks. No one smiles. Unless there's a "crazy person" babbling out loud, we travel together this way each morning, hundreds of us, locked in separate silence.

By the time the train pulls into the Montgomery Street station I feel I am at the bottom of a pile of bodies, barely able to breathe. Is it the airless train itself or the dread of our destinations that siphons the oxygen, the life, the humor from all these people, from me, before we've even had our muffins and coffee? I feel like screaming: *Does anyone on this train want to go to work today?*

But I don't scream. I just try to keep breathing. I plod within the herd through the station. I wait my turn to push through the turnstile. I ride the crowded escalator up to daylight. I am ejected with the others into the chilly, drizzly Financial District morning.

Vendors hawk the latest version of the news. Florists arrange overpriced bouquets for National Whatever-Hallmark-Calls-It Day. Coffee carts dispense caffeine and sugar: morning meds on Market Street.

And the homeless people are positioned in their regular stations, reminding us that we're the lucky ones.

"Mornin', ma'am," says Tom, tipping his hat and smiling at me as I stand on the outskirts of the crowd, waiting for the light to change on the corner of California and Montgomery.

I've never given this man a cent, never even made eye contact with him until a week or so ago, when I simply couldn't bear to look away any longer. (*Which is worse: ignoring him and his need, or acknowledging him and ignoring his need?*)

Ever since I spoke to him, Tom has been greeting me enthusiastically each morning, seemingly undaunted by my continuing failure to drop a coin into his cup. Often, Tom's is the warmest smile I see between leaving home in the morning and returning home at night.

(*Why doesn't he hate me for bustling by him, too rushed to stop and talk, too clenched to share what I have? Why don't I just reach into my briefcase full of the papers I earn good money to move from one desk to another, and give this man a dollar?*)

"Hi, Tom," I answer. I know his name because it's written on the sign he keeps propped on the wool blanket that covers his lap. Winter, spring, summer, fall, the same plaid blanket covers Tom's lap and the one leg that dangles from the folding metal chair he sits on. The sign says, "My name is Tom. Veteran Injured in WW II. Please Help. God Bless You and Have a Nice Day."

A woman in a pink suit and matching pumps edges up beside me and hands Tom a small white paper bag.

"Blueberry—your favorite," the woman says.

Tom beams at her toothlessly. "Thank you, ma'am," he says.

"You're welcome," the woman answers, and sprints across California Street against the light, dodging taxis and BMW's.

Tom pulls the muffin out of the bag. "Mary!" he calls to the woman who's always perched on a plastic milk crate on the opposite corner. Her sign says, "Homeless. Hungry. Please spare change."

Mary looks up, sees Tom waving the muffin at her, jumps to her feet. "I'll be right over," she shouts.

The light changes; I move on.

The woman who sits petting her fluffy white terrier in the Sanwa Bank doorway has a "Clinton/Gore" button on today. The button blurs the difference, shortens the distance between her and me.

Does she really think Clinton could help?

Do I?

"Hi," I say, looking the woman in the eye. She has no sign; I don't know her name.

"Hi," she says sadly. Four days a week for a year now I've been walking by without giving her any money. Why should she hope that I might give her something today?

Why don't I just give this woman a dollar?

I don't give her, or Tom, or any of the others, a dollar because I am afraid. Afraid of letting myself be flooded by the need, by the overwhelming needs of the homeless panhandlers I see and do nothing for every day of my life. Afraid of what I will lose besides the dollar: the wall—or the illusion of a wall—that the not-giving-the-dollar erects between the homeless people and me.

I used to avoid eye contact with Tom, and Mary, and the woman with the terrier, and the homeless people who crouch in the doorways of every main street in Berkeley, for that reason: to keep the wall—to keep the illusion of the wall—intact.

Then I realized that in denying their humanity, I was eroding my own. I felt the icy fingers of dispassion closing around my heart and I thought, *I can't bring myself to give them my money, but I can't go on pretending they're not there, either.*

Nothing makes this get better, or even feel better.

Why don't I just give this one woman just one dollar?

Why would I choose this one woman? Because we share a hope for the upcoming election? Because we both have dogs that curl up in our laps? Because Tom already has a blueberry muffin?

If I opened a window in the wall, decided to give someone a dollar, how would I choose whom to give it to? The World War II veteran or the veteran of Vietnam? The man whose sign says he's saving for a suit to wear to job interviews, or the man in the blue wool overcoat who screams incoherently into his matted beard? The couple with the sleeping children on the blanket beside them, or the woman who sits alone?

Each of them? What if I gave one dollar to each of them every day?

Opening to the compassion immediately triggers the rage. I pay my goddamn taxes, the government wastes my goddamn money. Why can't the people I elect and pay to run this country provide food and shelter for these people?

Guilt is nonproductive.

Why should solving this immense problem be up to me? I've got a family to support, dammit.

What kind of a human being am I?

The Buddhist in me imagines stopping to greet each homeless person I see, dividing the contents of my pockets evenly among them, dispensing respect along with spare change.

The homeowner in me wants the streets clean, property values elevated, the underside invisible.

The activist in me fantasizes organizing all the homeless people of Montgomery Street, Berkeley, the United States, into an unstoppable grass-roots movement for jobs, low-income housing, squatters' rights, free mental health care.

The mother in me imagines begging on Montgomery Street with Peter and Jesse barefoot in a rusty stroller beside me, feels that despair for just an instant and recoils from the picture . . .

The only kind of human being there is.

FEBRUARY 1993: BERKELEY

Tomorrow I'm going to New York to meet with publishers who want to buy my book. The dream of my life is unfolding; I pinch myself hourly but still it appears to be true: the dream of my life is unfolding.

Tonight Ann and I are going to see *Last Call at Maude's* at the UC Theater. It promises to be a big night in Berkeley for Sapphic-Americans: the movie's a documentary about the closing of the oldest lesbian bar in San Francisco. Assured by my agent that my book advance will more than cover two hours' worth of parking, I drive unhesitatingly to the twenty-four-hour meter lot near the theater. Impending wealth and fame notwithstanding, I can't help myself: I circle around until I find a space with a few minutes left on the meter.

"Good! We're twenty minutes early," I say, unbuckling my seat belt.

"I know what you're looking forward to," Ann teases me. "You don't care about the movie. You just want to cruise the girls on the movie line."

"True, so true," I agree. "And you . . . ?"

Ann laughs, squeezes my hand. "C'mon, Mer. We don't want to miss a minute of the action."

As we're locking our car doors a man steps out from the shadows.

"Wash your windshield, miss?" he asks, showing me the squeegee in his hand.

"Sorry," I say automatically.

"Could I watch your car while you're gone, then?" he asks. "I'm trying to get something to eat."

I start to shake my head. Something stops me. *My heart stops me.*

Never in my life have I felt such a richness, such an overflowing abundance of everything I need—want, even—as I do right now. I have healthy, great kids; a healthy, great relationship; friends all around me; a beautiful house and a thriving garden. And now, dangling before me: a chance to step off the BART treadmill, quit my job, turn my compost, write my book.

I feel a generosity of spirit. There's never been a better time for me to let down the defenses, give what I can, treasure the rest.

I have enough now. More than I need.

I reach into my fanny pack, pull out my wallet. *If you start you'll never know when to stop. You'll never be able to give enough. You'll lose everything you have and it still won't be enough.*

I remember a Ram Dass lecture on compassion Ann and I went to a couple of years ago. He talked about the difficulty of living compassionately in such harsh times as ours.

"We're afraid that if we give a dime to a beggar on the street," he said, "we'll go home and find the beggar in our living room."

I remember thinking, *And what would you say to the beggar in your living room? Don't you invite him there by giving him anything at all? How could you turn him away when you've given him reason to hope?*

Still I find myself unzipping my change purse, dumping the coins into the stranger's hand.

I feel like a human being.

"Thanks," the man says. A car parks a few spaces away; he hurries over, waving his squeegee at the driver.

Ann is staring at me in amazement.

"That's the first time I ever did that," I say. It's been a point of contention in our family that I refuse to give money to panhandlers; Ann, Peter, and Jesse do it all the time.

"I know," Ann says.

"Do you think we'll go home and find a beggar in our living room?" I ask her, only half joking.

Ann grabs me, hugs me close.

"Believe it or not," she says, "opening your heart a little bit doesn't make you a pushover. You did a good thing, Mer. Now let's just see what happens."

JULY 1993: BERKELEY

I have decided that I simply cannot stand to go on playing racquetball as badly as I play it. This forces me to choose between two almost equally unpleasant options: give up the only sport in which I regularly engage— or take a lesson, for once in my life.

And so tonight I will humbly present myself to the Beginners' Racquetball Clinic at the Berkeley Y. "I'm Meredith, and I have a Bad Racquetball Habit," I imagine myself confessing before the group.

As it turns out, no such introduction is necessary. The instructor looks the student bodies over, pairs us off for play, and dispatches us to the courts. My partner is a woman about my age who, it soon becomes apparent, is almost as inept as I. Like me, she seems to cope with her well-earned embarrassment by making nervous chitchat between serves.

"Have you been playing long?" she asks as we begin.

"No," I lie, denying the two years I've spent getting as bad as I am at the game.

"Is this your first time at Clinic?" she asks a few minutes later.

"Yes," I answer.

And then she asks the question I've been asked a lot this summer. "How'd you get so tan?" she inquires, as I limp to the back of the court to retrieve the ball from where it landed the last time I missed it—inside my spiffy new bike helmet, placed for safekeeping in the corner.

When I'm not as winded and disgusted with myself as I am now, and when I'm prepared to answer the questions that inevitably follow ("What's your book about? Have you found a publisher? When will it be in bookstores?", etc.), I explain the whole story: I'm writing a book, I have a laptop, I work a lot on my deck or at my cabin in the country. Hence—wrinkles and skin cancer be damned—my all-time personal best tan.

But, given the stress of this moment, I decide to offer my partner the summary version instead. "I'm kind of living outside these days," I say, tossing her the ball.

She raises her racquet to serve, drops it again, looks at me intently. I see her face register confusion, then Berkeley-style solicitude: the politically correct blend of empathy and respect (not, for Goddess's sake, pity).

"Oh," she says. "Are you homeless?"

I'm standing here in my $70 tennis shoes with my $50 racquet playing on a court I pay $30 a month to use once a week. And she thinks I'm homeless?

"No," I answer. "I'm writing a book. I'm using a laptop. I work outside a lot."

I watch my partner's face carefully. Am I imagining it, or does she look . . . disappointed?

This is what it's come to. We all want so badly to believe it's not as bad as it seems. That homeless people are living lives just like ours—playing racquetball, getting tans, wearing nice new helmets when they ride their bikes. There's just one little difference: they have nowhere to live.

SEPTEMBER 1993: SANTA BARBARA

Zoe wanted a break from New York, and we all wanted to see Zoe, but Ann couldn't take a break from work. So Zoe flew out and visited with all of us in Oakland for a couple of days, then she and I took Peter and Jesse down the coast for a four-day Surfin' USA/End o' Summer/Southern California Beach Blowout vacation.

Tomorrow we'll separate for points north and east. Tonight, our last night together, we're doing the tourist thing: checking out the surf shops and espresso bars on State Street.

Santa Barbara is beautiful, a scenic spit of land that joins the craggy Santa Ynez Mountains with the sea. Somewhere in those hills, Michael Jackson rides the carousel in his own private Disneyland, and Ronald Reagan gallops through the chaparral like a hero. The lesser local millionaires enjoy the endless summer in the sun-bleached stucco palaces that dot the foothills, their picturesque terra-cotta roofs a futile barrier against the fierce Santa Anas that whip voracious firestorms through their manicured landscapes every twenty years or so.

Santa Barbara's white sands are pristine; its palm trees sway invitingly in the soft evening breeze. But the dreamy blue horizon is defiled by an army of gunmetal-gray oil rigs that crouch menacingly above the surf.

"I'm surprised there are so many homeless people here," Peter says, as perhaps the fifth man in rags we've seen in the past half hour shuffles by us. "Is there a poor neighborhood in this town?"

"I don't know," I answer. "But I bet they do everything they can to keep the homeless people away from these stores and restaurants, so the tourists don't take their dollars somewhere else."

While we're deciding whether to eat lobster at Moby Dick's or fish and chips at Longboard's, the four of us duck into a cafe for some predinner Calistogas and cookies. Jesse and Peter were up till three A.M. last night communing with a couple of pubescent girls in the hotel Jacuzzi. Today they have required frequent infusions of liquids and sugar to keep their spirits at appropriately elevated vacation levels.

I hand a ten-dollar bill to the bronzed, ponytailed man behind the counter. I receive a few coins in change. Cheap, this town is not.

"How can they do that?" Peter asks, as we walk toward the beach, sipping our drinks. "How can they keep homeless people off a certain street? Can they bust them just for being where the cops don't want them to be?"

As Peter asks his earnest questions I watch a scene unfolding at the end of the block. A young barefoot man with stringy hair down his back, wearing tattered layers of faded shirts and brightly colored serapes, is walking toward us pushing a stroller full of crushed cans. A motorcycle cop headed in the opposite direction does a sharp U-turn, pulls up beside the young man, dismounts, and strides toward him purposefully.

"I think we're about to find out," I say to Peter.

As we walk by, the cop is talking to the homeless man. The homeless man is silent, unresponsive, staring straight ahead. The cop takes his phone off his hip and barks into it. The homeless man stands perfectly still, his bearded, dirt-encrusted face devoid of expression.

When we reach the corner, without exchanging a word, the four of us stop, turn around, look back. The cop is still talking into his phone; the homeless man is still frozen in place.

"I feel like I want to *do* something," I say. "But I don't know what would help."

"Let's go stand right next to the cop," Peter says. I glance at him. Sure enough, my older son has his now-familiar Warrior-for-Justice face on.

I know this mood of Peter's well: I was in it for ten years, starting at just about the age he is now. I know that in this mood it is possible to do almost anything in the name of what is right (or, more to the point, left). As the keeper of Peter's physical well-being and the provider of his bail, I have adopted the unexpected role of imposing upon Peter's newfound revolutionary fervor the cold, conservative voice of reason.

"Be cool, Peter," I advise him now. "You know you can get busted for interfering with an officer."

Like the homeless man, Zoe, Jesse, Peter, and I are immobilized: unable to walk away, unable to act. And so we stand, staring. Behind the cop's shoulder the orange orb of the sun is sinking below the mountains, casting filtered shafts of light onto the roofs and trees. When I turn around to face Zoe for an adult-to-adult reality check, I see the blue moon rising full and pale above the sailboats and yachts bobbing in the harbor.

"I'm going to walk by them," Zoe says now, "so the cop knows I'm witnessing what he's doing."

"Go, Zoe!" I cheer her on.

A few years after Zoe and I became best friends in 1963, the entire

world population was divided with surgical precision into the bad guys
(Part of the Problem) and the good guys (Part of the Solution). There was
no room in the equation for people like Zoe—who opposed the war, but
not in the all-consuming way that I did. I was outraged by Zoe's lack of
political passion and her lack of interest in drugs, certain that our
friendship would not survive the war, or even the Johnson administration (whichever ended first).

But somehow our relationship endured—in varying states of emotional and geographic proximity—as Johnson, and then Nixon, Ford,
Carter, Reagan, and Bush came and went. Now I realize that I'm still
hanging on to some outdated notion of me-as-activist and Zoe-as-
apathetic—long after the times, and our complex identities, have rendered ridiculous such a tidy distinction.

At the moment, in fact, I'm the one who's clutching at my son to
keep him from wreaking civil disorder. And it's Zoe who's taking action
in defense of a stranger's civil rights.

Zoe saunters deliberately by the cop and the homeless man, making unwavering eye contact with the cop as she turns and slowly walks
by them again.

"He's not busting the guy," Zoe says when she returns to our rebel-
outpost-by-the-sea. "Or even giving him a ticket. It's called harassment."

"Look, Zoe," I say, nodding at the cop. "He's giving you major dirty
looks."

"He leaned very deliberately and threateningly toward me as I
passed him," Zoe reports.

The cop mounts his motorcycle and roars off. The homeless man
gives his stroller a little shove and continues on his way.

We cross the street, walk out onto the pier that's lined with water-
front restaurants, candy stores, and gift shops. Gulls flap and dip above
us, swooping down to peck up sticky strands of cotton candy and paper-
wrapped ends of ice cream cones. On the beach below us several
homeless men are rolling out their sleeping bags for the night.

"Moby Dick's or Longboard's?" I ask.

"I'm too cold to eat outside," Zoe says, as we walk by Longboard's
outdoor patio.

"How 'bout Moby Dick's for dinner and Longboard's for dessert?" Peter says. "They show surf videos at Longboard's."

"Sounds gnarly, dude," I say.

Zoe and I need to act like New Yorkers to get a window table at Moby Dick's. Much to the eye-rolling chagrin of my sons, we do so.

"C'mon, guys," I cajole Peter and Jesse, who are grumbling now with embarrassment. "It's our last night on vacation. We're not eating in this tourist trap for the *food*! We want the view, the seagulls—the works."

The waitress hands us our menus; the busboy brings us a basket of warm sourdough rolls and foil-wrapped pats of butter. From my place at the table I can see moonlight dancing on the ocean and the last bit of twilight glowing behind the hills.

"Don't you think maybe we helped that homeless man just a little?" I ask. "Maybe the cop would've busted him if we hadn't been watching."

"Don't break your arm patting yourself on the back, Mom," Jesse says. "So the guy didn't get busted. Big deal. He's still homeless."

Guilt is nonproductive.

The waitress comes to take our orders.

"I'll have the lobster," I say.

Chop Wood, Carry Water,
Flip Pancakes

<hr>

SATURDAY, JULY 3, 1993

"Who's ready for more veggies?" Cornelia's voice drifts across the porch, borne on wisps of fragrant smoke from the hibachi she's tending. "Peter? Jesse? Steve? Anyone?"

"Hmm . . . ," muses Sue lazily. "Could I possibly swallow another bite?"

The only response from the forest is a woodpecker's rhythmic hammering high in a distant fir, punctuated by the faint hiss and spit of the vegetarian shish kebabs on the grill.

"What a feast," says Cornelia's husband, Steve, nodding at the potluck dinner strewn across the groaning board Sue has set up on the porch of her cabin, a quarter mile up the road from ours.

"Food always tastes so great up here," Cornelia says contentedly.

"*Everything* is always so great up here," I say.

Something like a zillion times since Ann and I bought our cabin five years ago I've sent thanks to Sue, Cornelia, and whatever goddess was smiling down on me the day I asked my old friend Sue, over happy-hour hors d'oeuvres at a Berkeley jazz club, where Ann and I should go to celebrate our fourth anniversary.

"Why don't you rent my cabin?" Sue asked. Ten years earlier Sue, her sister Francie, and Cornelia had gone in together on a hilly twelve-acre plot of fir and madrone and oak, and the four ramshackle cabins that a late-sixties hippie commune had built on it.

"Oh, and while you're up there," Sue added, "take a look at Francie's. She's moving back east, so we're looking for a buyer. There's another cabin for sale, too—it's in an incredible spot, but a long way from the road. Anyway, see what you think. I know you've always wanted a place in the country."

It took Ann and me about a minute to fall in love with the land and to choose Francie's cabin. And then it took six months of worrying about *everything* before the final decision was made. Could I, in my cyclically unemployed state, afford my half of the $250 monthly payments? Could our family live (even just on weekends and vacations) with an outhouse, without hot running water or Ben & Jerry's ice cream?

Sue and I had lived together in a Berkeley group house fifteen years ago, but would we make good land partners now? Ann and I had been lovers for five years, but in Oakland we still lived two miles apart. Were we ready to buy a mop, a mattress, *a home* together?

Would our video-addicted nine- and ten-year-old city boys want to take the three-hour drive to this no-electricity, no-phone, chop-wood cabin? More to the point: would I? There'd been a lot of miles logged on my thirty-seven-year-old body since the last time I chopped wood and carried water. Was I really ready to enter into that contract with nature again?

After another visit to Francie's cabin, to the idyllic waterfall-fed swimming hole below it and the unspoiled forest around it, Ann and I realized that the only appropriate response was yes, yes, a thousand times yes. Just before Thanksgiving of 1988, we signed on to the deed that made us co-owners with Sue and Cornelia of twelve acres and the structures on it.

Crossing the threshold of this semifunky, quirky cabin felt like returning to my roots, picking up the frayed threads of the commune-based life I'd left in the mountains of northern New Mexico, circa 1970. Everything about the place felt familiar, as if the train of time had rolled back several stations, opened the doors, and let me back in: the recycled barn wood siding and windows installed at crazy angles, the built-in desks and counters with stripped logs for legs, the shreds of marijuana that appeared in the dustpan every time we swept the unfinished plank floor.

Wrinkled and wiser, but no less in love with sunlight on leaves and the silence of mountain mornings, I felt I'd been given a second chance, a happy resumption of life as it should be after twenty years of dreamus interruptus. Finally the path that had led me running, at age eighteen, from Manhattan to Taos, and then dumped me—chasing lovers and jobs and excitement through the seventies and eighties—in one city after another, had brought me back to where I've always preferred to be: with dirt underfoot and quiet abounding.

There are miracles that happen here, miracles that could not and do not happen anywhere else. Here—subsidized by our paper-pushing labors the other five days a week—we earn the satisfaction of *real* work. Work that is performed not in pursuit of glamour, "advancement," or "security," but to keep ourselves warm and fed. Here Peter and Jesse, who in our city life demand payment for washing a car or mowing a lawn, stride ambitiously into the woods shrieking "Timber!" as they clear and cut skinny saplings into kindling.

And here—temporarily released from the estrangement imposed on our family by adolescent imperative—we do things we love to do, *together*. At this moment, for instance, I am watching a red-tailed hawk swooping above a hundred miles of pristine mist-shrouded mountains and sloping golden valleys, my belly full of great food, enjoying slow, easy conversation with my lover and friends, and—this almost never happens in Oakland—my adolescent sons are happily doing what I'm doing with me.

"Well, I guess we should talk about business," Cornelia says now, serving up heaping dollops of soppy strawberry cobbler. It's rare for all four of us land partners to be up here at the same time; whenever we are, we feel obligated to do something partnerlike together.

On the agenda tonight is the fate of our uninhabited, rapidly deteriorating fourth cabin—the one that's always been called "the Faraway" because of the half-mile precipitous hike required to get to it from the road. For years the Faraway has been standing empty, its dilapidated presence sparking the unfulfilled country fantasies of one visiting city friend after another.

Wendy envisioned herself hiking in on the wildflower-lined footpath with her yet-to-be-conceived baby in a Snugli and her arms full of weeks' worth of groceries. Bill fantasized about demolishing and rebuilding the place, starting over with lumber he'd haul in using an elaborate system of ropes and pulleys. Molly talked to bulldozer operators about cutting a road in, talked to contractors about restoring the cabin to livable condition, talked to Sue and Cornelia and Ann and me about becoming our fifth land partner. Then, after two years of investigating and negotiating, Molly decided to go in with some friends on a time-share, a former vineyard with electricity and a swimming pool an hour's drive from Berkeley.

"It's time we faced it," Sue says, spooning yogurt onto her cobbler. "The Faraway is going away. No one's about to buy it or even rent it in the shape it's in. I think we should pay someone to take it down before it falls down. Then we can use the lumber and stuff that's in it to fix up our cabins."

Ann sighs. "It's so sad," she says. "It was such a beautiful place."

"Beautiful . . . and hard to get to," Cornelia says. "I guess people just aren't willing to sacrifice convenience in the nineties the way they did in the sixties."

You can sure prove that by me, I think. When Paul and I built our house near Taos, we chose the site for its panoramic three-hundred-mile view and its isolation. We took pride in being hard to get to without four-wheel drive; we found it romantic that in winter, often, no one could get to us at all. Twenty years later, when Ann and I were offered the Faraway—far more enchanting but far less accessible than Francie's—we pictured ourselves lugging five-gallon water bottles and sleepy boys and, eventually, sleepy grandchildren along the dark trail when we arrived late on Friday nights. Quickly but regretfully we succumbed to the sensible choice.

Promises I couldn't keep, I think, remembering the days when I swore I'd never get old.

Sue passes around steaming mugs of Country Peach tea.

"The light is so beautiful at this time of night," Steve says. "That oak looks like it's on fire, doesn't it?"

We all sit contemplating the towering tree, backlit by the sinking sun. Jesse goes inside; through Sue's asymmetrical windows I watch him spill the pieces of a jigsaw puzzle onto her kitchen table.

"How on earth," Sue interrupts our reverie, "are we ever gonna get all that stuff out of the Faraway? There's no way anybody can carry a Wedgwood stove and a cast-iron bathtub up that hill."

"Maybe we should try doing it the way it was done in the first place," Cornelia says, grinning.

There are scattered chuckles. Cornelia has called up a collective memory of the reunion we held two years ago, when the mystery of our cabin's origins were revealed to us by the people who built them.

Pat and Elizabeth, who conceived and raised their kids in our cabin and still visit us the day after Thanksgiving each year, spread the word to their former fellow communards, now scattered throughout the backwoods, towns, and cities of Northern California.

At the appointed time, thirty graying doctors and disk jockeys, teachers and potters, pot-growers and social workers with names like Crow and Sage and Jasmine converged on our cabin with their teenage and adult children named Sierra and Dylan and Blue, and coffee cans full of pot, and our land's recent history to teach us.

That's when we found out exactly how our predecessors had built our comfy cabins, rutted but still-serviceable dirt road, and gravity-fed water system: exactly the way—and at exactly the same time—that Paul and I and our friends had built our houses in New Mexico. It was a classic hippie construction project, with enthusiasm, scavenging, and homegrown pot standing in for power tools, money, and know-how.

Their reasons for leaving the land—shortly after Paul and I left ours—were familiar, too. The pot economy and the pot culture weren't as satisfying or as life-sustaining as they'd once been. Their kids were growing up and the nearest school was twenty miles away. Couples broke up and reconstellated; sexual tensions shattered communal cama-raderie. The war ended; Sgt. Pepper was being piped into elevators;

suddenly no one was sure what they were for, what their lives were for, or against, anymore.

". . . We could put our work boots on and take our clothes off and smoke a bunch of grass and meditate the appliances up the hill." Cornelia giggles. Peter shoots me a shocked look. Cornelia's a *grand-mother;* he wasn't expecting to be invited to share a joint with her.

"Not a bad plan, Cornelia," I say. "Let's start with that, anyway. If it doesn't work, we'll just move on to Plan B."

Peter gets up and joins Jesse inside. Cornelia watches him go. Her own four grown children now bring their lovers and spouses and children to the cabin she bought when her kids were Peter's and Jesse's ages.

"What a weird thing for kids," says Cornelia. "To have people like us for parents."

In the deepening dusk the distant mountains are fading to smoky blue. The bats begin their nocturnal feast, swooping down on the mosquitoes that now flee our arms and ankles. Sue's screen door slams.

"Mom—we're going back to our cabin, okay?" Peter says. I see that Jesse has already started down Sue's steps.

"Do you need a flashlight?" I ask Peter, stalling for time. This is a first: the kids walking home alone in the near-dark, being in the cabin alone at night.

"Not if we get going now," Peter answers pointedly.

Bears? Rattlesnakes? Poison oak? My kids, I realize, will be safer on our dark dirt road than they are every winter evening when they walk the two well-lit blocks from the BART station to our house.

I nod at Peter. He murmurs, "Bye. Thanks," to the adults on the porch, and follows Jesse up Sue's path.

After another hour or so of desultory discussion about our eroding road, our decaying deck railings, and the success of our thrown-together meal, Ann and I gather our baking pans and pot holders and flashlight and bid our friends good-night.

My honey and I walk with our arms wrapped around each other, as we often do when we head for home, our favorite home, along this road whose turns and dips and curves we know and navigate wordlessly as in a much-rehearsed silent waltz. As we round the final bend to our cabin I see the yellow glow of kerosene lamps through the thicket of madrone and poison oak.

"Oh wow," I say. "Look! The kids lit the lamps by themselves!"

"Mer," Ann says, her voice registering a familiar mix of affection and incredulity, "did you really expect them to sit there in the dark?"

"I guess not . . . but . . . ," I stammer.

"They're growing up, Babe," Ann says.

As we step up onto the porch we peek through the window. Peter is lying on the couch; Jesse is bent over at the kitchen table.

"Mer!" Ann whispers. "They're *reading!*"

"They're growing up, Babe," I say. Ann elbows me, gently but firmly, in the ribs. I give her arm a conciliatory squeeze.

"Remember the first time these guys came up here?" I say. "Times sure have changed . . ."

Before we introduced Peter and Jesse to their new country house and their new (part-time) country life, Ann and I spent several weekends at the cabin, furiously scrubbing mouse shit off every horizontal surface, dragging beat-up mattresses and tattered Indian print bedspreads onto our growing dump pile, pulling out the nails that lined the ceiling at two-inch intervals—from which a few gnarled stems of marijuana, now certainly well dried, still hung.

The day before Christmas of '88 we loaded up Ann's "new" '68 Volkswagen bus and stuffed it with mattresses and dishes and firewood and groceries and two very excited little boys dressed in the first winter jackets and boots they'd ever owned. As we drove north through Cloverdale, the cold December rain turned to snow. Magic! On their first trip to their country house, Peter and Jesse were in the first snowfall of their lives.

Just past Ukiah traffic came to a standstill. A cop in yellow rain gear announced that cars without chains could go no farther. Of course we didn't have chains. We live in California! So we spent the first day of our new country life in Ukiah's last available motel room, calling around until we'd located Ukiah's last set of snow chains, and building the kids' first snowperson in the parking lot of the Ukiah Motel 6.

The next morning we filled up on gas and McPancakes and headed out into the area's worst snowstorm in thirty years. The chains got us onto the freeway and up the first mile of our dirt road, but—even with several hundred pounds of people and housewares for ballast—our valiant VW couldn't make it up the last hill.

So we spent the second day of our new country life lugging firewood and groceries and furniture up the steep snowy road, trudging from car to cabin and cabin to car in our soggy Goodwill mud boots and PayLess Thinsulate gloves and soaking wet secondhand down jackets.

When at last our possessions were piled inside, I built a roaring blaze in the potbelly and set a loaf of brown-and-serve French bread to bake in the oven. Soon the homey scent of yeast wafted into the room. Now! We were ready to start enjoying life in our cabin.

"Mom?" said ten-year-old Peter, peering under the claw-foot tub. "I hear a weird noise over here."

The weird noise was accompanied by a weird smell: propane. I rushed to the oven and turned it off.

"Ann," I said, "we have a major gas leak. I don't think we're gonna be able to use the stove."

Ann looked up from the box of dishes she was unpacking. "Hmm," she said. "Well, we can cook on the potbelly, can't we?"

"Sure," I said with false bravado, aware that my children had stopped what they were doing and were staring a bit wildly at me. "It'll be . . . an adventure. I'll make us some nice hot tea on the potbelly right now!"

I brought the kettle to the sink, turned the faucet. The pipes groaned. No water emerged. I touched the pipe. It was cold as . . . ice. "Ann," I choked out, "the pipes are frozen. *We don't have any water.*"

"No water," Ann repeated. Jesse grabbed a dry sponge from the sink and frantically began "cleaning" the windows. Peter burst into tears. "Of course we have water!" Ann said. "Look at all that snow! We'll just melt what we need on the wood stove!"

I was biting back tears myself. "We can't make tea *and* melt snow at the same time! And what about dinner? I can't make chili and corn bread on a *potbelly stove!*"

"I'll go get some snow right now," Jesse said, pulling on his soggy jacket and boots. "Me too," said Peter, swiping at his teary cheeks with a muddy glove. They each grabbed a bucket and clambered down the porch steps.

"I want to go home," I whimpered as soon as the kids were out of earshot. *"Now."*

"C'mon, Babe," Ann teased. "What happened to my hippie pioneer woman? We won't starve—we can always eat all those canned green beans you insisted on bringing in case of an earthquake."

Before I could resume whining Ann held her hand up in my face like a traffic cop. She wasn't teasing now.

"Meredith: I just spent two days getting here and half a day unloading the damn car. *I am not driving back to Oakland tonight.* If we're really miserable tomorrow we can talk about going home then."

But we weren't miserable tomorrow. Peter and I stopped sniveling, so Jesse and Ann could stop hypercoping, and in the morning we built a fire and cooked oatmeal . . . and then Ovaltine . . . and then coffee on the potbelly. And then we spent a glorious day sliding on snow saucers down our own private ski slope in the brilliant winter sun.

The next day I flipped pancakes on the potbelly and then we cut down our very own Hanuchris tree and made ornaments from cardboard and glitter and glue. And the day after that a neighbor from up the road took pity on us pitiful city folks and loaned us a Coleman camp stove, so we could cook macaroni and cheese and canned green beans, all at the same time.

Each night the fire kept us toasty as Ann read the kids to sleep and I lay in the platform bed, the only bed that was Ann's and mine together, listening to the mice scrimmaging in the pantry while I planned our potbelly-based menu for the day to come.

On New Year's Day we had to pry ourselves away. Splotched with poison oak, vowing never to eat another canned or boxed food item again, yearning for hot showers and TV, our family was knitted as never before. My own little commune! I thought, gazing proudly at my itchy, happy sons and my exhausted, exultant lover as we coasted back down the road in our family VW.

We'd survived! We'd had a great time! And we couldn't have done it without each other. In five days, we'd acquired a new shared notion of what we couldn't live without: water, heat, food, spirit, and love. And what "luxury" means: dry firewood, a camp stove, a battered aluminum saucer on a sunny, snowy hill. And what we *could,* as it turned out, live without: just about everything else.

Encouraged by the ecstasy engendered by our first big decision as a couple, a year later Ann and I risked making another one. We bought our Victorian in Oakland and began living together in the city too.

During that first chaotic year, when a print hung without preapproval on the wall or a plate improperly washed could and did catapult us into predivorce negotiations, our weekends at the cabin simply saved our relationship. Even when it seemed clear, in our "real" Oakland life, that Ann and I were utterly incompatible: our pairing a mistaken elevation of lust over reason; our love doomed to perish in the clash of our colliding neuroses—in our weekend life at the cabin there was undeniable evidence of the important things we valued and nurtured well together: the woodpile, the cantankerous water pump, our children, and yes, each other.

As time went on and Ann and I began to believe it reasonable to plan a future together, we promised ourselves the next time we move— when the kids have had their multicultural childhoods, when we no longer need a house big enough for four, when we're no longer city-bound by joint custody—it will be to the country. Full-time, this time.

We started fantasizing about making the cabin our real home. About *really* simplifying our lives: paying $250 instead of $1,600 each month for the mortgage, $12 instead of $75 an hour to the plumber, $6 instead of $120 a month for heat. Living nineteen miles from the nearest Safeway, a hundred miles from the nearest gay bookstore. Chopping enough wood each spring to keep us warm the next winter, and learning to stay put when the dirt road freezes over.

We joke sometimes, still, about installing a Stair-o-Lator up the side of the mountain so we can still get to the top when we're sixty-four. We imagine installing solar panels on the roof, a propane fridge in the kitchen, a cellular phone in the car. We wonder, together and separately, how well we would live with each other in such isolation, and whether we could construct the kind of interior lives we would need to replace the glittery distractions of the city.

But in more pragmatic moments we acknowledge that living full-time in the cabin might break its happy spell. That what we love most about the cabin—its simplicity, its remoteness—would cease to be magical if the cabin was no longer the place we escape to. Given our attachments to jobs, decaf lattes, film festivals, and friends, it seems likely that promoting the cabin to primary residence would turn it into the place we long to escape *from*.

Accepting all this, we now assume that our house in "the country" will translate to a cottage on an acre or two in one of the semirural counties within a hundred miles of the Bay area. Barring unexpected good fortune, we'll still need jobs to support the only slightly diminished expense of this new life. But Ann and I agree we'd rather spend hours commuting home to happiness a few nights each week than face the prospect of growing old in Oakland.

Some days I can hardly wait the six years it'll take to realize this modified plan. Other days I wonder if even it is realistic. Will we find a place as safe and welcoming for a couple of middle-aged lesbians as its hippie heritage has made the county in which our cabin was built? Will our grown-up kids be as eager to visit us in Jackson or Petaluma as they might be to return to the family homestead in Oakland? Will we make new friends? Keep the old?

I also mull over what vexed me in 1969, when Paul and I left underground newspapers and demonstrations and head shops and New York City behind and went off to build our dream house on the mountain. *What does it mean,* I asked myself then and I ask myself now, *for people like us to leave the cities?*

Then: Pot smokers had started shooting heroin; antiwar activists had begun building bombs in their basements. Garbage collectors went on strike and rats roamed the streets; Puerto Ricans and blacks drew turf lines on tenement walls. I got mugged at knifepoint twice in one night; a riot cop addressed Paul by name.

New York, and cities all over the world, were sinking like the

Titanic. And the youth revolution—our people, our culture, our hope—was drowning in the maelstrom. On their new album Crosby Stills & Nash sang, *"Horror grips us as we watch you die/We are leaving, you don't need us."*

We didn't know what it meant, our leaving: that the revolution would be fought without us, or that the leaving would be the revolution. But we knew we had to save ourselves before the cities sucked us under.

Paul and I packed up our bright red Volkswagen bus and joined the cavalcade of psychedelic schoolbuses and VW's headed for the rural escape destinations of the times: the green woods of Vermont, the scrabbly forests of Northern California, and the home we chose: the high plains of New Mexico.

An old lefty friend of Paul's lefty father "loaned" us fifteen acres to build on. Random House gave us a $3,000 advance to write a hippie back-to-the-land book. Paul and I formed a family with another refugee couple.

By day the four of us chopped wood, carried water, grew corn, built houses. By night we debated endlessly the value of what we were doing. Our old friends in the cities were still marching in the streets. Were we, on our mountain, part of the problem or part of the solution? Was there a necessary equation between changing the world and living unhappily in a city? In this state of alternating joy and antipathy, determination and boredom, the four of us lived on that land, on that money, until our little commune and our relationships broke up two years later.

I arrived in San Francisco on my twentieth birthday, which I spent on the steps of the city jail with some old friends from New York, protesting the murder of George Jackson. I was back in the city, back in the struggle. If I missed my mesa, at least I didn't have to anguish any longer about what good my living was doing.

Now: On weekends and vacations at least, I am once again someplace beautiful. Someplace my kids and my lover and I go to come back to our senses, to what is simple and real. Someplace my kids can shed their city slickness and Ann and I can stop worrying about what's coming through on the fax machine and the crack house on the corner and the chips in our Italian mugs. And the four of us, unfettered, can fall in love with each other again.

"Ann! Mom!" Jesse looks up as we walk into the cabin, his eyes sparkling, our *Wildlife of the West* book opened on the table before him. "Those birds we saw this morning? They really *were* wild turkeys. See?"

Peter puts down his surfing magazine; we all crowd around the lamplit table, comparing the pictures in the book to the birds that were gobbling near the porch when we woke up today.

"Amazing!" I blurt, before I think. "They look just like *real* turkeys."

There's a brief, what's-wrong-with-this-picture silence. And then all four of us burst into laughter.

"Which turkeys are real, Mom?" Jesse asks sarcastically. "The ones in the supermarket, or the ones in the woods?"

"Good question, Jess," I say. "I guess I'd have to say . . . both. Both are real."

Juneteenth

Today: June 20, 1993

I'm awakened by voices in the street outside my window. They are loud but calm; they don't push my panic button, don't trigger the all-too-familiar adrenaline rush that makes me roll over in bed and dial 911 in the dark with my eyes still shut and my heart in my throat.

The voices—a man's and a woman's—are saying, over and over, "This is *not* a through street. Go back. Turn your car around."

Tangled in the sweet sticky web of sleep, I try to ignore the voices, to slink back into slumber. But the windows of my second-story, street-facing bedroom are open to the warm June morning, so the words sound as if they're being spoken directly into my ear. Finally it's curiosity—not the usual hope of preventing or interrupting violence—that provokes me to get up and stick my head out the window.

Strange: Chia, the white woman from the south end of the block, the one whose front yard looks like a forest floor, is standing in the middle of the street, furiously waving her arms. Bob, the white guy who lives across the street, is talking to the driver of an old Lincoln Continental. Suddenly the driver pulls the Lincoln into Bob's driveway, backs it out again, and guns it to the corner.

"Hey!" Chia yells into the cloud of blue exhaust the car spews behind. "Slow down!"

"What's going on?" I call down to Bob. He looks up at me and grins sheepishly.

"It's Juneteenth," Bob says. "People are coming from all over for the party." He nods toward Adeline Street, two blocks away, where the commemoration of the Emancipation Proclamation is held every year. "We're trying to get them to use the main thoroughfares instead of our street."

I gaze at Bob quizzically. "They're taking all the parking places." He answers my unspoken question. "Plus they're screeching around waking everyone up."

I decide not to mention that it wasn't the traffic, but Bob and Chia's attempt to divert it, that awakened at least one resident of our block this morning.

"Uh-huh," I say, meaning to convey neither the approval Bob seems to want, nor the disapproval I feel. I remove my head from Bob's field of vision, flop back onto my tousled waterbed, lie there staring at the ominously cracked plaster on my ninety-year-old ceiling.

Oh, great, I think sourly. My white neighbors, who represent less than half of the people on our block, not to mention our city, not to mention our state and the whole fucking *world*, are out in the street at nine o'clock in the morning chasing away black people who are coming to our neighborhood to celebrate the abolition of slavery. Swell. Just swell.

"Bob! I just spoke to the cops." Chia's urgent voice invades my room once more. "They said they're gonna come set up barriers at both ends of the block."

What are my choices here? I wonder. Should I go downstairs and deliver to my neighbors—both of whom have lived on this block longer than I have; one of whom raised a son here; both of whose cars display bumper stickers promoting various progressive causes—a lecture on multiculturalism and the etiquette of living in a "mixed," mostly black neighborhood?

I consider pointing out to Chia that her own front yard—in which unkempt wildflowers and weeds sprout crazily from the carcass of a pepper tree left to rot where it fell—is a living monument to diversity and tolerance, surrounded as it is by the neatly manicured lawns, striped aluminum awnings, and tidily trimmed hydrangea hedges of her neighbors.

Our whole block is like that, actually: the architecture of the houses, and the distribution of people into them, embody the chaos and the triumph of cultural coexistence. A widowed African-American great-grandmother in shocking pink stucco beside a commune of graying hippies in peeling brown shingles. A Vietnamese family behind iron-barred windows, next door to a house full of grad students behind ornate stained glass. A retired African-American couple in lime green siding, across from aspiring yuppies in soft taupe clapboard trimmed in mauve. An African-American husband and his white wife of forty years in a gray-shingled Cape Cod, beside a couple of gay white men building their dream house from the ground up.

"No one's telling you to plant a lawn or paint your house pink," I imagine telling Bob and Chia. "So why can't you live with a little extra traffic once a year?"

Or maybe . . . maybe I should simply tell Bob and Chia the truth: that they are embarrassing me. That as white people demonstrating insensitivity toward black people, they are threatening the precarious equilibrium that makes it possible for me, for us, to live here—plopped down in someone else's community. A community that celebrates Juneteenth—the week in June 1863 when slaves in Texas finally learned that they had been legally freed six months earlier—as a symbol of its ongoing struggle for freedom.

I decide that regaling my fellow Caucasians with a more-politically-correct-than-thou lecture would be counterproductive. More to the point, it would be utterly hypocritical—given the murderous fantasies I entertain during long sleepless nights when the deafening accelerations of beat-up Oldsmobiles and Buicks interrupt my dreams. Hypocritical indeed, considering my equally futile fantasies about moving to some affluent enclave where late-model Saabs and Hondas purr quietly along tree-lined lanes, and the absence of a muffler on a car does not confirm the virility of its driver.

"Turn your car around!" I hear Chia again. "This is *not* a through street!"

I get up and close my windows. Surely, I tell myself, there are better ways to begin my Sunday than obsessing about the real or imagined transgressions of my white neighbors, and the real or imagined reactions of my black neighbors—most of whom, I realize, are unlikely to interpret as racist Bob and Chia's efforts to keep our block quiet today.

Sighing, I make my bed and head downstairs to make Sunday pancakes for my children.

As I pull the huge glass jar of Bisquick off the shelf, I enjoy an ironic chuckle at my own expense. I've never really admitted to myself before why I transfer the contents of each new Bisquick box into this unlabeled jar: I don't want my fellow food-snob friends to catch me with a box of *Bisquick, for God's sake!* next to the more culinarily correct tahini, rolled oats, and polenta on the open shelves of my pantry.

Not quite right with the black folks, I chide myself, and not quite right with the white ones, either. Maybe one of these days I'll give up anointing other people, whole groups of people, with the power to pronounce me acceptable, or (as is more often the case) not. *Yeah, right.* And maybe the plaster on the ceiling will defy gravity and stay up there forever.

The aroma of additive-enriched pancakes bubbling on the griddle brings Peter clattering down the stairs, followed by a series of thumps and small crashes. Those, I know, will be his Boogie boards and wet suit and fins, the stuff he needs for his trip to Santa Cruz today.

"Thanks for breakfast, Mom," Peter says, cutting his pancakes European-style, as my mother taught him to do. Chewing thoughtfully, he asks me, "Did you put vanilla in these again? They're good."

Extract of vanilla in the Bisquick pancakes; wet suits in the vestibule of our elegant Victorian in North Oakland. This life I have cooked up, I reflect, is nothing if not inconsistent.

The doorbell rings. Joe crashes down the hall, barking frenetically. "That's Carlos," Peter says, pushing his chair back from the table. Carlos Herrera and Peter, and Claudio Herrera and Jesse, have been best friends, off and on (inconveniently, the pairs are almost never "on" at the same time) since they met in preschool.

Today Carlos Senior will fill his van with as many of his sons' friends as his seat belts will contain, and drive them to Santa Cruz for a day of burgers and Boogie-boarding. Jesse isn't going, since he and Claudio are "off" these days; anyway, Jesse's basketball camp starts this afternoon.

I walk down the hall behind Peter, who's barking, "Joe: No barking!" with the usual lack of success. As Peter opens the door, Joe hurls himself down the front steps—past Carlos and Claudio and Carlos Senior, whom Joe knows, and past little Pablo Hererra, whom he doesn't know, and past Jeff, whom he doesn't know. A flying blur of teeth and fur, Joe lunges viciously at Aqualas—who just happens to be the only fully black person in the group.

Aqualas laughs as I grab Joe by the neck and toss him, squealing, into the house. Jesse, who's been awakened by the clamor, glares at me from the top of the stairs, his "You're abusing my dog again" accusatory look.

"Are you okay?" I ask Aqualas. He nods, seemingly unperturbed. That makes one of us.

"Our dog's a damn racist," I mutter at Jesse as the van drives off.

"I know," Jesse agrees glumly. "I can't believe a *dog* can be racist."

I can hardly believe it myself. But it's undeniably true: Joe is hostile toward African-Americans. The darker the person's skin, the more aggressive Joe's attack. Hence, without an instant to consider his choices, Joe bypassed Jeff, who is half black and half white—as well as the four Herreras, all of whom are lighter-complected than Aqualas.

Jesse shakes his head at Joe sadly and wanders back upstairs to pack for camp. I start scrubbing the puddles of Log Cabin (the kids won't eat real maple syrup) off the table and countertops, wishing dogs couldn't be racist. I wish people couldn't be racist. I wish race was not the day-in, day-out, life-and-death issue it is in my country, my neighborhood, the lives of my children and me. But that's what I wish. As usual, what is true is quite different.

Last Week: Peter's Graduation

It ebbs and flows, my optimism about the progress we're making in this complex, unglamorous experiment—this life-as-social lab struggle to find a way, as Rodney King cried, to "just get along."

Last week, I was elated by undeniable evidence that the experiment was succeeding. Listening to Peter naming the friends he wanted to invite to his junior high graduation, it suddenly struck me that my adolescent son has achieved what no white adult I know, including myself, has managed: deep, real friendships with people whose races and cultures differ significantly from his own.

A clear and direct result of growing up in this neighborhood, where ethnic diversity is not an ideal but a daily reality, the bonds between Peter and Jesse and their Chilean and Japanese and black and Jewish and Mexican friends have been forged effortlessly, naturally. These kids have simply grown up together—"in the same 'hood," as Peter half-mockingly says. Their relationships with each other have evolved without intellectual posturing, feigned tolerance, tokenizing or totemizing, blurring of differences, or sacrificing of ethnic pride.

This easy intimacy stands in sharp contrast to my own unsuccessful attempts to maintain and deepen friendships with nonwhite people—attempts that have proved more futile with the passage of time.

At Peter's age I had a black boyfriend. When I worked in factories in my twenties, my closest friends were the black women who worked on assembly lines with me. In my thirties and into my forties I worked on a gay and lesbian magazine and in a series of progressive businesses—all of whose methodically constituted multiracial staffs cleaved, ultimately, along racial lines.

As I have moved up the economic food chain, as I have aged, as workplaces and neighborhoods and cities have become more segregated, I have become increasingly disconnected—despite the neighborhood I live in and the friends my children have made—from people of color.

I am at once envious of and encouraged by my kids' friendships. They give me hope that despite the movement of society in the opposite direction, humans—especially young humans, who are, after all, the future—*will* do the right thing, given half a chance. It seemed—last week anyway—that snatching my kids out of the suburbs, transplanting them to Oakland, had produced exactly the desired results.

But then a few days later, my elation was flattened at the graduation itself. Sitting in the borrowed auditorium of Oakland Technical High School, where the ceremony was held because Claremont Middle School has no suitable room for such an event, surrounded by Peter's classmates and their families, for the first time in the nine years since I put my kids in Oakland public schools I got it: the reality of what my choice has meant for my sons.

I got it: that at their school, my kids are members of a small, shrinking, and highly unpopular minority group. I got it: that in their adolescent years—when nothing matters more than being "in"—my kids' skin color has put them out. I got it: that when white people move into a predominantly black neighborhood, neighborhoods like ours become "mixed"—but when white kids go to a predominantly black school, the school remains a black school.

And when that school holds its graduation ceremony, it only makes sense that the event would be "a black thing." That although white, Asian, and Hispanic students make up thirty percent of the school's population, the audience was ninety percent African-American. So there were polite smatterings of applause from their parents and siblings when white kids and Asian kids and Hispanic kids got up to accept their awards or their diplomas; but when African-American kids walked across the stage the auditorium erupted: aunts, uncles, cousins, church members, neighbors, family friends jumping to their feet, hooting, waving fists in the air, applauding.

I felt sad for Peter, and for all the kids who took that long slow walk from seat to rostrum accompanied by such a dramatic dearth of recognition. And I felt on the outs myself. I hardly knew any of these kids, and I hardly knew anyone in the audience. Where were all the white and middle-class black kids and parents I'd gotten close to throughout the years of meetings and potlucks and rummage sales at the elementary school that feeds this junior high? Not here: gone to private schools, nearly every one.

I felt even more disheartened, watching as the awards were distributed. In 1993, in this city that has become a national model of multiculturalism, still: each athletic award, with only one exception, was handed to an African-American child. Each academic award, with no exceptions, was handed to a white or an Asian child.

And so by the end of the ceremony twenty black boys and girls sat clutching their basketball and track trophies on one side of the stage, while on the other, twenty white and Asian kids held their trophies for academic achievement. I felt ashamed and outraged—for those children, for the school, for my country—by this blatant evidence of betrayal. Was this the progress that was promised when Martin and Medgar and Malcolm died, when the cities burned, when the wars on poverty and racial inequality were declared and funded with Americans' tax dollars?

The ceremony completed, I left the overheated auditorium with Peter's white-version extended family: two lesbian moms, one grandmother, dad, and younger brother. While my mother was loading film into her camera, I pulled Peter aside.

"I never really understood before today," I said, "what a black universe you guys live in. Has that been hard on you?"

Peter looked me in the eye and answered unhesitatingly, "Mom: it's a horrible time to be a white male. Black people expect me to be racist. Girls expect me to be sexist. And I don't feel like I should have to prove that it's not true."

Just then Ann tossed me a paper airplane she'd found on the ground. Before I tossed it on to Jesse I noticed it had writing on one side. I unfolded it and read a memo on Oakland Technical High School letterhead.

TO: ALL STUDENTS AND STAFF
FROM: W. Darrell Ovid, Principal
SUBJECT: The Passing of a Tech Student.

I have just been informed that Tech Student, Jessie Franklin III, was shot and killed on Friday, June 4, 1993.

Please inform your students to contact the Counseling Office, if they would like to talk to a counselor.

Please be alert to students in distress and contact the Counseling Office.

There the memo ended.

Stunned, I handed the unfolded flyer back to Ann, who read it and passed it to Richard. "Sounds like they print one of these every week," he said. "All they have to do is fill in a different kid's name."

He passed it to my mother. "This'll probably be the only graduation a lot of these kids ever have," she said.

I was stung by sharp recognition of my own denial. No wonder relations between the races have gotten so much worse, I thought. Black people's situation has gotten much worse.

I'd chosen, unthinkingly, to believe the opposite. To believe that because my kids had grown up seeing black anchorpersons on the news and learning black history in their classrooms and going to a black pediatrician, that black people's status had improved since I'd grown up watching *Amos 'n' Andy* on black-and-white TV.

But we're always the only white people in our African-American pediatrician's waiting room, and most of his other patients pay with Medi-Cal stickers. I get a glimpse of those other patients' reality once or twice each year, when Dr. Bean sits Peter and Jesse and me down and gives us the grim lecture he delivers regularly to all of his preadolescent patients, about crack and guns and AIDS and gangs and death.

Looking around at the 300 teenagers in Peter's graduating class, I wondered how many of them would still be alive to attend their high school graduation four years from now.

"It's like being at a gay event, wondering how many of the men will be here for the next one," I told Ann. "How do these mothers go on every day raising these boys, knowing the statistics?"

Suddenly those statistics—nearly eighty percent of Oakland's homicide victims last year were African-American men; fifty-five percent of them under the age of twenty-five—were not just numbers anymore. And suddenly these African-American mothers, strangers to me moments before, were my sisters. Sisters in loving our sons and sisters in the terror and rage and grief that comes with raising our sons in the city where we live.

Yes, my sons' odds of surviving their childhoods are better than their sons', I thought, as I watched Peter accepting congratulatory hugs from Ann, Richard, my mother. But my white Oakland boys could be standing on the wrong Oakland street corner some day, too. And what can I do about it? What can any of us do about this madness?

Two Weeks Ago: What Happened to Barbara

Despite my escape fantasies I know there are no guarantees to be offered, no risk-free groups or behaviors to adopt, no assurances of safety to be had. I know that with more certainty now, because of what happened to Barbara, my acupuncturist and Buddhist teacher.

Barbara is not a young African-American male, does not hang out on street corners in "bad" neighborhoods. The only drugs she buys and sells (at cost) are Chinese herbs. She always gives what she can to homeless people, especially homeless women. But none of this protected Barbara when the woman she was giving a dollar to—on a side street in the affluent, mostly white Piedmont area of Oakland—stepped aside as her male accomplice held a knife to Barbara's throat.

Two months ago Barbara and her lover moved to a rural Northern California town. After long deliberations they'd made the decision so many of my friends (and Ann and I) are wrestling with: to live peacefully in the country and commute long hours to work, rather than living conveniently but unhappily in the city.

In order to maintain her Oakland practice without spending four hours each day on the freeway, Barbara started spending two nights a week with a friend in Piedmont. So her car was full of her possessions when a black man came up from behind her and wrapped his arm around Barbara's neck and pressed the tip of a knife against her jugular vein and told her to give him her keys and her wallet.

Barbara did what he said, of course, and the man and the woman Barbara had given the dollar to jumped into Barbara's car and sped off. Later, the police told Barbara that the man—again, using the woman as a decoy—mugged several people the next night in the same neighborhood.

And the night after that, when the man used Barbara's credit card to fill up her car with gas, the station attendant noticed the card had been reported stolen and called the cops, who chased the man at high speeds through the streets of Oakland until the man crashed into a telephone pole at 100 miles per hour and died in Barbara's car, burned to ashes along with Barbara's clothes and wallet and Thich Nhat Hanh tapes and photos from her recent monthlong silent retreat with the Tibetan Buddhist monks in Nepal.

Listening to Barbara—the soother and container, these past two years, of my fears; this healing soul whose office is decorated with handmade thank-you gifts from men dying of AIDS and women dying of breast cancer, most of whom she treats for free—describing to me the terror she carries now in her body, I felt wounded. It was as though the knife that could have killed Barbara were twisting in my heart.

"It's been very interesting," Barbara told me—even in this, a model of compassionate detachment, "to observe the effect the fear is having on me. All the work I've done on myself around racism . . . since this happened, I've had to acknowledge that I am really afraid of black men.

"The feelings about race," she said, "are the most difficult to accept in myself. You know, a friend of mine, a black woman, told me recently that she won't take long car trips by herself anymore. She thinks the fear of black people is so intense in this country right now, she's afraid if she had car trouble no one would stop to help her.

"I like to believe I can be part of the solution, not part of the problem. It's painful to realize that may not be the case."

After talking to Barbara I went to sleep and had this dream:

I'm walking down a dirt road in the South with Bryant Gumbel. As we are passing a huge plantation mansion, a white man comes running out from between the columns of the house, up the driveway, to the road. He grabs Bryant by the neck, throws chains on Bryant's wrists and ankles, says, "You're my slave now, nigger."

The white man ignores me completely. I feel helpless, immobilized with horror as he leads Bryant, stumbling in the shackles, away from me. As I watch the man pulls a bullwhip from his belt, snaps it in the air near Bryant's face. Neither Bryant nor the white man looks back at me.

I decide I will somehow free Bryant. With no idea of how I might accomplish this, I start running through the brambles that surround the plantation, hoping a plan will occur to me. The only thing in my favor, I know, is the fact that I am white, and therefore not suspect, should I be discovered.

ONE YEAR AGO: THE VERDICT

I was at work in San Francisco on April 29, the day the first Rodney King trial ended in the acquittal of the cops who had beaten him. The radio in my office, usually tuned to the "greatest hits of the sixties," was set on "all news, all the time."

By noon there were increasingly horrifying reports—eerily reminiscent of 1968—of one American city after another erupting into flames.

Just after lunchtime Ann called from her office in Berkeley to ask me to come home.

"They're saying they might shut BART down if the rioting gets bad," she said. "I don't want you to be in the city and the kids and me over here. This is too scary."

Scary it was. And not one bit less scary once I'd made my way through the panicked crowds in the Financial District and the panicked commuters on BART and was sitting in my own sunny kitchen with my lover and my kids, listening to the bullhorn-amplified sounds of an impromptu rally that had convened nearby on Adeline Street.

Some of the speakers were pleading for calm: "Brothers and sisters: rioting has never advanced the cause of freedom. We only hurt ourselves. Please, stay cool." Others advocated militant action: "We must show the power structure that justice *will* be done—by any means necessary."

My 1968 self wanted to take my kids and my lover and walk around the corner to the rally and join it, whatever it ended up being: a peaceful gathering, a march to City Hall, a riot through downtown Oakland. An outrageous injustice had been done, and an immediate, powerful response was called for. Of course I would be part of that response, as I had been part of every protest against every social injustice that I'd been aware of since I was fifteen years old.

But my 1992 self was the mother of teenagers, not a teenage revolutionary. My 1992 self no longer felt I had nothing to lose, or that whatever I might lose would be well sacrificed to the "movement"—or even that the movement might result in actual progress.

My 1992 self was concerned, first and foremost, with the physical safety of my children and my lover and me. I knew that walking around the corner to the rally might not be "safe." That in fact, walking to the corner store just then might not be safe. That despite my own need to act on the outrage I felt, despite my history and my continuing commitment to activism, despite the fact that it was taking place in the neighborhood where we'd lived for eight years, my children and my lover and I might not be welcome, might not be safe at the rally around the corner.

And so I sat instead in my kitchen with the windows open, listening to the rally from a distance, feeling imprisoned in my own home.

Two Months Ago: The Verdict

I was in my office listening to the radio that day, too: the day the whole world was waiting for the verdict in the second Rodney King trial. At eleven A.M. there was a bulletin. It had been decided (who decides these things?) that when the jury reached a verdict, there would be a four-hour delay before it was announced.

"The purpose of the delay," the newscaster said, "is to prevent the kinds of random attacks that occurred after the first trial. This time everyone should have enough time to get somewhere safe."

Everyone? I thought. *You mean all the white folks should have enough time to get away from the black folks?*

Safe? I thought. *And just where might that be?*

The outcome of the second trial, I was certain, would be different. I couldn't believe that we'd need four hours to get somewhere "safe," because I simply couldn't believe that the cops in that videotape would be acquitted again.

So this time I stayed at work in the city all day, listening to reports of National Guardsmen being deployed in Cleveland and Atlanta; of gun and ammunition sales skyrocketing in East L.A. and the South Bronx; of Beverly Hills residents abandoning their mansions, taking preriot vacations at their "cabins" in Montana and Wyoming.

That night, driving Jesse down Shattuck Avenue to the Berkeley Y for our usual Monday-evening workout, I saw that my optimism was not shared by the merchants of Berkeley. Every store—Blockbuster Video, the International Deli, Harbert's Sporting Goods, even the clearance-sale bookstore—was barricaded behind sheets of plywood.

The stores were open and some of the storekeepers had spray-painted encouraging messages on the plywood: "Come on in!" "Open for business." Others had been visited by guest spray-painters: "Riot for Justice!" "Martin Luther King, Rodney King—It's All the Same Thing."

I remembered the first time the store windows on Shattuck Avenue were shattered by rioters: twenty-five years ago, when Ronald Reagan deployed the National Guard to seize People's Park from the radicals of Berkeley.

My children's father was one of those radicals, one of the fiery young UC Berkeley students who marched down Shattuck chanting anti-imperialist slogans and tossing bricks through store windows, choking under clouds of tear gas spewing from helicopters hovering overhead.

In those days, when the civil rights movement hatched white radicals by the dozen like fuzzy eager ducklings, we felt allied with our black sisters and brothers: the residents of Harlem, excluded by Columbia University from the fancy gym it built in their neighborhood. The black students of Jackson State, killed in their dorms by Mississippi state troopers. The conscripted black GI's on the front lines in Da Nang and Hue. And yes, the people of Harlem and Watts and Roxbury who exploded when Martin and then Malcolm were murdered.

In those days, we called riots "righteous rebellions." When plate-glass shattered and cities burned we chanted, "It's right to rebel!" and "No justice without peace; no peace without justice!"

On this night, I gathered my lover and my children to me and prayed for peace and justice once again. This time, two of the cops were convicted, and an uneasy peace prevailed.

TODAY: JUNETEENTH 1993

When I get in the car to drive Jesse to basketball camp, I see that there are, in fact, police barricades set up at our corner. I maneuver between them, turn right on Adeline Street, away from the Juneteenth party in progress.

Jesse twists his head around to peer behind us. "What's happening?" he asks. In the rearview mirror I see a bandstand outfitted with huge speakers, helium balloons bobbing, curls of barbecue smoke wafting from vending stands painted black, green, and red.

"Juneteenth," I say. Jesse nods knowingly. How many of my friends, I wonder, have ever heard of Juneteenth? I never had, until I moved to this neighborhood.

"I'd like to check it out," I say, thinking aloud. "But . . . I feel like it's for black people only. Like I'd be the only white person there."

"Tell me about it!" Jesse snorts.

I consider asking a probing question, decide against it. I know what Jesse means. He knows I know what he means.

As soon as we enter the hallowed halls of the UC Berkeley gym, I realize that Jesse will not have his usual ethnic experience at this camp, where Cal Bears coaches give intensive instruction to those boys whose parents can afford to pay for it. Although nearly all the star basketball players at his school, in our neighborhood, and in the Y league he plays in are African-American, the vast majority of the boys at this $350, four-day basketball camp are white.

I leave Jesse in his rather posh Cal dorm room and head back to "the 'hood." The house is empty and silent. Peter's in Santa Cruz. Ann's at an all-day karate workout in the Berkeley hills. The rare moment of privacy pulls me out to our sun-drenched deck to do a little unplanned Sunday-afternoon writing.

What a study in contrasts I find there. In my eyes: the beatific sights of the little haven Ann and I have created for our little family. A ruby-throated hummingbird hovers in place above the orange blossoms of the trumpet vine that cascades over the redwood trellis. The pink jasmine and the lavender pansies are in full bloom, nodding their happy little heads at me. Over in the vegetable garden, I see that the arugula is going to seed. The lawn is lushly green, evidence of the first good rainy winter in years.

In my nose, mixed with the perfume of jasmine blossoms: the pungent bite of barbecue smoke. And in my ears, mixed with the chirping of the birds that inhabit our garden: the booming voices of rappers and DJ's talking and singing into the sound system on Adeline Street.

"Are y'all having a *good* time?" a woman asks now.

"*Yeah!*" yells the crowd.

"Let me hear y'all saying you're having a *good* time!" the woman cries.

The crowd roars back at her.

"This is our day—our freedom day," the woman says. "And we're here to have a good time!"

And what am *I* here for? I wonder. To have a good time? To stay put and raise my kids here and work toward a better time? What is it that I might do, what contribution might I make, to help tip the scales toward justice? Maybe the best I can do for now is to learn, and to teach my children, the difficult lesson of otherness—to continue believing in the possibility of a better time, while living in the reality of these seemingly unending bad times.

WHAT IT'S LIKE
TO CHANGE
THE WORLD NOW

Election

<hr>

I'm still half asleep when the thought yanks me up from dreaming: it's election day. Sunlight peeks through the blinds; the autumn air on my still-tanned arms feels nearly balmy. Good omen! Good voting weather, at least here in Oakland. A surge of optimism pushes through me. Maybe something really good will happen today.

I roll over in bed and glance at the clock. It's already ten A.M. in Boston, where Ann's mother and brother will drive through freezing rain to vote for Bush, and ten A.M. in Miami Beach, where my Aunt Hazel and Uncle Morty will stroll through thick moist sunshine to vote for Perot.

It's nine o'clock in Chicago, where an African-American woman who's a county clerk this morning may be a senator tonight, and eight o'clock in Vail, where, during the next twelve hours, my kids' aunt and uncle and the ranchers and ski bums and migrant workers and millionaires will decide whether gay people are entitled to civil rights in their state.

I flip on the TV, eager for some early good news. *The Today Show* is running live footage of huge turnouts everywhere. This, Bryant Gumbel says dispassionately, is expected to work in Clinton's favor.

Just moments after the polls have opened in San Francisco, long lines of Asian, black, punk, Latino voters are overflowing armories and high schools, pushing up their sweatshirt sleeves and squinting into the bright morning. In Erie, Pennsylvania, pink-cheeked white folks in down jackets and plaid mufflers are stomping snow off their boots and breathing clouds into the frigid air, waiting their turn outside the VFW hall.

Maybe it's the flawless azure sky out my window, or the pollsters' authoritative predictions—but suddenly I am excited about this election. Suddenly I feel this election is happening to me.

Until this moment I hadn't considered the possibility of "winning," or what that might mean. Nothing in my experience has taught me a connection between an election and anything that matters to me getting better. But now anticipation hums through my body, as if it's my birthday or the first day of a long-coveted new job.

This electoral enthusiasm is unprecedented. I've voted in years past for local candidates and initiatives, but only once before have I voted for a president. A vice president, actually—Mondale didn't move me, but I took very personally the candidacy of Geraldine Ferraro, the first woman vice presidential candidate ever, for whom I cast my vote just months after I chose Ann as my first woman lover ever.

Horrified by the threat of a Bush/Quayle victory, a week ago I made the first electoral accessory purchase of my life: a "Clinton-Gore" bumper sticker. Unlike most of my friends and many of my neighbors, I did not affix it permanently to my car—but taped it ambivalently to my living room window.

This morning, I find myself unexpectedly unambivalent.

As though from a deep well long capped by the politics of pessimism, a stream of fantasies spews forth. I welcome them, allow myself to imagine the results of a good outcome today—the glittering possibilities of life out from under twelve years of Republicanism.

Might there be a few less homeless people to step around, to feel saddened—or worse, numbed—by on my way from the BART station to my office in North Beach every morning? I picture the kindly-faced, gray-haired woman who seems to live on the pile of rags she sits on in the Sanwa Bank doorway, endlessly stroking the shaggy terrier in her lap, whose mournful eyes and limp round body so eerily resemble hers.

In my wildest dreams a Democratic administration provides for this woman a bed made neatly with crisp, clean sheets, a twenty-five-pound bag of kibble for her dog, a mirror to sit before while she daydreams and brushes her long, freshly shampooed hair.

Dreaming on, I conjure a vision of more and newer textbooks, better-paid teachers in my kids' public schools . . . the reappearance of the disappeared goods and services—musical instruments, school nurses, art supplies, teachers' aides—stolen by thieving budget cuts in the long Republican night.

I imagine a day when slain first-growth redwoods no longer roll down Highway 101, strapped lifelessly to diesel-spewing flatbed trucks . . . a time when thrashing oil rigs no longer defile the Santa Barbara shoreline.

Dare I dream of walking, or at least driving fearlessly at night through the streets of the city where I live?

The fantasy is irresistible. It makes me feel patriotic.

I bounce out of bed, throw open the window. The air smells like spring, not fall. Like new beginnings. Am I getting too schmaltzy? Like a new day in America?

"Jesse—wake up," I whisper to my sleeping twelve-year-old son, our family's staunchest Clinton fan, who expressed at dinner last night his concern that Bush might fix the election.

"How do you know Bush won't go around and change all the votes?" Jesse asked. "We didn't want to have a war and he had one anyway. How do you know he can't make himself be president again, too?"

Rather than attempting to explain a process with which I'd had scant personal experience (and in which I'd historically had about as much confidence as my son), I invited Jesse to go with me to the polls tomorrow and see for himself. Maybe, I said, we'll both learn something.

This morning Jesse doesn't require the usual coaxing to get himself showered, dressed, fed. His eyes still soft with sleep, he strides out the door with great determination, his sweet jaw set as it usually is just before his basketball team faces a particularly tough opponent.

"I don't *believe* they have elections in somebody's *garage*," Jesse says as the two of us walk down Shattuck toward the polling place three blocks away.

"I like that, actually," I say, just now realizing why I've always liked voting in my neighborhood. "It feels like what democracy's supposed to be about. Regular people in charge. In a regular person's house.

"Anyway," I inform him, "it's all very official: little booths with curtains around them. They probably won't let you in the booth with me, but you'll get the idea anyway."

Jesse seems unconvinced. And I am disconcerted to find myself— an unrepentant, if slightly wrinkled, Yippie who refused to "Stay Clean for Gene," who chose instead to vote with my feet (among other body parts) to smash segregation, the Vietnam war, sexism—now defending the integrity of the electoral process.

"See that?" I show Jesse the signs marked "100 feet to the polls."

"No one's allowed to put up signs or pass stuff out near the voting place. They try to make it really fair, to make sure we make up our own minds."

"Sure, Mom—but what do you call *that*?" Jesse points to the house next to the polling place, whose windows and lawn are covered with a screaming profusion of red-white-and-blue Clinton signs.

"A good choice of candidates," I answer with a shrug, eagerly abandoning my ill-fitting role as apologist for bourgeois democracy.

The falling-down garage with the American flag out front is chock-full of my neighbors: mostly African-Americans in their sixties and seventies, some with grandchildren in tow; and whites in their thirties and forties, some with infants in Snuglis lolling against their chests.

The mood is festive. There are no curtains around the voting booths. My fellow voters are elbow to elbow, leaning over each other's shoulders and comparing notes on the party tickets that were hung on our front doorknobs early this morning by the Green Party, NOW, the Boxer-Feinstein Unity Team.

There's nothing and no one to keep Jesse from crowding into the tiny cubicle with me. He watches intently as I begin to punch holes in the ballot.

"This feels good," I murmur, surprised and pleased.

"Be careful, Mom," Jesse says, his finger keeping my place. "Don't make any mistakes."

A young black woman squeezes past us and into the booth next to mine. "Hey!" she says to no one in particular. "I don't know how to do this—I never voted before."

Jesse reaches around me, inserts the woman's ballot into its holder, and shows her how to use the stylus. Just then a snowy-haired black man who's been sitting in the corner hoists himself upright with the help of a cane, hobbles across the crowded garage, and stands directly behind the woman.

"Young lady," he announces in resounding tones, "there's only one thing you need to know how to do here today: vote for Mr. Clinton." He leans over, takes the stylus in his hand, and, with a dramatic flourish, positions it directly above the "Clinton/Gore" slot on her ballot.

"Okay, cool," the young woman answers, laughing as she takes the stylus. "That's all I'm here to do anyway."

I glance around to see if the officials are going to declare the whole election invalid, or what. But there aren't any officials—just the two elderly women, sitting behind a funky folding card table covered with rosters and stubby pencils, in whose garage this presidential election is being held.

Like everyone else in the place, these "election officials" are smiling and nodding. "Mr. Clinton, yes," one of the women agrees.

I'm half appalled, half thrilled. This is a new experience for me— feeling at one, if even for a moment, with my fellow Americans. *Everyone here wants the same thing—or at least the same president—I want!*

Jesse tugs at my sleeve. "Pay attention, Mom," he says. "Finish voting. This is important."

I look down at my serious son, and around at my jubilant neighbors. "You're right, Jess," I say. "This *is* important." I give Jesse's tightly muscled shoulder a little squeeze, and turn my attention back to the task at hand.

WEDNESDAY, NOVEMBER 4, 1992

Clinton, I think before I'm quite awake. *President* Clinton. And Senator Boxer and Senator Feinstein and Senator Carol Moseley Braun . . . and abortion rights, and gay rights, and jobs . . .

Without leaving my bed, I can tell the kids are happy today, too: through the wall between us I hear Jesse cooing at our dog, Joe, the way he does in the best of moods. Peter's step is light on the stairs as he heads down for his shower. In the kitchen a few minutes later, Ann's face is smooth and serene.

"I feel like things might really get better," says my lover, the queen of understatement. In our hug I feel her hope and relief.

"Now we don't have to move to Canada," I answer. Ann wasn't the only gay person who suggested that possibility to me during the days following the Republican convention, when we all believed that a Bush victory might threaten our ability to live—with our children, with our rights, with any measure of physical or psychic safety—in this country.

Waving good-bye to Peter and Jesse at the front door, I wave hello to our next-door neighbor, Minnie, who's on her way back from her daily walk to the corner store with the morning paper tucked under her arm.

"Good news today, Meredith," says Minnie, who has lived in the pink house next to ours, where she raised six children and now raises mustard greens and tomatoes, since she left Missouri in search of work and civil rights forty-five years ago.

"Great news, Minnie," I agree. She stops, rests her substantial shoulder against our redwood fence.

"For a while there," Minnie says, "I thought I was going to die before anything got better in this country."

I nod, struck by the similarity between Minnie's response and Ann's. Minnie, a sixty-eight-year-old African-American working-class grandmother from Steele, Missouri—Ann, a thirty-eight-year-old middle-class white lesbian from Boston. Both wanting "things to get better"—sure, don't we all, even those who voted, incredibly, for Bush? But who would believe that these two women would agree so closely on what "better" might mean, that these two women could be rendered equally optimistic by the same election?

Today is Wednesday, my day to work at home. Friends call and, uncharacteristically on a workday, stop by unannounced. It's like after the earthquake, when everyone needed to see and touch and remember our relationships with each other.

Brynn, just back from a six-week Himalayan trek, says: "The good guys won for once. While I was away my sweetheart decided to give us another try. Am I crazy for believing life might be okay after all?"

Tod says: "It couldn't have turned out any better. But I can't feel it. I guess I'm in shock."

Sara says: "Sure, it's better than Bush winning. But Clinton voted for the Gulf war. He has a horrible record on women. It's a big mistake, the left jumping into bed with the Democrats."

Stephen says: "This is weird, but I feel like I did when my parents died. Not the grief, but the . . . magnitude of it."

As the day wears on, I do my work and listen to the radio. Todd Gitlin, a fellow former underground newspaper reporter, says: "We will discover that a generation that had felt exiled from leadership can come home." An unnamed man-on-the-street says: "I'm fifty. I'm part of the generation that was going to change the world. Now for the first time since I was twenty-eight I feel like we're actually having an impact again."

I struggle to decipher my own reaction amid the din.

Like Ann and Minnie and Brynn, I feel pulled toward hope, toward believing that this election might be backdrop and metaphor for oppressive clouds lifting, not a thousand points but infinite beams of light breaking through.

Like Tod, I am numb, disbelieving. I hear the commentators talking about President-Elect Clinton and realize I can't remember a time when news has sounded good to me.

Like Sara, I question just how good this news really is—for me, for what's left of the left, for the woman in the Sanwa Bank doorway, for the ozone layer, for my children and the seventh generation of children.

Like Stephen, I feel, burning through my reluctance to believe the best, the certainty that something truly enormous has just transpired.

By nightfall I am more anxious and agitated than ecstatic or numb. What's worrying me?

I am transfixed by a TV special, *Behind the Scenes of the Clinton Campaign*. The camera scans the campaign team as they tease and joke and play gin rummy with the relaxed, laughing guy (my age) they call "Bill."

These people look like my friends. They're Jewish, they're gay, they're younger than I am. The women are in jeans and vests; they've got haircuts, not hairdos; they're not wearing makeup. The men are in T-shirts and Reeboks; they aren't wearing ties or slacks. Jesus, they're dancing to "I Heard It Through the Grapevine" in the aisle of the Clinton campaign jet! Tapping my own Reebok-shod feet to the familiar beat, I am suddenly tuned in to the chorus in my head that's drowning out the celebration.

What if, in the soft fuzzy happiness of winning for once, the left loses its edge?

What if there is no left?

What if the *government* is the left?

What about my current job, which entails mobilizing our company's customers to speak out against bad-guy legislation and bad-guy legislators? What will our action of the month be next month, and the month after that? Who and what will we move our customers against? Will our customers still feel the need to be so moved? Will I lose my progressive job in a progressive business to a progressive administration?

Is this election of a guy who's a lot like us a good thing? What if we count on this man and he betrays us? What if we—I—begin to believe in the government?

Will we—those of us who have defined ourselves since adolescence as the marginalized but cohesive "others"—lose our "usness" along with our "otherness"?

Will we be absorbed, assimilated into the undifferentiated mass of Americans—disenchanted Republican defectors, maverick Perot supporters, and scariest of all, suddenly satisfied liberals—who want, innocuously, to "change America"?

Maybe this high anxiety is just a flashback to my sixties training, when my brothers and sisters and I hoped, not so secretly, for a Nixon victory—on the theory that McCarthy would "co-opt the movement" and delay the revolution.

Or the Marxist-Leninist theories I absorbed in my communist cell throughout the seventies: since only the dictatorship of the proletariat could end the evils of capitalism, my comrades and I opposed liberal reforms as the opiate of the masses—far more strenuously than we fought the blunt, avowed forces of reaction.

And then, of course, the eighties, when suddenly there was no "us" anymore; when everything on every front got consistently and uniformly worse; when my friends and I started earning more money than we needed and spending it on therapy and child care—or dying of breast cancer and AIDS; and Abbie Hoffman killed himself with prescription pharmaceuticals and Jerry Rubin became an investment banker.

Or maybe . . . maybe this ambivalence in the face of apparent triumph is the product of older, even more pervasive training.

Maybe we wanted Nixon to win because we were most comfortable living with an enemy close at hand . . . because, as *Life* magazine claimed and we scornfully denied, we were a generation of malparented kids who unwittingly revealed ourselves when we vowed to "bring the war home"—where it had, indeed, begun. A generation defined by the struggle we projected from the battlefields of our families onto the wide, accommodating screen of the world in chaos around us.

Maybe I don't know how to live without that burning in my gut, that angry knowing that we, I, am not accepted, embraced, a part of . . . but separate from, different from, unwanted, rejected, on the fringe or at best the edge.

This line of thought makes me shiver, takes me deeper still.

How will I know who I am if I'm not locked in opposition?

It's as old as I am, this fear of not being in resistance. If we hadn't resisted the war, we would have been shredded between its voracious jaws. If I hadn't been in resistance to my family I would have been denied, diminished, disappeared.

It's ancient, too, the attraction and aversion to attaching hope to a person. It feels seductive and lethal to trust that a fatherlike person is benign, let alone benevolent—to put my fate, my kids' and grandkids' fate, my inner kid's fate in the hands of some tall handsome white man who promises to make things better for me, to make decisions that shape my present and my future, to take care of my needs as he sees fit . . .

Yikes.

And yet, there is another sound in there. Barely discernible, the soft chant of my own private peace movement.

Last night Ann said after Clinton's and Gore's speeches, in which AIDS was publicly named as the first of the country's problems and a day was publicly imagined when neither race nor gender would be relevant: "It makes me want to get up tomorrow and do something good right here in our neighborhood."

Barbara, my acupuncturist and a longtime peace activist, said she wants to call him up and say, "What can we do to help, Bill?"

Ann's words, Barbara's words, reach around and through the noisy angst to a quiet longing in me. A longing to finally finish the necessary, exhausting years of fighting and mistrusting—to let go of the bad stuff, embrace the good stuff, go out there and do good, be nice, contribute, add to, be a part of, don't tear apart.

Curling up around the edges of a lifetime of misgivings are visions of giving: people smiling at each other on the streets of my city because they're not stepping around homeless beggars anymore; my own and other people's emotional calluses softening, our humanness emerging because there's less suffering to be protected against.

From age fifteen I have believed this vision could only be created in a bubble, our bubble, the little world we made for ourselves and furnished with head shops and VW buses and mountain communes and rock and roll. We could be that good to each other, that peaceful with each other in the bubble, because we lived in isolation by the outlaw code.

Perhaps now I and my friends—"we"—have grown up, despite our sworn intentions to the contrary.

Maybe now we are too wise or too weary or too therapized to go on putting all our faith in no-faith, all our hope in hopelessness, all our energy into fighting, fighting, fighting. Maybe now we are simply too old for revolution—and old enough to envision a place for ourselves in or near the seat of our own, or this country's, power. And maybe our country has finally grown up with us.

Last night, watching a handsome, ruddy-cheeked young Democratic hero stride to the podium to make his acceptance speech, Ann and I tensed at the same moment.

"Don't shoot him, please don't shoot him," I blurted. Ann looked at me knowingly; my children looking at me unknowingly, and in that instant the history of my country in my lifetime flashed before me. The cheers, the napalm, the chants, the tear gas, the gunshots, the rage, the blood, the blood, the blood.

I want for my children a history of this country in their lifetimes that brings them better memories than this. I want for my children a life in the bubble, but I want the bubble . . . bigger.

This is how I sit tonight, in the aftermath of the first election in which I voted and was enthusiastic about a president. The first election in which the majority of Americans and I voted for the same candidates. The last election in which my oldest son was too young to vote and too young to be sent to war.

This election in which a man my age who demonstrated against the Vietnam war and married a woman lawyer was elected by the people of my country to lead us. Along with a vice president who is more of an environmentalist than I am, whose prescription for healing this country incorporates the concepts of codependency and Alice Miller. These men who chose for their convention and for their victory party the rock-and-roll music of Fleetwood Mac.

Whatever else it all means, this much I know: This is the beginning of an era that brings with it the hope and the risk of integration—when us becomes them. When there is no easy enemy. When we—when I might begin to live, for the first time in my life, within my country and at peace with my soul.

Will Work for Food

Much to my surprise, I love this job. Whatever qualms I had about sacrificing my political integrity for a regular paycheck have been overpowered by the sheer amount of fun I am having every day.

When I was a freelance writer, the mailman was the only adult I could count on seeing every day. It was up to me to keep myself warm (in the lean years, never quite warm enough), fed, and entertained. Now I go to a place called "work" where all of my basic needs—and then some—are satisfied. There are bottomless pots of decent coffee in the kitchen, three kinds of muffins on Fridays, boxes and boxes of pens and printer ribbons in the supply room—and a paycheck twice a month, whether I stay up all night working or not. In appreciation for catalog copy well written and profits amply earned, Banana showers its award-winning Creative Department with goodies intended to maintain our creative edge: we take company-sponsored field trips to clothing outlets and airports and museums; eat expense-account lunches, work in Bay view offices in San Francisco's grooviest neighborhood; hire top-notch freelancers and consultants.

In return for this embarrassment of riches—and despite my utter lack of experience—I am expected to edit the Banana Republic catalog, and to "supervise" the whiz kids who write it. By acting as if I am a person who can do these things, I somehow become a person who can do these things. I love editing a particularly clever piece of copy, conceptualizing a catalog cover, and then finding it in print in my mailbox six weeks later. I love filling my closet, and my friends' closets, with the eight-dollar pigskin shirts and fifty-cent felt hats I scarf up at employee sample sales. Amazingly, I even love being a "boss," which mostly entails praising and doling out hefty raises to the talented young writers who "report to me."

Khaki is hot; sales are strong; spirits are high. My worklife, once politically fulfilling but lonely and poverty-stricken, brims with productive brainstorming, good news, shared laughter. My boss, Susan, obliges the needs of a single mother by agreeing to let me work at home on Wednesdays. How did I get lucky enough to be having this much fun, and $36,000 a year, too?

The only thing that isn't fun is the fear. There's this ripple of anxiety that reverberates through Editorial every time we send out a batch of catalog copy for approval.

What if Mel (Banana founder and ultimate authority) *doesn't like it? What if the buyers* (who procure the "merch" about which we write such witty, if nondescriptive descriptions) *don't like it? What if the customers don't like it?* The fear fever spikes when copy comes back with "Weak," or "College humor—do better" scribbled in the margins. *For every one of us, there are ten hungry copywriters out there . . .*

But hey—this is on-the-job training for me. A bit of high anxiety is a small price to pay for the education I'm getting at Banana U. Almost every day I do something interesting, learn something interesting I've never done or known before. Almost every morning I look forward to getting to work; almost every evening I tear myself away and speed back across the bay before Peter and Jesse's after-school center closes.

Plus, there's this other thing I love about my job: the company I work for mails catalogs to several million people several times each year. There is evidence that many of those people actually read what we write. And the company has, at last count, ninety-two stores in cities all over the country. The unrepentant (if temporarily co-opted) radical in me can't help imagining: what if we could sell all those Banana Republic loyalists something more than safari fantasies and washable wool sweaters? What if we could sell them . . . political consciousness?

After all, every American is bound to do three things: pay taxes, die, and . . . buy stuff. What if every one of them had to *think about what's going on in the world* every time they thought about what to buy? What better place for consciousness-raising than in the marketplace?

One of the many perks of my job is the plethora of magazines the company supplies. In the December *Esquire*, my eye is caught by a photo of two grinning hippie guys, Ben Cohen and Jerry Greenfield. I read on. Ben and Jerry have an ice cream company in Vermont, and a vision of merging business with social change. Unlike me, these guys don't seem to think they've sold out by going into business. They seem to think that their kind of business is a continuation—not a violation—of what we were all doing in the sixties.

Sounds good to me!

I rally the willing troops of the Editorial Department behind our new mission. Soon, subtle and not-so-subtle political messages begin to turn up in the pages of the Banana Republic catalog. We name an otherwise nondescript garment "The E.R.A. Skirt," attributing to it such virtues as a back vent "that allows there's still much ground to cover." An Indian cotton shift becomes "The Gandhi Dress . . . sense its peaceful revolt against constraint."

With the encouragement of my boss, I appoint myself Banana Republic's "Minister of Corporate Ethos." I write and distribute an eight-page "Conscience Report" that describes all the wondrous, world-changing uses to which ninety-two stores and a hugely read catalog might be put. Banana Republic could be—should be!—raising money for community groups and nonprofits. Educating customers about current political issues. Turning our workplace into a nurturing home away from home. Mobilizing our 2,000-person workforce into an army of activists.

I'm on fire! Maybe I *can* have my free lunch and my politics, too!

While senior management is mulling over my wide-eyed suggestion that they "evaluate the conditions under which our products are manufactured and sold, and compare those working conditions to the principles with which BR would like to be identified," I'm home at night taping a PBS series called *Growing a Business*. Some soft-spoken guy named Paul Hawken has visited companies all over the country—Ben & Jerry's among them—to report on the emerging trend of people-centered, socially responsible business.

I institute a new Creative Department lunchtime ritual called "View 'n' Chew." Every Thursday I fill the conference room with the enticing aroma of microwave popcorn, then force-feed my hungry co-workers episode after episode of *Growing a Business* while they munch. Witnessing the glowing reports of Patagonia's on-site child care center, Ben & Jerry's "Joy Team," Springfield Remanufacturing's employee ownership program, my cohorts begin to grumble. Why isn't Banana Republic as groovy as those other companies? Why don't *we* get to bring our kids to work with us every day, or have a say in corporate decisions, or own stock in the company?

Six months after I am hired, Susan calls me into her office and closes the door. An industry survey undertaken by Human Resources, she explains, has indicated that I am grossly underpaid. My salary is raised nearly twenty percent to $42,000 a year. The people whose "boss" I am buy me drinks after work to celebrate.

It sure wasn't like this when I worked on the line at Ford Motor Company, where I spent four years of mandatory ten-hour night shifts installing rear brake lines and gas tank floats.

Early in 1988 Mel Ziegler launches his long-imagined travel magazine, *Trips*. In the galleys for the first issue I read a story about South Africa—a story that I, as self-styled guardian of the corporation's conscience, deem insufficiently critical of apartheid. Bristling with righteous indignation, I rush into Mel's red-walled office to persuade him to kill the story, or at least have it rewritten.

Mel says: "The story's okay. We can get away with it. We're Banana Republic."

I say: "That's another thing I've been meaning to talk to you about. The name of the company is offensive."

Mel says: *"The name of the company is offensive?"*

I respond, haughtily, "I'm not the only one who thinks so."

Mel says: "You don't seem to mind the name of the company when it appears *on your paycheck.*"

The conversation ends. I return to editing catalog copy and helping to transform Banana Republic into a model workplace.

Banana Republic is to be transformed, all right. And quickly. But not in a Ben & Jerry's kind of way.

It seems that we go to sleep one night working for a booming, top-of-the-curve business and wake up the next morning chukka-deep in doo-doo. The fall line isn't selling. K Mart has racks of cut-rate khaki. The cost of producing and mailing catalogs is skyrocketing. The stock market crash has disposed of disposable income. Catalog and store sales plummet. Employee morale follows.

To finance expansion, Mel and Patricia Ziegler had sold Banana to The Gap years ago. As long as Banana was raking in the bucks, The Gap was an absent, beneficent parent: funding the opening of ninety new stores (complete with antique steamer trunks, Jeeps extruding through display windows, and two-story papier-mâché giraffes); underwriting start-up costs for *Trips*; providing sumptuous office space and seemingly unlimited cash to keep its eccentric prodigy child happy.

But as the bottom line begins to bleed from black to red, The Gap's generous open hand becomes an angry punishing fist. The Zieglers are the first to go. The second issue of *Trips* is yanked off the press. Panic-provoking emergency meetings replace creative brainstorming sessions. In the space of six months the carefully assembled Creative Department is dismembered. The bakery that used to deliver muffins to us every Friday morning now delivers afternoon Bon Voyage cakes with equal frequency. The friends I used to laugh and write copy and share dreams with are scattered to the winds.

Midcarnage, our new Gap superiors "ask" Susan and me to go to lunch with a buttoned-down guy we're told is visiting from J. Crew. After two hours of polite chitchat about the vagaries of catalog production, our "visitor" beckons for the check and whips out his credit card.

"But you're our guest," Susan says graciously, putting her credit card on the table.

"Oh no—this is on me," he smoothly disagrees, handing Susan her card with an unmistakably pitying glance, and scribbling out a generous tip for the waiter. Susan and I exchange worried looks.

A few weeks later, after sending Susan off on a business trip, our new boss asks me if I'd be interested in Susan's job, "should it open up." Susan, she complains, is "so difficult, and insubordinate, too."

"I could never stab Susan in the back that way," I say, watching the Gap executive's eyes glaze over as I speak.

I had it right in the first place, I think. *Capitalism sucks. There is no room to be a human being in this setup.*

When Susan returns she and I are informed that the man from J. Crew has been brought in to replace us both.

On August 15, 1988, I share my own double-chocolate fudge cake and tearful going-away party with three others fired on the same day. I surrender my parking sticker, pack up my Conscience File and souvenir safari helmet, and return to the jungle of the unemployed from whence I came, it seems, just a few short happy days ago.

1990–1991: SMITH & HAWKEN, MILL VALLEY

Fifteen minutes into my first day as editorial director at Smith & Hawken I place a call to Ann at work in Berkeley.

"I love it here!" I whisper, lest my embarrassingly unbridled enthusiasm be overheard. There are hardly any offices at Smith & Hawken; like most everyone else's desk here, mine is one of many in a big open room.

From the moment I enter the wisteria-draped, beam-and-glass ark of a building that houses Smith & Hawken's Art Department, I am thrilled (I'm working for Paul Hawken, the guy I used to watch on TV!), and dizzyingly, gratifyingly in love.

I'm in love with Mill Valley, this hidden-away foothill fairyland of a village. Birthplace of Banana Republic in the seventies, Mill Valley in the eighties became the company town to Smith & Hawken, which now occupies seven of the town's buildings, subsidizes the town's annual film festival, and ensures that a profusion of narcissus blooms along its redwood-shaded roads each spring. For this New York–Jewish–Oakland girl it's like shopping at Disneyland to shop at Mill Valley Market, where affluently attractive blond people say "Excuse me" as they glide past each other in the aisles, and Smith & Hawken's account pays for companywide treats—baguettes, brie, berries, and pastry for two hundred—every Friday. I feel I've sneaked into an exclusive country club that hasn't yet noticed that I'm not qualified to be a member.

I'm in love with the fifteen bright, gorgeous, high-spirited women in the Smith & Hawken Art Department, who have, in the years preceding my arrival, created the work environment of my dreams.

Each morning, while the computers are booting up, the French doors are being adjusted for climate control, and the fresh flowers freshened, the day begins with an exchange of the previous night's dreams, therapy sessions, and sexual or near-sexual encounters. Haircuts, new clothing purchases, and signs of emotional or physical distress are also noted and discussed; scarves imperfectly knotted are adjusted, shoes swapped or removed.

Later, when the phones are jangling incessantly and it's too foggy to shoot the cover and the buyers change the product mix *again* and we've got to send out for lino *tonight*, someone might whisk a sample-sale damask dishcloth off a sample-sale Italian platter of homemade scones or banana bread. Someone else might offer up a jar of homemade plum jam. And then garden stools and teak tea chairs are gathered 'round and food is shared, breaths are taken, energy renewed, teamwork restored.

Special attention is paid each day to the person upon whom the bulk of that day's work has fallen—in Smith & Hawken parlance, the one who has, like a python that's bitten off more than it can chew, "swallowed the pig." A pink pig is placed on the appropriate person's desk so that support may be properly directed; the pig and the sympathy are relocated as the workload shifts.

For everyone, every day, there are backrubs, Pepperidge Farm cookies, dirty jokes, and clean arguments that flare, are tended, and then extinguished. As there was at Banana Republic, there is a palpable pulse

of paranoia that throbs through our department every time we're awaiting approval of our work by the higher-ups; an expectation of criticism
to follow whenever praise is offered. In defense we protect our bond
fiercely; like siblings in an unstable family, we look out for each other
with near-desperate fervor when disapproval snakes its way through the
chain of command and threatens to strike one of our own. In fear and in
joy we grow ever closer. In and around these most loving of labor
relations the fifteen of us manage to produce twenty-plus garden, furniture, clothing, tool, and holiday catalogs each year: an average of one
full-color catalog every two or three weeks.

At first I chalk up my sense of being a stranger in a strange, if
wondrous, land to the difference between WASPs (nearly all of my
coworkers) and Jews (I was the third one hired at headquarters; the
woman who hired me was the second). "Just try to think of yourself as an
exotic, dark flower in a field of calla lilies," my boss advised me during
my interview, when I fretted that I might not fit in. Not only is the
workforce predominantly female—there are so many beautiful blue-
eyed women in this company it's hard not to believe they were hired for
their looks.

But after a while I realize that there's another explanation. Smith &
Hawken's corporate culture is best described by one word: emotion.

In this beauty-driven company, love—or its dark side—is the
currency that underwrites each transaction. Love—or its dark side—is
the current that charges each interaction. Love and beauty, beauty and
love: the scent of dried roses in the halls all year-round; a company-
sponsored child care center opened next door because a favored employee wants to nurse her first baby.

Love, and its dark side. Everything—job descriptions, salaries,
hirings, and firings—*everything*—is personal. Everything is about relationships. Relationships, and the power they confer, are reconfigured
hourly. Policies don't count; even the written ones are routinely ignored.

The same brilliant, impulsive man who hired all these wonderful
people because he loved them has built a company as manic as he is.
Paul Hawken's moods soar and plummet—when sales rise or fall; when
a catalog fails or succeeds; for reasons unknowable to the rest of

us—and his tremors reverberate through the company. His irresistible affection and laser attention dart from this department to that, from this person to that; those who hope to hitch their career wagons to a star spend a lot of time hitching, unhitching, surveying the ever-shifting landscape, and hitching again.

Like its founder, this company is more emotional than most people I know. It weeps, exalts, sulks, coos, rages. It puts its arms around me and squeezes tight. Breathless, I surrender. For the first time I imagine myself working somewhere—working at Smith & Hawken—forever.

As enlivened as I am by the magic of my new workplace, though, I soon find myself numbed by the mundane nature of my task at hand: to discover—and then rediscover, over and over and over again—the twenty-five (or less) informative, clever, vaguely British-sounding, yet accessible words that have not yet been written about paperwhite narcissus.

In one catalog alone: *Paperwhites in a green crate; paperwhites in terracotta; paperwhites in blue glass; paperwhites in green burlap; paperwhites in an English-style bird bath.* Whatever artistry might survive the sheer repetition is squelched by the pace of catalog production. In one fall alone: *the Spring Garden catalog, Spring Garden Two, Retail Furniture, Trade Furniture, Spring Clothing, Bulb, Sale.*

Predicting this problem when the editorial director's job was offered to me, I negotiated a second, juicy set of responsibilities that I hoped would offset it. Paul agreed to appoint me Smith & Hawken's first social mission director. I would help him scout new ways for Smith & Hawken to walk its environmental/socially responsible talk. I'd work to integrate the company's politics into catalog copy and editorials. And, along with Paul, I would represent the company at meetings of the Social Ventures Network—an elite association of progressive entrepreneurs (including my heroes Ben and Jerry).

Having edited plenty of (far more interesting) catalog copy at Banana Republic, there's not much growth for me in editing catalog copy at Smith & Hawken. But I resolve to do my job with all the enthusiasm I can muster, spurred on by the yummies I already feel I can't live without: the daily joys of working with exceptional people; the satisfaction of having a hand in the making of beautiful catalogs; a passport into the otherworldly gentility of Mill Valley; the chance to learn the art of socially responsible business at the side of Paul Hawken.

Then one day in a new product meeting—four months after I've been hired—I notice that the buyers are rolling their eyes at every suggestion I make. Paul stops returning my calls. Some copy I've circulated for review comes back covered with scathing Post-its. After avoiding me all week, my boss calls me into her office and tells me that there are questions (she can't say whose) as to whether I'm the best "fit" for the position, after all.

I am terrified, enraged, distraught. If I lose this job, in this economy, how long might it take me to find another one? I've been schooled in the company lore; I know that far more entrenched souls than I have been lost to Smith & Hawken in exactly this manner. Old-timers still grieve for the good parent they lost in the wrenching divorce, a few years before my time, of the legendary Smith (Dave) from Hawken (Paul). Early on, my coworkers warned me that I was the latest in a long series of writers who had been deified, then discarded. Now, it appears, my number is up.

I take the advice I am given by those who have weathered these episodes before. I swallow my terror, treat this like a small but dangerous earthquake, hide beneath my desk until the temblor stops. And it does stop, or at least, it does stop for me. The mucky-mucks stop frowning at me and start frowning at someone else; my boss starts talking to me again; I get warm voice mail messages from Paul again. I breathe a sigh of relief, dust myself off, assess the damage, and go on. Even if my job— like everyone else's in this intense, unpredictable company—is on shaky ground, my heart has taken root here. I am determined to survive.

A few months later, employee dissatisfaction reaches critical mass. People are fed up with the fear and the inconsistencies; with the contrast between "the book" (Paul's reputation as a new age business guru, as embodied by *Growing a Business*) and "the movie" (real life at Smith & Hawken). While Paul is off accepting awards for environmental and social responsibility, his employees are at home working long hours for unglamorous wages; feeling insecure, unheard, unappreciated. Groups of disgruntled S&H'ers gather in Mill Valley cafes at lunchtime, over after-work margaritas; from these kvetch sessions arises a movement to make Smith & Hawken a less volatile, more democratic workplace.

I muster my courage and tell Paul that people are afraid of him— too afraid to tell him so. He says he wants things to be different. He encourages staff people to form task forces, conduct employee surveys, hold special meetings, create a People and Practices Committee to establish personnel policies uniquely suited to Smith & Hawken's temperamental soul. The chief operating officer, a former Zen priest, prints and distributes buttons in tasteful forest green that say, "Blame Less." In response, many people sport handmade buttons that say, "I'm Not Less." I take a dab of Wite-Out to my own button so it reads, "Blame-Less."

At a companywide meeting on Earth Day 1991, against the beatific outdoor backdrop of the Mill Valley Outdoor Art Club, with daffodils and iris blooming and blue skies overhead, Paul declares his commitment to repairing Smith & Hawken's "internal ecology." He proclaims this "The Year of the Company," and promises that on Earth Day '92 we'll be celebrating breakthroughs yet unimagined. His words are greeted with grateful tears, skeptical snorts, and riotous applause.

I've also been given Paul's approval to start a committee called C.A.U.S.E.: Community Action Unites Smith & Hawken Employees. The idea is to make the resources of the company available to employees who are doing world-changing work—to give the staff a chance to help shape the company's social priorities, long the private domain of its founder. Anyone can come to the monthly meetings, present a favorite cause, solicit support. Twenty-five people from all over the company show up at the first meeting. We agree to take up a collection and buy Christmas presents for kids in a battered women's shelter. C.A.U.S.E. quickly becomes a Smith & Hawken institution.

Work is exhilarating. I bring all of me to Smith & Hawken every day. All of me is welcomed here. My forthrightness with Paul has earned me a gratifyingly close relationship with him, and a special place in the hearts of my coworkers. Even the editorial part of my job is becoming more satisfying: we're working on what we affectionately call the "P.C. insert," a few pages in the upcoming Holiday catalog offering products from companies owned by friends of Paul's—socially responsible and women-owned small businesses.

The biggest problem I'm having is balancing work with the rest of my life. Actually, I'm having a hard time *having* a rest of my life. My connection to Smith & Hawken is compelling and consuming. I feel more appreciated, more known, more loved in the Smith & Hawken family than I ever have in any group in my life—and my lifelong hunger to feel that way all the time is distracting me from finding it in my own family. There are Smith & Hawken parties on the weekends, Smith & Hawken friends calling every night, Smith & Hawken dramas to lose sleep over, Smith & Hawken triumphs to rejoice over and analyze, endlessly.

Then, suddenly, I have another problem. A really scary problem. Once again, there are rumors that someone "up there" doesn't like me. Once again, my work is inexplicably found wanting. Somehow I know it's serious this time. Two months after she gave me a stellar review and a ten percent raise, my boss takes me out for coffee and tells me there is "concern" about my "priorities." The same unnamed people who once questioned my qualifications now worry, she tells me, that I'm too busy with Social Ventures Network and C.A.U.S.E. to do my real job. "You need to stop everything else you're doing and focus on your editorial responsibilities," she says. "I understand that this may not work for you."

I stare at her, stunned. *Who wants me out of here, and why?* I ask. She averts her eyes. I don't ask the bigger question: *How could you betray me this way?* Easily, I realize, and for what must seem to her an excellent reason: to please the person or people who told her to get rid of me. To keep her job. To get a better one someday, if she's hitched her wagon to the right star.

This is the Big One—the Smith & Hawken crisis I won't withstand. I spend weeks arguing, grieving, looking for someone to reason with. But no reason is available. Paul says, "You belong here," assures me again and again that he wants me to stay, but still the untenable ultimatum stands. Word gets out; support is mustered. Day after day people take me aside and whisper, *What can we do to stop this?*

But there is nothing my coworkers can do to stop this. Their initial surge of outrage is followed by bitter resignation: *So much for the Year of the Company. So much for making this company safe and sane.*

The runaway train of my leaving is roaring down the tracks. I could jump out of the way. I could duck for cover once again: give up the most important, social mission part of my job; accept my demotion to Editor-Only. But the work of making progressive business progressive is as much a part of me now as my fingers. How ironic: it appears that all the affirmation I've been soaking up while I've been dodging bullets in this crazy company has had some positive effect on me. Thanks to Smith & Hawken I'm too healthy to subject myself to Smith & Hawken anymore. *I'm forty years old. I won't be infantilized. I can do better.*

I mourn in the arms of the Art Department while negotiating my severance package. At night I mourn in the arms of my lover, who soothes me while wondering not so secretly if this separation from Smith & Hawken might redirect my straying attentions to her and to our family.

On my last day I am called to a special company meeting in the conference room. Towering bouquets of lilies nod in handpainted ceramic vases as Paul presents me with a huge "seed packet" conceived by him, produced by the Art Department, and circulated throughout the company. "Seeds of Change: Sprinkle Through the Garden of Life," it says. It is filled with love notes, memorabilia, gift certificates, and trinkets from the coworkers I have loved and lost. Earth Day '92 will have to happen without me.

As it turns out, Earth Day '92 will also happen without Paul: he leaves the company a few months after I do.

At a Social Venture Network meeting a few months ago, Peter Barnes offered me a job in his company. Working Assets offers three services: credit cards, a travel agency, and a new long-distance phone service, all of which generate huge donations for nonprofit activist groups. I call Peter and tell him I'd like to be considered for the position—which is now, he tells me, on the verge of being offered to someone else. I fear that I won't get the job at Working Assets—*and then what will I do?* I fear that I will get the job at Working Assets but that I will never again experience the ecstasy and the agony that I have known at Smith & Hawken.

Immediately after beginning my new job at Working Assets in downtown San Francisco, I realize that this is true.

1992–1993: Working Assets, San Francisco

Instead of listening to a meditation tape in the car each morning as I cross the Richmond Bay, curve into the sheltering crevices of Mount Tam, and arrive at a destination so desirable that I wish I could afford to live there—now I cram myself onto BART, elbow my way through the bustling cement canyons, and ride an elevator to an office that smells of new carpets and Melamite furniture and reverberates all day with screeching sirens and car alarms. Now, I can't wait to get home at night to the relative calm of Oakland.

Love and beauty are not priorities at Working Assets. Progressive politics, social activism, altruistic goals may enter here, but hearts are best checked at the door. Employees are hired and valued—not, as at Smith & Hawken, for their good looks and extraordinary personalities—but only for those parts of themselves recorded on their résumés.

What is familiar is the chronic low buzz of worker discontent. Just as employees flocked to Smith & Hawken in search of Paul's promised brave new workplace, refugees from the corporate world arrive at Working Assets expecting an island of socialism. People want to know: why does Peter Barnes, the president, get to work at home and work erratic hours, when everyone else is expected to be present from eight to five, Monday through Friday—and then some? Just because Peter founded the company, why should he get to change his mind—and a week's worth of work—at the last minute? Why do he and the CEO make decisions that affect the whole company without consulting the staff, or often even the top managers? If Working Assets is socially responsible, shouldn't it be a democracy?

My taste for the aesthetic and the genteel, nourished in the green-house of Smith & Hawken, is seen by the activists who work here as proof that I am superficial, snobbish, uncommitted. My few failed attempts to make soulmates of workmates and improve the office ambiance—to serve meeting muffins in baskets instead of plastic bags; to hang a Smith & Hawken wreath or two on the walls—leave me feeling foolish, vulnerable, and lonely.

Overnight, I've gone from Shangri-La to urban jungle. From folk hero to distrusted interloper. From house radical to house yuppie. Finally, I'm working with people whose politics match mine. And I can't find more than one or two among them who want to go to lunch with me.

On the other hand, my new job—creative vice president, they call me—has eliminated the biggest problems I had at Smith & Hawken: the repetitiveness of the work; the continual effort to imbue high-priced, largely nonessential products with social value; the dissonance between the company's (Paul's) tony editorial voice and my own; the subjectivity with which my work was judged.

At Working Assets I don't have to sneak political messages in around selling cotton skirts and teak benches. The company's product is social change. The services it offers are merely tools to accomplish that end.

Here, I am given a high-stakes task with a measurable outcome. In its first year Working Assets Long Distance has signed up fifty thousand customers; they want to have twice that many a year from now. My mission is to invent a direct-mail package that will convince fifty thousand people to switch from AT&T, Sprint, or MCI to this upstart, unproven but unquestionably p.c. phone company.

The task is challenging but doable. I know how to appeal to Working Assets' potential customers, because (unlike the upper-class Connecticut Republicans who dominated Smith & Hawken's customer base) those people are just like me. Highly invested in my success, management gives me what I tell them I need: the freedom to work at home one or two days a week; the budget to hire my favorite designer; the authority to strategize, conceptualize, and implement the project.

Working Assets' competitors are offering big prizes to people who switch phone companies: up to $100 in cash, a free month of long-distance calling, complicated money-saving calling plans. What kind of small-ticket, alluring, yet consummately cool bribe would work on people like me—while clearly communicating the difference between AT&T and Working Assets? What about some kind of yummy food . . . some kind of yummy food that costs enough to make it a real treat . . . some kind of expensive yummy treat that screams socially responsible business . . . of course! *We'll let them eat Ben & Jerry's!*

Ben Cohen agrees to let us give a coupon good for a free pint of Ben & Jerry's to anyone who switches to Working Assets. We agree to pay B&J's the going rate for each coupon redeemed. Ben writes an irresistible letter on his own letterhead endorsing our phone service; my designer, Jim, produces an irresistible direct-mail package into which we insert Ben's letter.

The mail drops. The package is wildly successful. New customer service reps are hired to handle the deluge of orders. We sign up nearly twice as many customers as was projected. A second floor of office space is leased; a new commercial long-distance service is launched. Working Assets is dubbed "The Ben & Jerry's of phone companies." I am given an unexpected $5,000 bonus for "saving the company."

Still . . . after a year at Working Assets I have yet to experience the kind of collaborative breakthroughs or loving laughter that made catalogs effective and life worth living at Banana Republic and Smith & Hawken. My bright ideas are conceived at home alone, or on the phone with Peter Barnes—who also works best at home, alone. One day, in the middle of a fax-and-phone brainstorming session, me in my house and Peter in his, he shares with me his vision of the ideal workplace: a room full of modems interfacing with each other. I know he isn't kidding.

The company's management style grates against me like fingernails on a chalkboard. I feel oppressive as manager, oppressed as managee. I wear my VP title with discomfort; it draws distrust from "below," less respect than I'd hoped for from "above." People don't make friends with their bosses here. The Smith & Hawken Art Department still gathers monthly for "Girls' Nights" at one of our houses or another, but I have yet to socialize with a single Working Assets coworker after hours.

Despite my "successful career," despite my position of "power" on the Working Assets management team, despite my juicy salary and my dedication to Working Assets' lofty mission, despite my awareness that most people who are fortunate enough to have jobs at all do them under far more onerous circumstances for far less money . . . I am still unhappy here.

I believe in the product, but the process is bringing out the worst in me. As the company grows larger, I feel myself growing smaller.

What's my problem, anyway?

Why can't I be more like Ann? For eight years now, since right after she got to California, she's worked happily at the same company— beginning as a part-time publicist, now as a software marketing director. What's the difference between us that led Ann quickly and permanently to a groovy yet steady company—and keeps leading me into these impossibly unstable job situations?

Maybe if I'd had a different family I wouldn't need my workplace to be one. Maybe if I weren't a woman I'd care more about the reward than the journey. Maybe if I'd stuck with companies like Ford Motor I would never have expected to find spiritual, economic, creative, social, and political gratification in a workplace: bizarre idea, but one that is epidemic among those of us who seek sanctuary in the promised land of socially responsible business.

I want work that makes me happy. Work that has obvious, unquestionable value. When I chop wood with Ann, our bond grows stronger and our cabin grows warm. When I write a poem or a letter, I am better understood. When I pull a baked-from-scratch pie from the oven, my kids and my lover come running from all ends of the house and we eat it happily together.

When I come home from work in the city my muscles don't ache; there's no flour on my nose or dirt dug into the calluses on my hands. But it's hard to know what I've accomplished. I'm thrilled to work for a company that gives thousands of dollars to groups like Planned Parenthood and Greenpeace each year. But it's easy to lose sight of the end product amid the tedium of producing it. Did that two-hour argument about which typeface to use in a direct-mail letter help convince one more person to vote prochoice? Did that frenzy to meet a print deadline help save an ancient forest from clear-cutting? If so, it was worth it. If not . . .

Big surprise: it turns out that I have not escaped the harsh reality I hoped to leave behind when I fled Marxism and the Ford assembly line and landed on the soft, inviting shores of new age business. Too bad, but true: the laws of capitalism still apply. Working for a living is still working for a living. Whether the boss is Mel or Paul or Peter, whether there are advertising awards or hydrangea wreaths or Greenpeace posters on the walls—wherever there is a boss who controls the paycheck of a worker who needs it, there is imbalanced power, and there cannot be democracy.

Progressive companies vow that their employees need not "leave their values at the door." Yet no matter how truly progressive the owner, no matter how assertive the worker, no matter how beneficial the product, the very nature of business requires us all—owner and worker and everyone in between—to leave some portion of our selves—of our *value*—at the door.

Companies like Smith & Hawken and Working Assets offer their customers a real alternative: a chance to "shop for a better world," to "vote with their wallets." But when it comes to their employees, the best that Paul or Peter and the people who work for them can do—the best that "socially responsible business" can do—is tweak the formula. Create a workplace that minimizes fear, or one that escalates it. Hire people who want to reach for the stars and give them a ladder; or squelch people beneath the steel-toed boots of mediocrity. Reward teamwork, or promote individualism. Encourage laughter, or silence it.

Just like the guys who started these companies because they were too twisted by the sixties to work for anyone else, I am not cut out to be an employee. The older I get, the less willing I am to be "supervised," "reported to," "reviewed." A child of upwardly mobile Jews, a teenager of the youth revolution, I can't help but look for what might be better than what is.

I am plotting my next move. And feeling there is nowhere else to go.

I don't want to get another job until I figure out how to have one. I don't want to gather up the stinky, untidy bundle of my nirvana fantasies and my outsized expectations yet again, just to dump it on the doorstep of yet another well-intentioned but imperfect company.

And then a miracle happens: I get a book contract. So I can quit my job and I don't have to get another one. Not right now, anyway.

FEBRUARY 1994

Since I left my job I've been doing some work for a few Social Venture Network companies, including Working Assets. But I'm a part-time consultant now, instead of a full-time employee. In Monopoly terms, I've gone from "In Jail" to "Just Visiting."

It's not a perfect escape. I miss the engagement, the urgency of a real job. I miss the medical benefits, the social and psychic benefits of working full-time, full-on. But this is what works for me. For now.

The slogan of my consulting business is "Will Work for Food." These days I mostly work for companies that make things my family and I like to eat: Odwalla Juice, Stonyfield Farm Yogurt, Ben & Jerry's ice cream. When I can, I arrange trades: juice for a slogan, yogurt for a brochure, free ice cream coupons for a consultation.

They think it's funny, the hippies—now millionaires—who started these companies, when I tell them why: thanks to the safety net of my book contract, I have a chance to simplify my life, get back to basics, exchange labor for food. They think it's funny because that's what they were trying to do fifteen years ago—before it all got so complicated—when they started squeezing oranges in a garage, or milking cows in a barn.

But my slogan is more than a joke. It's also a statement of intention. I want to feed the socially responsible business movement because these are the companies, this is the grand experiment that will teach business—if indeed it can be taught—how to feed its employees, its customers, its communities. And I want to be fed—to find joy and camaraderie and meaning in the work I do.

Bring the War Home

I'm driving up to the cabin by myself for four days. Not alone by choice, but in abandonment: my girlfriend's abandonment of me (her flimsy excuse: a business trip); and my own abandonment of any number of friends who would have happily come along for a weekend of sun, conversation, and avocado sandwiches shared on the sandy bank of the swimming hole.

Apart from Ann there's no one I feel really good with these days. I'm caught between craving companionship, mirroring, shared laughter—and longing for soothing solitude. But nothing soothes. I feel lonely with other people; I feel lonely with myself. I don't fit anywhere. Is that my choice?

I love listening to music in the car when I'm alone. I howl along, my unmusical voice disguised by four speakers blaring good sound. I pretend I might still be a rock star someday. I pretend I'm a rock star right now. I'm not forty-one years old, those aren't wrinkles on my face, I'm not in a Honda station wagon by myself on Highway 101. Anything is possible, even still. I'm singing into the mike with my eyes shut against the glare of the footlights; I'm losing myself in the song; my backup band and my own strong, sure voice fill the hall; the fans are screaming . . .

But I can't find a radio station that plays my kind of music. I don't *have* a kind of music—at least not a kind of music that's been recorded within the past two decades. Driving north through Richmond, San Rafael, Santa Rosa, Ukiah . . . soul, oldies, heavy metal, easy listening. None of it is easy to listen to for me. I station-surf the way my kids do at home with the TV remote, driving me crazy and, ultimately, out of the room.

The soul station plays Smokey—yes!—but then, some slow song I've never heard. Hit the button. The oldies station is playing some awful early-seventies bubblegum—switch. Heavy metal: hate it. Easy listening: Neil Diamond, give me a break. I'm not *that* old.

I want the connection to the present, to the outside world that the voices on the radio provide. But what choice do I have? I rifle through the glove box, pull out a tape, stick it in the deck without reading the scribbled label. My tapes are all homemade concoctions: I roll my own, since I can't find any I like enough to buy.

Janis Joplin, *Pearl*. Ah, good. A woman for these times, if only she'd lived that long. I belt a few out with her. I never was moved by "Bobby McGee" or "Mercedes Benz," but "Get It While You Can" always got me. Still does.

The side is over too quickly. Just like Janis's life. The tape auto-reverses and suddenly I'm listening to the Red Star Singers, a Berkeley band whose lead singer, Bonnie, lived in a big house around the corner from Danny and me in the early seventies. They recorded one album; I was one of maybe a thousand people who bought it. Probably one of ten people who still have it, taped it, still listen to it.

The guitar player: Ron Rosenbaum. I used to baby-sit for his infant daughter Carey while he was out at gigs and grape boycott meetings. Now Carey's in college and Ron is "Mr. Rosenbaum," head guidance counselor at Peter's high school.

I had a little crush on Bonnie. I can picture her on all those makeshift stages at all those benefit concerts, slamming the tambourine against her muscular thigh, her long brown hair and unrestrained breasts flopping against the beat. I still see Bonnie around Berkeley sometimes, but she doesn't seem to recognize me. Her hair is cut short now, and she appears to wear a bra.

I sing along as Bonnie pumps out "Still Ain't Satisfied" in her fierce soprano: "*They liberalized abortion/but I still ain't satisfied/cause it still costs a fortune/and I still ain't satisfied./They call me Ms./they sell me blue jeans/ call it Women's Lib/they make it sound ob-scene . . .*"

Then my favorite song on the album comes on. The song that always makes me cry, even when I'm not feeling lonely and displaced.

"*Let the struggle and resistance begin/like a fire being spread by the wind/while the peasants lead the people again/behind the guns of the Viet Minh . . .*"

"Vietnam Will Win," it's called, and for me, that song is it. The whole thing. That time. Those places. Those feelings. The outrage. The urgency. The rage. The certainty. We knew who we were. We were doing what had to be done. We were doing it together. And only we could do it.

1966

I wanted Paul for my boyfriend because he was the leader of the hippie pack at school, the kids who stood on the corner before, after, and sometimes during classes smoking unfiltered Camels and joints, wearing torn jeans and super-short miniskirts and peace buttons and long tangled hair parted down the middle, or not parted at all.

I loved having Paul for my boyfriend because we had hot hand sex in doorways on our way to school every morning, and because he loved me, really loved me. And because our names appeared together on the masthead of *Sansculottes,* the underground newspaper we cranked out with our friends on the mimeograph machine in Paul's bedroom at his groovy lefty parents' house, then sold for a nickel in the bathrooms at school. And because Paul rescued me from everything I'd hated since birth about my parents and their world, rescued me from the life I would have been condemned to if Paul hadn't taken my hand and walked me away.

A month after Paul became my boyfriend the principal of the Bronx

High School of Science called my parents in for a conference, to which I was also invited. The principal told my parents that I had fallen in with a bad crowd, "known communists and opium smokers." In order to protect me from a fate worse than, and possibly including, death, he said, my parents must take action immediately to sever me from these undesirables. The teachers and administrators of Bronx Science, he offered magnanimously, would be happy to help enforce the separation.

That night, my father informed me that I was, from that moment forward, forbidden to see Paul and my new friends.

Thus the war began.

1967–1969

Watching the eleven o'clock news every night, falling asleep to nightmares of children's faces melting, blinded mothers screaming, heroes in black pajamas. Being chased through city streets by cops on horseback, being Maced, gassed, cornered, beaten, busted . . . could that, could *anything* be enough to do when every moment we slept another baby was napalmed in our names?

"*One people from Saigon to Hanoi/reunifying what could not be destroyed/Vietnam/Vietnam . . . will win.*"

I'd never sewn anything in my life, but I hand-sewed a tote bag I wore slung over my shoulder everywhere I went. Each side was yellow corduroy on the top, blue corduroy on the bottom, a brilliant red velour star in the middle. The National Liberation Front flag.

"*Like the songs that the people sing/like the flags that they wave in the wind/let the thunder and the echo ring/Vietnam/Vietnam . . . will win.*"

"Hell, no/We won't go!"

"One, two, three, four/We won't fight your fucking war!"

"Bring the war home! Bring the war home!"

"Ho, Ho, Ho Chi Minh/The NLF is gonna win!"

None of this namby-pamby civil disobedience—nonviolent passive resistance—Martin Luther King—Gandhi—Buddhist Peace Delegation shit for us. The Vietnamese people had a war to win. And so did we.

We appointed ourselves the Western division of their liberation army, doing our paltry share from within the belly of the beast. I was terrified every single time I put on my gas mask and my water-soaked bandanna and my football helmet to go to a demonstration—absolutely bone-chilled terrified, every single time.

I must have gone to two hundred of them—street-corner confrontations, marches on Washington, induction center picket lines, Wall Street riots. There was never a choice not to go. Wherever the action was, it found me like a heat-seeking missile, loaded me on board, and delivered me to the scene.

Grand Central Station. The Statue of Liberty. The baseball field across from Bronx Science. Tompkins Square Park. The Pentagon. Throwing marbles beneath police horse's feet. Throwing plastic bags of red paint against the walls of Dean Rusk's hotel. Throwing hissing tear-gas canisters back at the riot squad. Throwing our bodies into the grinding gears of the war machine.

The thwack of the billy club on the barricade just as I leaped over it. The jab of the bayonet an inch from my belly. The tug-of-war with the undercover cop who was dragging Paul by one arm to the paddywagon, me hanging on to Paul's other arm screaming until some fellow demonstrators helped me wrench Paul safely back to our side. Watching as a riot cop grabbed Abbie Hoffman out of the crowd, calmly bent Abbie's arm behind his back until it snapped, broken in two places, then handcuffed Abbie's mangled arm to the other and stuffed him into a waiting cop car.

Each time I thought: This will be the time it won't stop with broken arms and noses, head wounds, gas, jail. This will be the time they start killing *us*, too. Nothing inside or outside me gave me a reason not to die that way. I had no vision of the future except more of this—until we died or won. There was no choice but to go, each time. And so I went, terrified, and went and went again.

There was a war to stop, a war to bring home, a war to win.

What *was* the war, really?

1982

I wake up sobbing from this dream: *My parents and I are having a screaming fight. The argument is: did I become a terrible person because of them (bad childhood) or me (I was born that way)? My father starts taunting me about the protests I used to go to, how much I loved fighting in the streets. He says that proves I'm an inherently sick person. I yell at him: "Don't you get it? Yes, I loved fighting the war! Those demonstrations were great for kids like me who had so much hurt and hate to express—at least then we had a target for it. If it wasn't for the war, we might have killed our parents."*

1967–1969

The so-called liberal media were our most insidious enemy, dismissing with their two-bit psychological analysis the worldwide youth movement that was shaking every Western nation to its core. *Life* magazine said we were just typical teenagers rebelling against our parents. Were Danny the Red in Paris, Bernadette Devlin in Ireland, Bobby Seale in Oakland just rebelling against their parents? Didn't those fools in the media know there was a war to stop, a revolution to win?

We scorned the haughty, head-tripping liberals whose intellectual musings never opened them to what we felt in every throbbing cell of our bodies. While reporters invented newsstand explanations and our parents consulted shrinks and lawyers, we were in the streets changing the world. There was a war to stop. A war to bring home. A war to win.

1969

The war was escalating, and on the Lower East Side things were getting ugly. People weren't having gentle acid trips anymore; we all kept Thorazine in our stashes. Some of the raving friends we had to bring to Bellevue never really came back. Some friends disappeared to Canada, some disappeared into the Weather Underground. Some disappeared into Eastern religion or California encounter groups. Some just disappeared.

Nothing was working. There was no reason not to try anything.

Paul and I went to New Mexico. We built a house on a mountain, grew food with Trippy and Lee, smoked pot, wrote a book, got bored. One day a guy with a crew cut knocked on our door: an AWOL GI who'd hitchhiked down from Fort Collins in Colorado. He'd heard there were hippies around Taos who might take him in, save him from a second tour of duty in Nam. Every night Ed woke us up, screaming in his sleep. One morning we woke up to eerie silence. Ed was gone. No note, nothing, just gone.

A couple of times each year Paul and I drove to one coast or the other to get our fixes of adrenaline and new records and underground newspapers and other people. Sometimes friends or fuck buddies would come from New York or San Francisco to stay with us. The second winter I started sleeping with a guy from a nearby commune. It wasn't the first time I'd exercised our agreement, mine and Paul's, but our agreement wasn't keeping Paul warm at night. Paul took his typewriter and moved to Santa Fe.

It was December, forty below zero for two weeks. My honey jar was frozen solid, the woodpile was low, and I could see another blizzard blowing in across the mesa. Trippy was leaving Lee, moving to San Francisco. The whole country thing was blowing apart. I gave away the goats, packed a few clothes, bought a Youth Fare plane ticket, and I left, too.

1970–1972

I went to Europe, hitchhiked around, fucked around, got into kundalini yoga, fell in and quickly out of love. Came back to New Mexico. Didn't get back together with Paul. Went to live with Trippy in San Francisco. Had an abortion. Moved in with Danny. Moved to Berkeley, lived in Sue's driveway with Danny in the red Volkswagen bus Paul and I had bought together.

The war was ending. While I'd been away, a women's movement had begun. I joined the Berkeley Women's Health Collective. The women I worked with were all becoming lesbians and nurses. I had the hots for a woman in my "Psych Emergency Function Group," but I was still in love with Danny. I confessed my crush to Danny; he promptly broke up with me.

I moved in with a friend I'd met at the Red Star Singers' house and went to nursing school for free at Merritt Junior College in Oakland. Every night I came home from the hospital crying about the babies born too soon, the dying old men whose children never came to see them, the diabetics with their crater wounds. I couldn't eat or sleep. I lost twenty pounds in six months.

At Merritt College, where the Black Panther Party had been founded a few years earlier, my sociology teacher used the Little Red Book as our class text. I loved the poetry, the simplicity, the inarguable truth of Mao's words. Being Jewish, I was especially responsive to his generous use of food analogies. *"To know the taste of a pear you must first change the pear by eating it." "You can't make an omelet without breaking some eggs."*

Mao's koans made everything make sense. Of *course* an antiwar movement couldn't end war; only class war could end war. Of *course* women and blacks were oppressed; their exploitation benefited the capitalists. We had to eat the pear, break some eggs, smash imperialism, build a workers' state. Put the wealth in the hands of those who create it. Only the proletariat could lead the way to a truly just, peaceful society. *Of course.*

1973–1980

I joined the October League, one of several national communist organizations that sprang up in the floundering aftermath of the sixties. I quit nursing school, shaved my armpits, pledged to tithe ten percent of my income as long as I should remain a member, and went to work for $2.20 an hour in a notebook factory beside Rich, my new Marxist-

Leninist boyfriend. Egged on by the revolutionary zeal of the communists, the workers in the plant walked out on a wildcat strike. Every one of us—the Chinese and Mexican women who didn't speak English, the white revolutionaries who didn't speak Cantonese or Spanish—was fired, blacklisted by the Teamsters Union, and denied unemployment benefits.

Rich and I got married on December 21, 1974. Presiding was a friend, a fellow cadre and Universal Life Church "minister." During the sixties, he had received from the Church a mail-order certificate of ordination—the draft-dodging ploy successfully used by many of the white middle-class guys who might otherwise have sought psychiatric or student deferments.

Rich and I wrote our own Little Red Book–inspired wedding vows; the ceremony and the reception were held in the three-room Oakland apartment we'd shared for the past year. Our comrades ordered our cake: a big red revolutionary star. The bakery, understandably, misunderstood. And so our wedding cake was a big red Star of David, inscribed in white icing with the requested stirring message: *Rich and Meredith, the future is bright.*

I got a job installing brakes on the line at Peterbilt Trucks. (My male coworkers, in whom I was placing my hope for the aforementioned bright proletarian future, started calling the company "Pussybilt" in honor of me and the three other women who were the first females hired there since World War II.) The day before my ninety-day probation was up, my FBI file came to visit and I was fired again.

Electronics shops, cookie factories, tortilla factories, canneries. In and out of Bay area factories I went: attending study groups and cell meetings as my day, swing, and graveyard shifts allowed; passing out leaflets at plant gates at daybreak and dusk. And then my final assembly-line job: fifty-eight mandatory hours a week, through three years and two pregnancies, at the Ford Motor Company plant near San Jose.

For eight years every time I laced up my steel-toed boots and stuffed leaflets and Little Red Books into my lunch pail, every time a worker I'd been working on showed up at a union meeting or a Workers' Defense Committee meeting, every time an unemployed black woman

or a former member of the "old" Communist Party joined our organization, I became more convinced that I was once again doing the only
thing that would work, the thing that had to be done.

Until 1980.

1980–1983

When I got pregnant with Jesse in 1980 the auto industry was in chaos.
Ford was working us fifty-eight hours one week, laying us off the next.
Whole assembly operations were being moved to the Philippines, Mexico, Taiwan. I clambered around installing carpets in sixty-one trucks
per hour while my belly swelled and I tried not to inhale too many toxic
new-carpet fumes.

When I was six months pregnant, Rich's mother—the woman
whose loving of her four children, and me, had made me eager to have
my own children so they might know that love—died suddenly and
horribly. Rich unraveled. Choking on my own unexpressed grief, I was
working six nights a week, caring for my ailing husband and one-year-
old son, pregnant with my second child, who would never know his
grandmother. I took an early, unpaid maternity leave to try to nurse
myself and my family back to health before our fourth member arrived.

With the money Rich's mother left him, we bought a house in San
Jose so I'd be closer to the Ford plant and the Ford workers when I went
back to work. But by the time Jesse was born, the plant was history.

And so was the October League. Internal squabbling, ideological
uncertainty, and—as my obstetrician pronounced at the surgical end of
both of my labors—"failure to progress" aborted our organization and,
with it, my political and social universe.

As the bonds that once bound us frayed and snapped, Rich and I
found more and more to fight about and less and less to love in each
other. Our support systems—his family, my job, our organization—had
disappeared like a tablecloth yanked off a fully set table. Our life still
looked the same, but the underpinnings—our reasons for living in San
Jose, working in factories, living together—had vanished.

It was simply too much loss to face. So I didn't face it—not yet. Bulldozing through the debris, I joined a grass-roots group in San Jose that hoped to unionize the burgeoning electronics industry. I took a job at National Semiconductor, one of the many parcourse-lined, nonunionized Silicon Valley "campuses" on which Trident missiles were being built where plums and cherries had blossomed just months before.

But the assembly-line workers at National were inaccessible to me, locked inside soundless "clean rooms" and languages I didn't speak. Many of the clerical workers were virulently antiunion, grateful refugees from union manufacturing jobs that had abandoned them for Third World countries. The engineers just wanted to toot their coke, get their Beemers detailed, and change companies every few months. My boss warned me to stop wearing knee socks and sandals and start wearing more "professional" nylons and pumps. I couldn't find anyone to eat lunch with, let alone organize. I gained fifteen pounds in six months.

It seemed to me that one night I'd gone to sleep happily married, happily pregnant, and happily ensconced in a loving extended family, a tight-knit revolutionary organization, and a meaningful if strenuous job—and the next morning I woke up in a city and a house I hated; unemployed, disenfranchised, and fat, with no friends, two needy babies, and a husband with whom I was clearly heading straight through disillusionment to dissolution. And—for the first time since I was fifteen years old—I had no viable means of political expression.

In flat-out desperation, I'd even tried dosing myself with the panacea I'd long scorned as the opiate of the petite bourgeoisie: I'd begun therapy. If I couldn't save the world, or my marriage, I hoped at least to save myself. But even that didn't seem to be helping. Nothing seemed to be helping.

What *was* the war, really?

The war was in my disoriented, weary head. In my disheartened heart. In my once-happy, now tension-strafed home. And there seemed to be no stopping it. No one to help me fight it. And no way to win it.

1984–1987

Feeling as trapped and alone as I had as a child drove me back to the coping strategy that saved me then—when I wrote my way out of my unhappiness with a flashlight under the covers. Now I was writing my way out of my unhappiness in the women's bathroom of National Semiconductor, with my feet up on the toilet seat so my boss couldn't peek under the stall door and find me.

Much to my surprise, the first story I wrote—about born-again Christians in Silicon Valley—was published in *Mother Jones*. Writing exposés of Silicon Valley led me to writing more: investigative articles about the Ford plant shutdown, my new friend Wendy's cancer support group, incest, eating disorders, AIDS.

The sword had failed me, but I was rescued in the nick of time by the pen. Easing out of Silicon Valley and into freelance journalism helped ease me out of my marriage and out of San Jose, into the arms of the woman I met at a publishing conference and a cottage near the Berkeley border.

Better now. I was struggling by on $12,000 a year, buying my kids' clothes at thrift stores and bread at the Orowheat outlet, settling in for a second shift at the computer after I tucked my kids into their bunk beds and set the burglar alarm each night. But I was writing stories that had some meaning, for magazines and newspapers that real people read. Researching them was bringing me to interesting people and places. I was in love and I was loving being a lesbian as the gay wave was swelling.

Compared to lots of my sixties friends (still searching, or bored, or dead) and fellow ex-cadres (starting from career scratch, but this time at thirtysomething with kids and mortgages to support), I was doing really well.

But not all better. It just wasn't the same.

There were gays to save from bigotry and cancer patients to save from misdiagnosis and molested girls to save from their fathers. But the urgency wasn't the same.

I was becoming a better writer, writing about important things. But the satisfaction wasn't the same.

I couldn't tell what good my work was doing, or if it was doing any good at all. My labor power, my attention, felt diffused, desultory. AIDS this week, incest the next. I had causes, but no cause. And I was working all alone, all the time.

Suddenly I was building a career instead of a movement. I missed knowing that what I was doing with my life was the best possible thing to do. I missed the joy of doing it with my friends. I missed the days when it was honorable to be poor, when it was "better to have dope in times of no money than money in times of no dope." I missed "us."

I missed the war.

1987–1992

I was thirty-six years old. My kids wanted Air Jordans. I wanted to have a conversation with an adult once in a while. I decided to get a job.

Where would I fit? I hadn't acquired a taste for the long-avoided nylons and pumps—nor would any "normal" corporation have me, with my dubious past and eclectic skill-set. The only jobs I'd ever had were chosen for their organizing potential: the more mistreated and exploited the workers, the better my chance of winning them over. Being a communist had taught me how to find a bad job, but I didn't know where to look for a good one—if, indeed, such an entity existed for an unrepentant if somewhat unfocused hippie/commie/writer like me.

My old friend Alan—the editor in 1967 of the youth culture book Paul and I wrote, now a Berkeley therapist—told me that Banana Republic was looking for a catalog editor. It's more like a magazine than a catalog, he assured me. Not like a real job. They're all journalists over there. They've got cool office space. And their politics are pretty good.

A company? With good politics? Having received my training at the Marxist-Leninist School of Business, and having consequently been employed by some of the worst-politics companies in America, the concept seemed oxymoronic, downright blasphemous.

So this is how co-optation works, I thought a few weeks later, sitting in my new office in an old slaughterhouse in the hip San Francisco SoMa district with a shit-eating grin on my face and my lunch dates for the week scribbled into my leather-bound Day-Timer.

Think of it as R&R, advised my fellow journalist friend Michael, when I worried aloud about the effect on my revolutionary vigor of all the fun I was having. You've paid your dues, he said, now cash your check and enjoy yourself.

What is the absence of the war, now?

JANUARY 1991

I'm in a new-product meeting in the conference room at Smith & Hawken, mapping out the next catalog, when a coworker runs in, sobbing. "We're bombing Iraq," she cries.

We? I think. Even in this moment of horror, I am reminded that my past has rendered me irreconcilably different from ninety-nine percent of the people I now know. I still think "us versus them." Worker versus company. People versus government. Doves versus hawks. Good guys versus bad. But my coworkers, colleagues, even close friends use the word "we" in ways I never would. "We're changing our product line." "We've got to solve this health care problem." "We're bombing Iraq."

Everyone rushes out of the conference room, gathers around a portable TV someone has brought from home in anticipation of the start of this war. A haggard, bleary-eyed reporter is narrating live footage of bombs falling on people's houses, of Israelis huddled in bomb shelters strapping gas masks to children's faces, of young Americans in uniform tumbling out of fighter jets like matchsticks from a box.

What is the war, now?

The reporter is talking about the possibility of random terrorist acts against American citizens. Beefed-up security measures are being put into place at stadiums, conference centers, airports. Ann is in Chicago for work, flying home tonight. I'm stabbed by fear, then anger: is there real danger, or are the media just trying to drum up even more racist anti-Arab sentiment than already grips this nation?

A coworker puts her arm around me, rests her head on my shoulder. I feel her body shaking. "It's so awful," she says. "I can't believe we're at war again."

We failed, I think. We were out to end all wars, to turn bomber jet planes into butterflies, to build a beautiful loving world. And now here we go again.

At dinner that night Jesse asks me what I would do if he was eighteen and there was a war and he got drafted. Peter tells me he wants to go to the protest march in San Francisco tomorrow. Jesse asks me how Bush could start a war when no one wants there to be one. Peter asks me if I can get him some spray paint so he can paint slogans on the Chevron building when we march past it. Jesse asks me if I think the war will be over by the time he and Peter are eighteen.

The next morning Peter and I take BART across the bay, join thousands of demonstrators gathered on Market Street. It's a reunion of the class of '68—most of the demonstrators are graying people my age, many of them accompanied by their children. *They must not be expecting violence,* I think, realizing then that without thinking about it, of course, I do expect it.

"No war for oil! No war for oil!" we chant as the march begins. The fear has evaporated, now that I've thought it through. *This isn't that war, those times.* I feel proud and certain, thrilled to be marching with my son at my side.

When there's a war, at least, I know what to do.

"Mom," Peter mutters between chants, "I hope this doesn't mean I'm gonna end up wearing bell-bottoms."

Two or three demonstrations, a few bad news nights. It's over in a flash.

SUMMER 1993

Peter has a job this summer with a program that's helping cops and teens make peace on the perennially plywooded streets of Berkeley. He works from five to midnight, sleeps till noon.

"You call that working?" Peter teases me, watching as I type away on my laptop, reclining on our deck in the sun. "What are *you* contributing to the community, Mom? C'mon, keep a teenager off the streets. Take me surfing now!"

What are you contributing to the community, Mom? Not much. I go to neighborhood meetings—but only when I feel resilient enough to handle the latest reports of robberies and murders. I go to demonstrations for gay rights and city council meetings to oppose school cutbacks and conferences to build the progressive business "movement."

Bring the peace home.

The peace begins where the war began: at home.

I do take Peter surfing. I take Jesse shopping for Air Jordans when he needs new shoes and to the Y to play basketball when he wants to go. Because for the first time since I became a mother fourteen years ago, I can do that much, at least.

For the first time in my children's lives I can stop working in the middle of a sunny Monday and spend some time with my sons, both of whom were in day care from the time they were three months old and both of whom will be gone from me soon. I can cook dinners that take longer than fifteen minutes to prepare and stand on line for an hour to buy the best blueberries at Berkeley Bowl market. And then I can sit with my children and my lover at our kitchen table while my blueberry pie stains their teeth deep purple and they talk to me about everything that fills their pulsing brains and their strong, sure hearts.

My children are proud of their parents' history. And they are well on their way to making some of their own.

Despite the beating of the drums, despite the irretrievable loss of a time in my life—in this country's life—that made eternal disappointment inevitable, the truth is: my life has never felt as good to me as it does now. I write those words and the drumbeat becomes a thunder. *What are you contributing to the community, Mom?*

I sleep in a T-shirt that says, "I want what I have." I bought the shirt as a joke. I thought Ann would laugh: Meredith always wants, always wants what she used to have, what she's never had, what she'll never have. But Ann didn't laugh when she saw the T-shirt. It's true, she said. You want what you have. You've changed.

I don't want war anymore.

In 1967 Martin Luther King nominated the Vietnamese monk Thich Nhat Hanh for the Nobel peace prize. We were outraged. What good was meditation in the face of napalm bombs? *Bring the war home!* The Buddhist Peace Delegation wanted peace, not victory. They were sellouts, betraying their own people. *"While the peasants lead the people again/behind the guns of the Viet Minh."*

What *was* the war, really?

It was the voice of Thich Nhat Hanh that comforted me as I drove to work every day with a lump in my breast. It is his voice that comforts me now as I lie awake in my bed at night listening to gunfire. *Peace is every step.*

Can I live with the absence of the war, now?

Too early Sunday morning, driving south toward Santa Cruz on High-way 17. Fog and drizzle and sun peeking through, then fog and drizzle again. Eight o'clock was too early to rouse myself from my warm bed, my warm lover, the one morning this week Ann and I could have had a little full-body contact, a little pillow talk, a spark of connection before the day sets us running on separate tracks again.

But Wendy's been wanting more time with Jesse and Peter, and they've been missing her too. So Jesse spent the weekend at her house last month; this weekend is Peter's turn. The deal was, Wendy would do the Friday-night pickups in Oakland, and Ann and I would handle the Sunday return trips. I know that four hours on the freeway is a small price to pay for what my kids get from Wendy on these weekends—a massive infusion of her special love potion: unadulterated attention; unbridled hilarity; surfing and shopping, or drawing and movie sprees; custom cooking, heart-to-heart talks, chocolates on their pillows at night.

I know this and yet as I am driving south through the suburban wasteland that spreads from Hayward to San Jose, past the strip malls and semiconductor factories and concrete industrial "parks" erected on the graveyards of cherry orchards and lettuce fields, I'm getting crankier by the mile. Ann and I really could have used some time in bed together today. I hate this ugly drive. I hate what greed and indifference have done to this landscape. I hate this distance between Wendy and me.

Last time I drove to Santa Cruz was a couple of Thursdays ago. Wendy asked me to go with her to the doctor's appointment she'd been putting off since 1992, since her periods ended along with her breast cancer treatments. She'd tried everything she could think of to get her body to right itself naturally: Rosen body work and acupuncture and homeopathic "remedies." But still there was no period, no baby. And no remedy for the pain Wendy has been in since the doctor told her that the chemotherapy that saved her life had thrown her into irreversible menopause. That her body would never hold a baby.

My heart softens. This is the seesaw of my feelings for Wendy these days: the fear and the grief and the rage of losing her from my life as she was once in it; the tenderness of loving her just the way she is. Already Wendy is saying she'll adopt. I can't bear the thought of her raising a child ninety miles away from me, but still, I hope she can have a baby—however she can, wherever she lives, whatever it takes. I hope some young pregnant woman will be convinced to give her baby to an unmarried, self-employed, two-time cancer survivor who will probably be the best mother in the history of the world. "Personally," Peter wrote on the card that Ann, Jesse, Peter, and I sent to Wendy when her menopause was diagnosed, "I think you should be everybody's mom. We should make you the Universal Mommy. You are the most beautiful person that I will ever know."

I'm through the worst of it now, past San Jose and into Los Gatos, where the road narrows and curves into the forested foothills, moistly green from the February rains. In my good moments—and there are more and more of them lately—I can let go of the need to have things, people, relationships just-the-way-I-want-them. I can swaddle myself with knowing that the universe is benign, if not always benevolent. That Shit Happens, and Miracles Happen, and occurrences of both are mercifully out of my control. That even people who can't give me everything can give me a lot. When I am able to do this the squalling quiets; the prosecution rests; contentment settles over me like a soft quilt. Things with Wendy, things between Wendy and me, are not the way I want them to be. And I feel blessed to have Wendy in my life.

Muffins, I think, as the day's first hunger pangs nip at my innards. *Maybe Wendy will bake muffins for breakfast.*

It's ten-thirty when I pull into Wendy and Michael's driveway. Peter's surfboard is sticking out the window of Wendy's Toyota like a big yellow tongue. The front door of the house is wide open, as it almost always is. I don't feel as jealous as I used to of Wendy's safe Santa Cruz existence—since the murder I overheard from my bedroom a year ago, our own neighborhood has become inexplicably less dangerous. Lately the gunshots I think I hear sound indistinct, far away. I can't remember the last time one of our cars got broken into, or the last time we called 911. The quieting of the streets seems to echo the quieting in my head— or maybe it's the other way around.

"My Merry!" Wendy squeals, flying across the porch, enveloping me in a hug. "Thanks for driving all this way," she says between kisses.

Over Wendy's shoulder I check out my older son, on whose lips I detect a telltale blue hue. "Did you take him surfing this morning?" I ask Wendy. I pull away from her, notice the puffiness around her eyes. "Peter and I were real early birds today," she confesses. "We got to the beach at seven-thirty."

Who else but Wendy? "Hey, Babe," I say to Peter. He pulls me against his hefty chest. My head comes to rest in the crook of his neck. "Did you guys have fun?" I ask. Peter releases me, then leans over to pat the top of my head. "Yes, little Mommy," he says. "We had a great time." Michael comes out of the bathroom toweling his hair. We exchange half-hugs. It feels weird to hug a man my age who's shorter, narrower, smaller than my son.

"What's that good smell?" I ask hopefully. Wendy smiles. "Muffins!" she says.

I follow her into the kitchen. "How are you?" I ask. "Sad, still," she says, bending to open the oven. "I cry every day." She taps the muffin tin against the countertop; eight perfect whole-grain muffins tumble onto one of her grandmother's plates. On the refrigerator behind her are photos of some of the children Wendy has already adopted: Peter and Jesse, her one-year-old neighbor, Naomi, her friend Kathleen's three kids, her brother's newborn daughter.

The four of us stuff our faces with muffins smeared with home-made kiwi-lemon jam. Then Peter transfers his belongings from Wendy's car to mine, and he and I hug Michael and Wendy good-bye. It's eleven o'clock; we're right on schedule to get Peter to his job in Berkeley by one. "Let's do better than this once-in-a-blue-moon stuff, Mer," Wendy says, leaning in through the car window as I'm fastening my seat belt. "I want to see you more often." "Me too," I say.

As we're approaching the freeway Peter pulls a cassette out of the pocket of his baggy jeans, slips it into the tape deck, and turns up the volume. It takes me approximately ten seconds to identify the music that comes blasting through the speakers. "That's Jimi Hendrix!" I gasp. Peter nods brusquely without looking at me, the nod that means *Don't make a big deal out of this, Mom.* I take a deep breath, attempt to eliminate all traces of emotion from my face and my voice. "I didn't know you were into Hendrix," I say casually.

Peter digs into his jeans, pulls more tapes from various pockets, spreads them on the dashboard. *Electric Ladyland. The Jimi Hendrix Experience.* And a couple of homemade ones. "Bob Dylan," Peter says, nodding at those. "Michael and I stayed up late last night listening to Hendrix and Dylan. Mom: if you ever want to know anything about Jimi Hendrix, just ask Michael. He's the man."

Hendrix? Dylan? The screaming assault of Jimi's "Star-Spangled Banner" fills the car. "He's amazing, isn't he?" Peter says reverently. I nod, bite my lip to keep from saying more. Peter has taken a distinct turn, these past few months, toward the values and accoutrements that defined me when I was his age. His hair is wild and long—I laugh when I catch myself starting to brush it back from his face or (Goddess forbid!) suggest a haircut. He scorns conspicuous consumption, disdains alcohol, worships Bob Marley, has a wardrobe consisting of five T-shirts, five pairs of jeans, and a couple of sweatshirts. For his fifteenth-birthday shopping trip, he asked Ann to take him to Haight Street. He came home with handmade pillar candles, incense, psychedelic posters.

And Peter is an activist. Since last summer he's been employed by a City of Berkeley–funded group called RESPECT: Racial and Ethnic Sharing Providing Empowerment to our Community Today. During evening rush hour Peter and his coworkers keep BART commuters safe, escorting them from the station to their cars or houses. On Sundays they work on developing an ethnic diversity curriculum for the Berkeley public schools. In the course of his on-the-job training—not to mention his life—Peter has learned more about racism and diversity than I'm likely to know, ever. He instantly recognizes and critiques every "ism" there is—in the media, in his classrooms, at the dinner table, in himself—including several per day that would have slipped right past old radical me.

All of this, of course, pleases me enormously. Makes me feel gratifyingly bonded to my son, and to my history. And yet I know I need to conceal my delight, relinquish my old claim on my son's new turf. "If you want to see Hendrix in concert," I can't resist saying, nonetheless, "there's this movie called *Monterey Pop* . . ." Peter nods dismissively again. "I rented a bunch of Hendrix videos last week," he says. I didn't know there *were* any Hendrix videos.

Peter falls asleep as we're heading north through Los Gatos, as I'm singing along to "The Wind Cries Mary." (I discover that I still remember every one of the lyrics—and also, that they make no more sense now than they did then.) I take in my son's closed eyes, his slackened jaw, now speckled with wiry black hairs, and I feel the familiar disappointment. I'd hoped to bond with Peter on this long ride home; to hear just a few of the many secrets that protect his privacy, to widen by just a bit the narrow slice of his life that he makes visible to me. But Peter has no such agenda, no such need. He sleeps all the way to Berkeley. I drop him at work, wave hello to his boss—a former Black Panther—and head for home.

"Doctor J," I greet Jesse. He mutters an indecipherable greeting, barely looks up from the college basketball game he's watching. I feel the familiar annoyance. Should I interrupt his sports-induced catatonia to point out to him, for the billionth time this year, that a grunt is neither friendly nor courteous? And then I hear the familiar flapping of the family chickens coming home to roost. How can I expect Jesse to be "courteous," when the word "manners" was never spoken in our home; when I taught him and his brother to shun hypocritical social conventions—to be honest, not polite?

Anyway, I tell myself, he's thirteen years old. And besides, he's not just watching TV. He's studying. Jesse has devoted himself to basketball this past year with the same single-minded concentration he's applied to his artwork since kindergarten. He plays on his school's eighth-grade basketball team—currently in second place in the Oakland league. He plays pickup basketball with men twice his weight at the Y on Monday and Wednesday nights. And since Ann (with Richard's help) put a basketball hoop in our driveway, Jesse shoots alley-oops with anyone (usually Ann) who will toss the ball to him, over and over, for hours at a time.

On Saturdays Jesse plays from nine P.M. to midnight in a high school league modeled on "Midnight Basketball," a Berkeley program that encourages young men to stay off the streets and "shoot hoops, not each other." Ann, always the trooper, stays up long after I've crawled off to bed, drives out into the night to pick him up. Then the two of them stay up even later to cackle together over *Saturday Night Live,* their favorite show.

And still he finds time to draw and paint and cartoon and sort and resort his baseball cards and even, occasionally, do a little bit of home-work.

"Ann?" I call. "In the kitchen," she answers. I find her bent over a mixing bowl. "I'm making *plain* corn muffins for Jesse," she says with a smile. She need say no more. A few nights ago I made corn bread with the intention of pleasing my younger son. He sniffed at the pan suspiciously—recalling, no doubt, the Erewhon Brown Rice Crispies I tried to substitute for the Kellogg's; the organic applesauce that didn't taste as good as "the regular kind"; the fresh-squeezed Odwalla lemonade that wasn't sweet enough after a lifetime of Minute Maid. "What's in this, Mom?" he asked. I answered encouragingly, "Just corn, Jess." He took a big bite, then spit it out in disgust. I meant kernels of corn. He thought I meant cornmeal.

I come up behind Ann, put my arms around her waist, rest my chin on her shoulder. We fit. After all these years, we still fit. "That's so nice, what you're doing for him," I say, tasting the batter with my finger. This is what Ann has always done for Jesse and Peter, but for Jesse, especially: interpreted his needs when Richard or I haven't understood them; met them herself when that was possible. I've felt threatened, at times, by the special bond between Ann and Jesse, envious of their easy compatibility and all the things they share: their pace (one moment at a time); their ability to be in the present, their taste in food, their taste (or lack of it!) in puns.

But mostly I've felt grateful. Jesse has had his Mom Two, and I've had a partner in parenting. A coparent ("trans-parent," Ann used to call herself, in the early days when the kids still let us drag them to lesbian-mother-and-child picnics) who has helped me clear away the prickly underbrush of my own childhood deprivation, so I could love my children as boundlessly in deed as I do in my heart. Thanks in large part to Ann—and despite my sneaky attempts to lay my footprints all over Peter's path, and inject Jesse's rapidly growing body with nutrients—even through these distancing years, my relationships with both of them are strong and deep.

And so is my relationship with Ann. For the past several months we have skidded toward and skittered away from the realization that our tenth anniversary—our tenth anniversary!—is approaching. That we had promised ourselves a commemoration of that event, should it, in defiance of all odds, occur. Two months ago we got clear that we wanted, at least, a vacation together for our anniversary week. We booked the vacation. One month ago we got clear that we wanted to have a party. (Always the guardian of parity, Ann said, "Straight couples get six blenders when they're just starting out. Why shouldn't we get six blenders after ten years together?") We printed the party invitations—their only ornamentation a tiny yin-yang: symbol of Ann's continuing commitment to martial arts; of my darkness and her lightness; of the merging and the opposition and the balance between us.

Then there was the matter of a ceremony. We were both pulled to have one, each in her own way and for her own reasons. And we were both uncertain about the content. I vowed that I would never take vows I couldn't be sure I would keep. Ann said we didn't need to talk about the future; we could just affirm the values that shape our relationship now. I said I didn't want it to be an imitation of a straight wedding. Ann said she wasn't comfortable with the "W-word" at all. We looked each other in the eye and asked each other if we would choose to get legally married if that was an option. Both of us answered honestly that we wouldn't. There were other things, too, that we agreed about: we wanted it to be small, we wanted it to be officiated but not officious, we wanted the kids to be part of it.

When we were driving back from dropping Jesse at the Y two Saturdays ago, Ann said, out of the blue, "Whatever we decide to do about a ceremony—let's exchange diamond earrings on our anniversary." I fought my urge to control this: to debate the merits of amethysts versus diamonds, to query Ann about the size of earrings she had in mind, to remind her of the importance of shopping around for the best price, to come up with an alternative plan yet unimagined. Instead I said, simply and satisfyingly, "Great idea." To my surprise and delight, it turned out that my rare abdication of control left room for Ann to assume some. "We'll go get our ears pierced tomorrow," she said. "That way the holes will be healed by our anniversary."

The next morning—the day before Valentine's Day—Ann and I left the kids still sleeping at home, went to a local jewelry store, bought the tiniest diamond studs in the place, and held each other's hands as we had new holes punched in our left earlobes. Then we went across the street to Just Desserts and drank Peet's coffee (Ann) and a latte (me) and made jokes about penetration and studs and whether we should register at Crate & Barrel or the vibrator store. And Ann let me eat the cheese out of her Danish and I didn't force her to taste my bran muffin, and we bought heart-shaped chocolate-dipped cookies to bring home to the kids, who stared at us wide-eyed when we showed them the diamond earrings and the temporary posts in the new holes in our ears. I think it was the most romantic morning of my life.

And next Thursday we have an appointment with a Buddhist priest from Berkeley Zen Center, a woman whose daughter is a lesbian, who says yes, Zen Center will support a wedding between two women, and yes, she'd love to help us design a ceremony appropriate for us and for our family.

"Want some corn muffins, Jess?" Ann calls into the living room. No response. Again, I am annoyed. Again, I wish I'd done whatever magical thing other parents do that makes their kids answer when they're spoken to. Again, I am choosing my battles. If I scold him now, will that ruin the rest of our day together?

I am saved by the click from the TV remote, which silences the sounds of the basketball game. "Corn muffins?" Jesse asks guardedly. "From a mix," Ann says, graciously avoiding reference to my recent from-scratch, whole-kernel fiasco.

Jesse ambles into the kitchen, folds his lanky five-foot-nine-inch frame into one of our creaky wooden chairs, and eyes the muffin on his plate. He breaks it in half, inspects each piece, takes a cautious bite. In the time it takes me to blink the muffin disappears. "Another one?" Ann asks. Jesse nods enthusiastically. "Mer?" Ann offers me one. I've already had my muffins today. I'm not even hungry. And who knows what kinds of chemicals and fat and sugar went into that mix? But . . . but I can't miss this unexpected chance to sit at the kitchen table and break (corn) bread with my lover and my son in the middle of a Sunday afternoon. Who knows how many Sunday afternoons are left before it's just my lover and me at the table?

"Thanks," I say, and Ann drops a muffin onto my plate. "Mmm," I murmur appreciatively. All those chemicals and fat and sugar really do something for the taste of a muffin.

"Mom: how tall do you think I'll get?" Jesse asks, a question we've discussed about a hundred thousand times in the past few months. The problem is, Jesse doesn't like my answer. ("Your father is six foot four;

the men on my side of the family are under six feet. Odds are you'll end up around Dad's height, maybe shorter.") Before I can recite it to him one more time, Jesse says, "Shaq O'Neal's dad isn't that tall, and Shaq's like seven foot two."

Ann interjects what she has interjected every other time we've had this conversation. "Jess: you can be a lot shorter than Shaq and play pro basketball, if you're really good—if you keep working at it the way you've been doing." And Jesse shakes his head impatiently, as he always does. "I've *got* to be taller than Dad. I just *know* I will be."

Ah, the tightrope walk of mothering teenage sons. I don't want to smother, or dominate, or encroach upon Jesse's—or Peter's—precious private territories. But I don't want to send them out into the storm unattended, either. I don't want to give Jesse false hope, but I don't want to stunt his dreams. What does he need more right now: a reality check, or the pleasure of a fantasy? Do I really need to remind Jesse yet again that Shaq's mom is six foot one, that Jesse has a better chance of making a living as an artist than as a basketball player, that half the thirteen-year-old boys in Oakland, not to mention the rest of the Western world, go to sleep every night, as Jesse does, with the three magic letters—NBA—forming and re-forming on their tender lips?

Anyway, who am I to say that dreams don't come true? Two years ago I barely dared to imagine a life as good as mine is now. Ten years ago my odds of feeling as happy as I do these days seemed as good as Jesse's odds of ending up seven feet tall. Twenty years ago I wouldn't have believed that I'd know this much peace and this much pleasure in a family that is far more—and far less—traditional than the kind of family I'd imagined. In a life that is far more—and far less—traditional than the kind of life I'd imagined.

What has made it possible for me to sit still and write a book; to eat muffins twice in one day; to forgive myself for leaving some of the work of changing the world to my capable sons and their friends; to say and do nothing every once in a while? What has made it possible for me to stay close to Wendy for thirteen years, to stay . . . married to Ann for ten years, and to *feel* every bit of it, nearly every minute of nearly every one of those years?

Was it the good nutrition and social advantages that came with my middle-class childhood? The magic of sperm, at last, meeting egg; of eye, at last, meeting eye? The book contract, the therapy, the meditation, the passage of time? No doubt my blessings are owed to all of those things—and to the random shit and random miracles that have happened and will continue to happen along the way.

"Anything's possible, Jess," I say. "You never know."

Acknowledgments

To the people in my life who sacrificed their privacy; agreed to live with the differences between how they saw it and how I wrote it; and stayed close despite having to sort our daily intimacies into "those-for-publication" and "those-not-to-write-about": thank you for forgiving me, challenging me, and loving me throughout.

For life support, I am grateful to Wendy Traber, Diana Schweickart, Drew Maran, Zoe Gold, Phoebe Bixler, Jeremy Sherman, Christy Shepard, Alan Newman, The Girls of Girls' Nights, Barbara Wilt, and "Miranda."

For writerly support, Kathryn Olney, Sue Moon, Nancy Friedman, Mariah Burton Nelson, Craig Neal, Michael Castleman, Geneen Roth, Alan Rinzler, Jeffrey Klein, Katy Butler, and Eric Utne.

Thanks to Cori Wells Braun for the cover photo and much, much more.

My agent, Felicia Eth, earned her alias ("The Saint"), by refusing to consider anything less than the best, and pushing me (and everyone else concerned) to make sure that's what we ended up with. Felicia is a top-notch editor and a shrewd businesswoman; she also anchors me to earth, using nothing flashier than honesty for mooring.

I could not have imagined an author-editor relationship as suppor-tive, as growthful—or as loving—as the collaboration I've enjoyed with Toni Burbank. Toni's enthusiasm and encouragement have contributed enormously to the joy of writing this book; her skills—and those of Alison Rivers, Barb Burg, and Amanda Mecke, my Bantam team—have contributed enormously to the end result.

Peter and Jesse did for this book what they've always done for me: kept it real. I am boundlessly grateful for their insights, their wisdom, and their sparing use of the veto.

My lover, Ann, is my sharpest editor and greatest champion; the most loving trans-parent two boys could ever find; the bravest and the most ethical human being I've ever known; my home and my hero.

About the Author

MEREDITH MARAN has been: co-publisher of the nation's first high school underground newspaper at the "prestigious" Bronx High School of Science (circa '67); a back-to-the-land hippie in Taos; a union organizer on Bay area assembly lines; a suburban wife and mother; a freelance journalist for magazines ranging from *Bride's* to *Mother Jones,* from *Parenting* to *New Age Journal;* an urban lesbian mother; and editor/creative vice-president/creative consultant to a host of socially responsible companies including Banana Republic, Smith & Hawken, Working Assets, and Ben & Jerry's Homemade.

Meredith Maran is now: forty-three years old, living in Oakland with her two teenage sons, Peter and Jesse, and her lover, Ann. Anything else you might want to know about her is in this book—every last detail.